Purists and Peripherals
Hip-Hop and Grime subcultures

the **Tufnell** Press,
London,
United Kingdom

www.tufnellpress.co.uk

email contact@tufnellpress·co·uk

British Library Cataloguing-in-Publication Data
A catalogue record for this book is
available from the British Library

paperback ISBN	*1872767494*	
ISBN-13	*978-1-872767-4-99*	

kindle edition

ISBN-13 *978-1-872767-54-3*

Printed in England and U.S.A. by Lightning Source

Purists and Peripherals
Hip-Hop and Grime subcultures

Todd Dedman

To Maya and Erin—dream up!

Acknowledgements

This book would not have been possible without the guidance, expertise and patience of Professor Shane Blackman. Without his support and unerring confidence in my abilities I would not have been able to continue my work—he made the seemingly insurmountable possible. My doctoral supervisory team of Shane, Professor Les Back and Professor Grenville Hancox were intimidating, challenging but ultimately enthusiastic and encouraging. I am grateful for their positive criticism and suggested avenues of investigation. Also, thanks to Robert Albury at The Tufnell Press who has been a reassuring presence throughout the transformation of this work from a thesis to a book.

An earlier version of the purist and peripheral concept was published in the Journal of Youth Studies in 2011, thanks to the editorial team for allowing me the chance to develop it further in this book. At various stages of this work I have been helped by Emma Elwood, Rob Henry, Andrew Bligh, Andrew King, Matt Barton, Zachary Cooke, Rob Forsyth, Deborah Kee Higgins, Peter Crascall, Sarah Butler, Ben Grant, Tim Slight and Luke Moysey. Thanks are due to them all. I am indebted to the individuals who gave their time and offered their considered opinions in the focus groups, as well as those individuals who were willing to engage with me at rap shows, parties and festivals. The original scope of the research has resulted in many elements being necessarily omitted from this book yet the contributions of all those in my fieldwork allowed me to move forward positively with this project.

Huge thanks to Brian Pain and Alistair Brownlow at Rochester Independent College for funding my Ph.D and for their constant support throughout the process over the years. Cheers also to Nicki, Pete and Ed for their help in designing the cover. My partner, Louise Allen, has been a constant source of support and her patience seemingly knows no bounds and for that I will always be grateful. Finally, to all my family and friends, for their tolerance in listening to me go on and on and on about this work over the years and their support and encouragement. I love all y'all.

Contents

Introduction

A book about hip-hop and subcultures is, you would imagine, unlikely to begin
with an anecdote about John Shuttleworth, a comedy character whose routines
are largely based on the minutiae of life in Yorkshire, England. Shuttleworth's
shows debate the complications of one cup of tea not being enough, but two
being too many, and the challenges faced by being offered savoury food once
already onto the sweet course and they are therefore as far removed from debates
of the representation of ethnicity or notions of authenticity in rap music as is
perhaps possible. A close friend has a spare ticket for a John Shuttleworth show
but he is going with work colleagues. I often feel socially anxious meeting new
people and my level of trepidation is not helped by the fact that my friend and
colleagues are psychologists and so I presume they will be analysing my every
move. I take my seat in the group next to a nice lady in her early 60s who I get
talking to and after some time we realise that I knew her daughter, Cara, whilst
in the sixth form at school. I then remember a story where I am 15 or 16 and
talking to this girl at a disco at the local rugby club. Cara is quite an imposing
figure as she is a year older than me but also about six inches taller. Her dyed
black hair is spiked upwards, adding another few inches to her height. Her
heavy eye-liner and black lipstick suggest an aesthetic debt to Siouxsie Sioux
and Patricia Morrison. In passing I call her a Goth. 'Fuck off!' she shouts 'I'm a
punk!' before storming off. This previously buried memory is now fixed in my
mind as the social mistake which led to my general interest in (sub)cultural
affiliation; how we label ourselves and wish others to perceive us.

This book is an exploration of five youth cultural groups based in the South
East of England with a preoccupation for American hip-hop and British
grime culture. I examine how they view themselves, their participation in the
subcultural groups and their views on the imagery and lyrics in the music
they consume on a daily basis. This is a multi-disciplinary piece of research,
encompassing sociology, media and cultural studies and popular music studies.
In Sociology, subcultural theory is a major approach in the literature for studying
young adults. It has theoretical heritage and the power to explain young people's
actions, practices and values (Brake, 1980) although its relevance and academic
applicability has been debated in recent years. It became clear in my own
reading that there were gaps in the literature which this book goes some way
to addressing. The most significant of these gaps was that much of the work

viewed young people as homogeneous, easily labelled and in many instances as a dichotomous form (subcultural or 'mainstream'/not subcultural). This, to my mind, is an oversimplification of the lives of young people and is not a satisfactory or accurate portrayal of the groups who took part in my own research as their lives were much more complex and dynamic than much of the previous writing in the field would have me believe. The most frustrating stumbling blocks that I came up against when I started delving into this academic area were threefold and, in my opinion, somewhat related. First, there was the overly simplistic determination of young people as either belonging to a subculture or not. There exist a number of books that differentiate between those who perceived themselves to be members of a subculture and the part-timers but such relationships between 'full-time' and 'weekend' tend to be portrayed as fractious and, in some instances, hostile. When I was undertaking my own research this was not a true reflection of what was becoming evident to me in the field. Second, there were the persistent disagreements and intellectual contests in the literature over what I can only describe as the 'academic naming rights' to the term which could/would/should replace 'subculture' in light of varying paradigmatic shifts in the last fifteen years or so. Third, why does so little of the literature in this area explore how the people involved in the research understand and interpret the cultural commodities that were seemingly so closely tied to their identities?

As a result of these aspects, the basis for this book is around three questions:

Does the term subculture still retain academic value and if so in what way?

Do young people commit to cultural engagement in different ways?

How do these people perceive the products of the industry that they consume?

These questions underpin the structure of this book. Due to the central role of subcultural theory as one of the major approaches to studying young people I will examine the relevance of this theory as a mechanism to explore and understand the practices and ideas belonging to five groups of people involved in hip-hop and grime. I first look to assess the applicability of the concept of subculture in order to meet the overall aim of the book. Hodkinson's (2002) notion of subcultural substance is utilised using the data from the fieldwork to elaborate on his attempt to reformulate subcultural theory. Using the qualitative data from the fieldwork the significance of the term subculture became apparent during the research.

This book introduces the conceptual purist/peripheral model of subcultures into academic discourse. This model varies from previously presented theoretical concepts in this area as it does not merely present a bifurcation between those deemed subcultural and others who are seen to have only a partial engagement in forms of cultural activity or, as Hebdige defined them, the originals and the hangers-on (1979: 122). The purist/peripheral model illustrates the complexity of contemporary subcultural existence by presenting a non-essentialised portrait of subcultural groups and asserts that each individual and subsequent collective possesses relative though varied degrees of agency as well as self-imposed judgements on their position within the subculture. It was found in the research stage that a number of varying subcultural positions could be interpreted in the fieldwork according to the literature of subcultural studies. The concepts of 'purist' and 'peripheral', therefore, do not solely relate to hip-hop subcultures but could be applied to other substantive youth groups to help establish variations of subcultural affiliation and commitment between its members. As will be discussed later in this book, the purists were more actively engaged in the culture when compared to the peripherals and were also, perhaps surprisingly, less likely to use visual signifiers such as dress code as a way to express their subcultural membership — I term the purists as 'inward looking' as their interests are more on cultural capital than spectacular style.

Purists and Peripherals contributes to the growing work on how hip-hop helps establish identity formation for many people but also does something different as a key focus here is on the audience's interpretations of representations inherent in the texts, whilst also framing these responses within the field of subcultural theory. There is currently a lack of research relating to the decoding of audience responses to hip-hop and grime culture. The study seeks to fill a gap in the literature through the incorporation of the interpretative readings of the audience. Writers such as Rose (1994, 2008), Perry (2004), Quinn (2005) and Ogbar (2007) assess the ideological messages inherent within rap music but do not take into account the interpretive mechanisms of the people at the forefront of the commodified variant of the culture, namely the consumers. Riley states that '... much of the literature on rap is ... unconcerned with attempting to empirically locate the interpretive communities and reading formations of the increasingly diverse hip-hop audiences ...' (2005: 297) and this book attempts to address this factor by incorporating the opinions and attitudes of hip-hop consumers to construct an exploration of consumption. The work here is multiperspectival (Kellner, 1995) in line with more recent work in this area by Wilson (2006), Gunter (2010) and Haenfler (2010).

Chapter 1 of this book focuses on the literature in the field of hip-hop studies. I start by discussing the growing field of Popular Music Studies before moving on to an historical overview of hip-hop culture. A discussion of empirical studies on hip-hop is then presented and I demonstrate the lack of studies in the area which examine the reading positions and decoding capabilities of young people.

Chapter 2 demonstrates that subcultural theory is a recurring, though contested, means to examine youth cultural practices (Frith, 1978; Brake, 1980). It is therefore important to put forward an overview of subcultural debates, from the Chicago School work of the 1920s to contemporary postmodern explanations. In recent research there has been an increasing degree of scrutiny of the validity of earlier positions in the study of youth culture and this chapter presents the paradigmatic shifts in this area. The focus here is on the discourse which closely links subcultures to musical consumption. The discussion of key terminology in this chapter should be seen as part of the theoretical underpinning of the study and relates to the research participants' cultural engagement.

Chapter 3 utilises Paul Hodkinson's (2002) notion of subcultural substance as a central theoretical position to assess the validity of the varying discourses on subcultural theory. In this chapter I also introduce the individuals who took part in the focus group discussions, a significant aspect of the research process. The fieldwork data is incorporated here to assess the value of the concept of subculture, in terms of its relevance and application to groups affiliated with hip-hop and grime. Four determinants are used to confirm a sense of subculture. They are consistent distinctiveness, identity, commitment and autonomy and are applied to the research subjects in order to demonstrate that the term subculture is germane for the individuals within this study. The first three chapters in this book, therefore, not only discuss the theoretical elements which underpin the work that follows but also address the first of the three main questions of this book which relates to the continued validity of the term subculture in the academic study of young people.

Chapter 4 further develops the focus on subcultures. I argue in this chapter that varying degrees of subcultural agency are evident in contemporary hip-hop subcultures, thereby addressing the second of the book's main questions. A descriptive model is presented which differentiates between subcultural members according to a sliding-scale of agency and creative activity within the culture. The research participants are divided into two descriptive sets—the purists (Canterbury, Lewisham and Ashford groups) and the peripherals (Rochester and Brighton groups). These differential positions are developed further in the study as they describe the varied reading positions of subculturalists evident in the field. Aspects such as musical knowledge, relative engagement in the culture and the notion of unspectacular style are discussed to demarcate between the purist and the peripheral positions. This chapter seeks to add to academic debates in the discipline and examines the term subculture within the context of early twenty-first century cultural practices. It was found that different aspects of subcultural theory, from seemingly competing paradigms, can help explore the varying behaviours, attitudes and values of the research groups.

Chapter 5 focuses on an examination of grime culture at a subcultural level. The appropriation of a localised musical form is suggestive of increased agency in the subcultural groups (Gidley, 2007: 149) and consists of a three staged process — adoption, transformation and retrenchment (Webb, 2007: 175). The grime culture of London, with its roots in dance hall and UK garage, is one notable recent musical phenomenon which has gone largely unrecognised by academic research and so this chapter looks to address this. The origins of grime are considered before an analysis of subcultural engagement by the research subjects.

Chapter 6 presents an analysis of the representation of black culture in mediated aspects of hip-hop and how the respondents in the study use, interpret and understand such imagery. During the course of the fieldwork and analysis, issues surrounding the interpretive capabilities of the young people involved in hip-hop and grime became central to the research. The grounded theory approach allowed for the development of an appreciation of the distinct reading positions of identifiable collectives in the field, hence the focus on decoding capabilities and the demarcation in the study between the purists and the peripherals. Many previous studies have discussed the portrayal of gender and ethnicity in hip-hop, yet few studies detail the reading positions of the audience from a grounded theory perspective. It was found in the research that this was a significant area for consideration for many in the focus groups and led a number to reflectively assess their own cultural engagement. This chapter details the quantitative data and the qualitative findings from the focus groups. The aim here is to evaluate the interpretative mechanisms utilised by each group in order to determine whether any observable variance is in evidence between the purist and peripheral positions. The qualitative data on the representation of femininity, masculinity and ethnicity are analysed to develop an appreciation of subcultural uses and understanding of mediated cultural images, an aspect which is lacking in the current literature. The data from the groups informs this chapter and, as a result of the voiced opinions of a number of the respondents, issues relating to hegemony and the commodification of musical artefacts are also considered. White people make up 75-80% of the global market for rap music, a figure often repeated in the literature of hip-hop studies.

Chapter 7 critically examines the notion of authenticity which is a key feature of the popular discourse of rap and grime music. Using data from the field I explore how authenticity is an intangible and contested concept. Debates of authenticity are used within the machinations of the marketing of popular music and within the discourses of the audience. The research findings from the quantitative and qualitative data are presented to further an understanding of contemporary notions of the authentic in popular culture and, more importantly, how such a concept is incorporated into subcultural being. Four dimensions of authenticity were raised by the focus groups and are presented in this chapter: locality, biography/narrative, vocal delivery and ethnic identity. Through the application of grounded theory I draw on the data to examine the nature of authenticity from the perspective of the research respondents and the importance of this concept to their cultural consumption. Chapters 6 and 7 address the last of the book's main questions, that which relates to the perception of cultural products by consumers.

Biographical issues and methodology

In the tradition of biographical work established by the Chicago School under Park and Burgess, I used my experience and familiarity with the setting of the culture to set up positive research relationships with the respondents (Anderson, 1923; Becker, 1963). Feminist studies have also been influential in the use of such an approach in this study as they sought to bring their research set out of invisibility (McRobbie and Garber, 1975; Pollert, 1981; Oakley, 1981). The feminist approach challenged conventional research approaches which were seen to be patriarchal, favoured relationships between researcher and researched that were hierarchical in structure and treated research subjects as subordinate (Merrill and West, 2009). The research process not only encouraged a sense of reflexivity from the respondents but also enhanced my own understanding of my cultural activities and experiences with the research participants.

Miller (1997: 101) suggests that a researcher's personal biography not only influences the area of investigation but also frames the specifics of the research questions. The decision to conduct research on hip-hop comes from a personal interest in global cultural forms and their incorporation into individuals' sense of personal identity, coupled with a longstanding engagement with varying forms of hip-hop culture. Hodkinson (2005: 131) discusses the idea of researchers, particularly at doctoral level, who have some degree of association to that which is being investigated. The implications of 'insider research' are addressed from a practical and an epistemological stance. Hodkinson raises issues that concern the interpretation and understanding of ethnographic detail from a researcher with some relative cultural proximity to a subculture and its activities. The degree to which the sociological fieldworker is considered either an 'insider' or an 'outsider' by those under investigation will vary depending on their behaviour, including speech, movement and dress, and to the extent to which the researcher considers it significant to be either seen as an 'insider' or 'outsider', which would depend on the context and the group under scrutiny. For example, during the focus group interviews my behaviour was regulated and adapted in order to make the participants feel more comfortable. It was occasionally necessary to adopt the role of somebody with less cultural knowledge; somebody on the peripheries of the phenomenon being studied compared to the research subjects. In this sense the fieldwork strategy was for my role to be that of an apprentice so I could be instructed by the research group (Coffey, 1999). However, this differential approach was not appropriate at a rap gig or club as it would be necessary in order to gain data that would be more pure to appear as a collective member of the audience, following the same ritualistic behaviours as the rest of the attendees. My age during the fieldwork (mid-30s), ethnic background (white) and preferred styles of hip-hop (and, thereby, the acts used as a reference point in conversations) may have acted as determinants of whether co-actors within given situations would perceive the researcher to be inside or outside of their culture. I have engaged at a personal level with aspects of hip-hop culture for many years and although I do not incorporate signifiers of such an involvement in my day to day existence, in terms of dress code and patterns of speech for example, I have a history of consumption of rap records and attendance at hip-hop events. In this respect, this study may be considered to be from an insider-in perspective (MacRae, 2007: 54).

The ethnic background of a social scientist incorporating a focus group methodology has been addressed by Briggs and Cobley who state that from their experience such an approach '... yields a specific kind of data irrespective of the racial identity of the moderator ...' (1999: 339). They maintain that, on occasions when the ethnicity of the researcher and the respondents differs, the task is to facilitate free-flowing discussion with the group at the centre as opposed to researcher-led interviews. This was an issue that was not seen to be significant in my own research as positive relationships were established with all focus groups very quickly.

There are many variant genres within hip-hop, from gangsta rap, through to party rap and conscious rap. My own preference was offered in conversation when deemed necessary, perhaps to illustrate a point with some clarity or to offer an example of my own knowledge and experience in order to further the relationship between researcher and the object of the research. It became clear within the focus group interview process that many of the acts that I had knowledge of were unknown to a number of the participants from the Rochester and Brighton groups who were, for the most part, very much consumers of mainstream hip-hop. Whereas I choose to listen to acts such as Immortal Technique, Clipping, MF Doom and Latyrx these groups were very much more interested in mainstream, corporate acts such as Kanye West, Eminem, Jay-Z and Drake. Had I used my favoured artists in focus group discussions this would have undoubtedly led to a degree of alienation for the respondents with no prior knowledge of these acts.

Brewer states that an effective ethnographer, in gaining trust from the subject, must '… eat like they eat, speak like they speak and do as they do …' (2000: 85). This is a common line within the literature of ethnography and follows on from the anthropological writing of Malinowski who perceived the need to fully immerse oneself in the culture in order to gain an understanding of the subtle complexities of the matter being investigated. However, it was decided that total immersion within the hip-hop culture, incorporating a variant form of speech and dress code, would only hinder my understanding as the participants would likely see me as a 'faker' and would therefore cease to engage with me in a positive manner. There does need to be some demonstration that the researcher has some background understanding, some form of cultural competence (Bourdieu, 1986) and subcultural capital (Thornton, 1995) of the lifestyle choices made by the individual participants, and therefore an introductory conversation with each focus group included an historical overview of my own personal involvement with rap music. The fact that I have regularly attended hip-hop events and concerts since 1991 made the participant observation aspect of the fieldwork uncomplicated inasmuch as there was a familiarity with the expected customs and behaviour patterns at such happenings so as not to stand out in the crowd when undertaking research whilst also maintaining '… rigorous standards of objective reporting designed to overcome … potential bias …' (Angrosino and

Mays de Perez, 2003: 108). It was decided that during the research I would not dress in a spectacular hip-hop style nor incorporate vernacular speech patterns or walk using hip-hop mannerisms. During the fieldwork I dressed in the manner that I always have when engaging within the cultural sphere of hip-hop. This conscious notion of self-presentation reflected the significance of impression management to the research (Hammersley and Atkinson, 1983). The approach taken in the research was that I would demonstrate basic understanding, experience and knowledge of the culture but that the group members, as the focal point of the interviews, possessed a more enriched and perceptive interpretation of hip-hop and grime. It is argued that insider status enhances the quality and effectiveness of qualitative interviews (Hodkinson, 2005: 138) and therefore acceptance of my own experience and knowledge by each focus group aided the research.

In regards to the methodologies used in the research for this book, I used a mixed methods approach combining both quantitative and qualitative data. The quantitative data came from 132 questionnaires which were completed from a range of sources including educational institutions and internet music forums. I sought the opinions of fans and those who declared no particular fandom or affiliation to hip-hop or grime culture in an attempt to establish whether variations existed between these sets of respondents with regards to their views on the culture. The qualitative aspect of the research centred on five focus groups who met regularly. This approach allowed the respondents the opportunity to discuss aspects of the culture that they were aware of rather than address a prescribed set of criteria established by the researcher. Both the quantitative and qualitative data demonstrated that the research respondents declared a preference for American performers and, therefore, the focus in this book is largely on the consumption of American rap artists by young adults. British rap and grime acts were mentioned during the fieldwork by a number of the respondents and the relative positions of popularity of artists from the States and the UK in terms of consumption is reflected herein.

I also attended a range of parties, concerts and nightclubs where hip-hop was a central component to further enhance my knowledge of the field although this book largely centres on the focus group interviews, with reference to the quantitative data where appropriate. The research process began (slowly) in 2008 and ended in 2012. I also spent a considerable amount of time and effort in trying to secure interviews with a number of recording artists and other practitioners in the field of hip-hop and grime and managed to speak to a significant number of artists. This book, however, centres on the young (and not so young) people in the research who live and breathe hip-hop and grime. In my opinion a book such as this, one which privileges the voices of those engaged at a subcultural level with hip-hop and grime as opposed to the academic musings of a scholar far removed from the grassroots level, is long overdue.

Chapter 1

Popular music studies and Hip-Hop

"Know your history ... "[1]

Introduction

I begin by looking at the field of Popular Music Studies and the chapter then moves onto a brief history of hip-hop in the UK before a more in-depth focus on hip-hop's origins in the United States of America. A detailed history of British rap artists is perhaps overdue but as a result of the research respondents in this study favouring American artists this book is not the right place to offer such an overview. The chapter then moves on to a discussion of academic research in the field of hip-hop studies. Both empirical and textual studies are considered and I highlight the contribution that this research offers to the field. An historical overview of grime music is detailed in Chapter 5.

Popular music studies

The study of popular music is a recently established, though still marginalised, interdisciplinary academic area which has seen researchers in musicology, ethnomusicology, sociology, anthropology, media and cultural studies, psychology and cultural geography react against the traditional precepts of their disciplines in order to politicise music (Hesmondhalgh and Negus, 2002: 6). Historically there has been a degree of hostility to, and a trivialising of, popular music in academic discourse and this has been an ongoing issue for writers in the field of popular music studies as much of their work has lent itself to a defence of their analytical approach (Moore, 2003: 7). Popular music has long been seen by theorists as devoid of creative artistry. Theodor Adorno's (1991) rubrics of mass production, standardisation, false differentiation and the regression of listening are at the centre of such an approach. Adorno argues that the culture industry centred on popular music produces formulaic commodities which are fetishised in order to assume significance. This results in impotence for the listener wherein '... an approach in terms of value judgements has become a fiction for the person who finds himself hemmed in by standardised musical goods ...' (ibid.: 30). Adorno presents the audience as passive and easily manipulated by the machinations of the culture industry. There is a lack of agency in his theoretical conceptualisation of popular music listening, a notion which is contested at the theoretical centre of this book. Krims argues for a move away from a reliance on an Adornian perspective, stating that '... Adorno constitutes one of the single greatest obstacles to developing a Marxist analysis of music ...' (2003: 131). This is seen as a result of Adorno's relevance to a particular historical moment and it is argued that his theoretical position lacks longevity. The process of flexible accumulation, or post-Fordism, has markedly altered the capitalist structure to such an extent that Adorno's work becomes increasingly irrelevant. The relatively inexpensive nature of musical production and distribution in contemporary culture has disabled the notion of standardisation as an increasing number of people have access to tools such as home computer music software packages as well as autonomous distribution via the internet without the need for a record company. Middleton (1990: 61) argues that Adorno's ideas are strongest when applied to production practices but are considerably weaker when concerned with the dissemination and reception of popular music by its audience.

Hall and Whannel's 1964 study *The Popular Arts* is credited as being the first cultural studies examination of popular music culture (Storey, 1996: 99). They argue that there is often a difference between the use intended of a musical artefact by the producers and the use made of that product by the consumers. This is an important idea for this book as later chapters show that the focus groups demonstrated varying reading positions and interpretative perspectives, highlighting the contested nature and contemporary values placed upon musical consumption and subsequent identity formation through group affiliation. Many of the research respondents were critical of the output of mainstream rap music, thereby challenging Adorno's notion of a passive, unreflective audience.

Murdock and Phelps' (1972) pioneering study of British teenagers and popular music consumption argued that there was a correlation between 'taste clusters' and age, social class and school commitment. The notion of taste clusters was categorised by the dichotomous markers of mainstream/ underground and activity-potency/understandability. Activity-potency refers to black music stressing beat and rhythm, whereas understandability is defined as music performed by whites which stresses the lyrical aspect of the song. They found that '... many middle class pupils largely rejected this 'mainstream' pop and preferred the various minority styles, generally lumped together under the umbrella heading of 'underground-progressive' rock ...' (ibid.: 8). This form was embraced by the middle class research respondents who used music to encapsulate values and roles undervalued by schools. They were largely isolated from street culture and therefore utilised music to form aspects of rebellious and anti-establishment identities, whilst retaining a conformist approach to their academic life (Coleman and Hendry, 1990). The working-class members of the respondents tended to favour mainstream cultural products which served as the background to other collective activities centred on street culture. This was an area that particularly interested me in my own work and I was sceptical as to whether such demarcations would be possible in my own research. As will be shown in later chapters, there were some very interesting findings relating to socio-economic position and hip-hop consumption. The term underground is used in this book to refer to forms of hip-hop and grime culture which contain elements of '… anti-corporate production practices and … anti-materialistic music messages …' (Harrison, 2009: 165). It is within the underground spaces that purist subcultural activity occurs, where agency exists for those in the centre of hip-hop culture.

In 1981 the academic journal *Popular Music* first appeared and the concept for the International Association for the Study of Popular Music (IASPM) was developed at a conference in Amsterdam (Horn, 2011: 471). Although many writers in the field claim that this was the beginning of 'popular music studies', Middleton states that a genealogy of the study of popular music can be traced back to the 19th century (2011: 472). Three waves of academic concern can be identified in popular music studies literature from 1981 onwards. First, the journal *Popular Music*'s main focus in the early years was on theory and the political dimensions of theoretical debates. Second, the study of popular music in the 1990s became increasingly diversified and included a focus on music scenes, local music-making practices and the role of new technologies (Bennett et al, 2006: 5). Finally, an interest in, and investigation of, the mundanity of music and its uses within the context of everyday life established itself as a key focus in the early years of the twenty first century (DeNora, 2000).

Definitions of the term popular music centre on the commodified nature of the form. Burnett states that '… when we speak of popular music we speak of music that is commercially oriented …' (1996: 35). Tagg (1982), however, argues that the manner of distribution is significant and that focus on the recorded aspect of the sound, as opposed to oral transmission or scribed notation, allows for a better understanding of the term. Shuker suggests that '… a satisfactory definition of popular music must encompass both musical and socioeconomic characteristics …' (1998: 228). The focus for Shuker is on both the musical specifics as well as a consideration of the audience. When related to rap music,

Burnett's definition fails to fully address aspects of underground hip-hop which is a significant component of the culture as a dichotomy between commercial and underground is perceived by rap consumers (McLeod, 1999). Negus suggests that the relationship between independent labels (i.e. underground) and major labels (i.e. commercial) is symbiotic rather than oppositional as the major companies use underground producers '... as an often optional and usually elastic repertoire source ...' (1999: 96). There exists a commercial aspect to underground rap (Asante Jr., 2008) which is not considered in McLeod's analysis and which can be seen as romanticising the role of artists that are perceived to be within the realms of the underground scene.

Hip-Hop culture in the UK

Hip-hop is now a key genre within the popular culture industry in the UK. Bramwell (2015) notes that there are few studies which focus on how both hip-hop and grime are used by youth groups to form aspects of identity. He argues that the production of both musical forms is more complex than many authors suggest as their roots in British consumption and production do not solely rely on aspects of black culture mediated through Caribbean culture. In this respect, UK hip-hop is a localised variant of globalised US musical forms (Bennett, 1999b). UK hip-hop and grime should be seen as amalgams, echoing the very foundations of hip-hop culture in the Bronx in the early 1970s. For example, hip-hop has been appropriated into the hybrid genre musical scene of *desi*, a popular mash-up of tastes and music popular amongst South Asian youths in the UK (Kim, 2014). In the desi scene, hip-hop is just one of a number of diverse musical forms which is used by youths as a marker of identification. Kim's study focuses on the concept of scene and she does not therefore see her research participants as existing within a subculture.

Rap music initially became popular with British reggae audiences as a result of its links to Jamaican sound systems. The pioneering British rap artists and collectives grew out of the reggae and soul scenes of the early 1980s (Gilroy, 1992: 258) with artists such as Smiley Culture incorporating a 'fast chat' form of reggae toasting, very similar to forms of rap delivery. Much in the same way that artists such as the Last Poets and The Watts Prophets can be seen as proto-rap in America, many reggae toasters and dub lyricists can be seen as early incarnations of UK rap artists and MCs. Radio DJs Tim Westwood, Dave Pearce and John Peel played a central role in the dissemination of hip-hop culture to British audiences as all regularly featured rap music in their respective shows, with Tim Westwood in particular becoming a major player as a promoter for American rap artists coming to the UK to play shows. The American hip-hop films *Wild Style* (Ahearn, USA, 1983) and *Beat Street* (Lathan, USA, 1984) were significant in informing a British audience of hip-hop culture as did the performance of *The Message* by Grandmaster Flash and the Furious Five on Channel 4's music programme The Tube in 1983. Two documentaries by film-maker Dick Fontaine, *Beat This!* (BBC, 1984) and *Bombin'* (Channel 4, 1987), illustrate how American rap music and graffiti were attractive to British youths and are useful resources to develop an appreciation of how American cultural products were introduced to audiences in the UK through the incorporation of workshops which taught youths how to spray paint as well as demonstrating various scratch techniques on turntables. The first British magazine to solely focus on rap music was *Hip-Hop Connection*, first published in 1988.

Many pop artists in the early 1980s used raps in their songs as a way of appropriating the latest musical trend from America but the first British rap tune to be released was *Christmas Rapping* by Dizzy Heights (1982, Polydor). UK rap has been marked by an initial reliance on the American template. For example, the British rapper Derek B, amongst others, used an American accent on much of his work which led to accusations of inauthenticity. As UK hip-hop flourished there developed a reluctance to be seen as a facsimile of the rap scene in the States. This reaction led to the creation of a number of sub-genres such as hip-house, trip-hop and to contemporary artists such as Roots Manuva's occasional use of Jamaican patois, a means of establishing ethnic heritage. The accents used by UK rappers remains to be an important means of determining a sense of authenticity as can be seen in the work of early rappers such as Monie Love and Rodney P of the London Posse and later artists such as Skinnyman, Scroobius Pip and Braintax.

Debbie 'Cookie' Pryce, one half of hip-house pioneers The Cookie Crew, stated in an interview I conducted with her that rap was very much a South London phenomenon:

DP: … when we started in the 80s there were just lots of people and hip-hop groups doing their stuff that were from South London. You had the Cookie Crew, Monie Love, Cut Master Swift … there were loads. All the groups came from South London. You had a few from the East, from the North or whatever but we always got on. We always had that territorial thing, I'm very territorial about South London. I still am, but it was more, we were like, unified. We came more together when we met at Covent Garden or we met at a hip-hop jam. It was, I don't know, it was just like a small community. And it was amazing.

Most significant from the above quote is not so much the historical accuracy, or otherwise, of placing South London at the epicentre of the UK rap movement, but the sense of ownership that Debbie felt of the culture and community within it. Dürrschmidt (2000) uses the concept of milieu to describe how people living in London are culturally dis-embedded and re-embedded and thereby seek 'normalcy' through routines and stable, identifiable and measured actions. This idea of milieu can be applied to Debbie's quote as although degrees of territoriality existed there was still a strong bond of unity amongst the different London factions when they congregated. The re-embedding in Dürrschmidt's work can be related to the altering of the American form of hip-hop culture into its British variants via adoption, transformation and retrenchment (Webb, 2007). In this sense, for UK rappers to be taken seriously by their audience they needed to somewhat transform rather than copy the template set by American artists. As will be shown in later chapters, many in the focus groups for my own research favoured American rappers as they were perceived to be more authentic whereas many British acts were often, perhaps surprisingly, seen as redundant due to their reliance on a generic formula which they did not help to establish.

Morgan's (2008) study of hip-hop culture is rare in the literature as it includes a genealogy of UK hip-hop and the subsequent variant culture of grime, although he does not examine the relationship between text and reception as his work is historical in impetus. The focus in my own study is primarily on rap acts from the United States with some consideration of British grime artists. The research group consumed a range of hip-hop; a significant number listened to commercially successful mainstream rappers whereas others actively sought out records that they perceived to be within the 'underground'. Gangsta rap was discussed extensively in the focus groups as this was seen to be the most visible sub-genre form in the mainstream.

The origins of Hip-Hop

The history of hip-hop and rap music has been chronicled in numerous studies, including works by Lipsitz (1994), Rose (1994), Bennett (2001), Perry (2004),

Quinn (2005), Schloss (2009) and Harrison (2009). Hip-hop sprang from the Bronx district of New York in the early 1970s and is omnipresent in contemporary Western culture (Rose, 1994; Negus, 1999; Ramsey Jr., 2003). Schloss (2009: 5) states that the term hip-hop relates to three different, but overlapping, categories. The first of these refers to a group of interconnected, mostly unmediated, creative aspects in different forms—sound, visual and movement. This includes such cultural practices as breaking and graffiti writing. The second relates to hip-hop (or rap) music and the third to an identifiable collectivity, a loose demographic designation for contemporary African American youth. The main focus in this study is on the second of these categories.

Rap is a narrative form of vocal delivery which is spoken in a cadenced patois (Bennett, 2001: 89), accompanied by highly rhythmic, electronically based music (Rose, 1994: 2). Krims (2000) develops a typology of rap genres based on musical style, vocal delivery and the issues addressed. He contends that the culture is dynamic and therefore such categorisation should be understood as existing within a state of creative flux and that such terms are often contested by artists and audience alike. Party rap, mack rap, jazz/bohemian rap and reality rap are not seen by Krims as mutually exclusive and each contains sub-categories, such as gangsta rap as a sub-set of reality rap. Party rap relates to the earliest form of rap where the onus was on the MC to create a positive atmosphere for the audience and links to the Sugar Hill sound of the late 1970s. Mack rap relies on R'n'B musicality whilst the lyrics and imagery centre on ostentatious displays of wealth and a celebration of hegemonic masculinity. Jazz/bohemian rap is perhaps best exemplified in the 'daisy age' sound of De La Soul and A Tribe Called Quest who combined a sense of Afrocentricity with messages of peace and unity. Reality rap's core themes revolve around the ghetto and toughness, usually manifested in terms of physical masculinity. The jazz/bohemian and party rap forms have all but disappeared from mainstream hip-hop whereas both mack and reality are evident in the work of recent commercially successful acts such as 50 Cent, Snoop Dogg, Jay-Z, Lil' Wayne, OFWGKTA, Kendrick Lamar and Schoolboy Q. Williams (2011: 54) states that such distinctions are analytically useful but should not be seen as absolute as there are a number of artists who utilise many of the varying sub-genre forms in their work.

The precise dating of an emergent cultural form is epistemologically problematic, yet 1974 is the date given by three pioneers of the form, Afrika Bambaataa, DJ Kool Herc and Grandmaster Flash, as the birth date of the culture (Perkins, 1996). However, August 11 1973 is also cited as the date of the first hip-hop party, hosted by Kool Herc at 1520 Sedgwick Avenue. The term hip-hop was coined by Bambaataa who, in turn, took the phrase from DJ Lovebug Starski. The original four elements of hip-hop, namely breaking (later termed breakdancing), graffiti, DJing (or turntablism) and rapping, were interlinked although the DJ, the most essential component of hip-hop block parties, was often celebrated as the star of the nascent form. The pioneering years of hip-hop were concerned with celebratory aspects wherein lyrics were often either not incorporated or contained word play as opposed to specific messages. The eventual use of lyrics would become important '... as a community-wide means of addressing and negotiating the extreme socio-economic circumstances which characterised everyday life in the Bronx ...' (Bennett, 2001: 89). The spotlight shifted around 1978 from the DJ to the MC, later to be known as the rapper. The MC (microphone controller or master of ceremonies) hailed from a long tradition of black radio disc-jockeys from as far back as the 1950s who would use repetitive phrases and slang terminology to entice a crowd to dance. Grandmaster Flash was one of the first DJs to assemble a crew around him so that he could solely concentrate on his mixing abilities. Keith Wiggins (aka Cowboy), Melvin Glover (Melle Mel) and Nathaniel Glover (Kid Creole) became the focal point of the group known as the Furious Five and their emergence was swiftly followed by others who would perform battle raps in an attempt to claim microphone supremacy. Key protagonists at this time included Grand Wizard Theodore and the Fantastic Five, DJ Breakout and the Funky Four, Cold Crush Brothers and Afrika Bambaataa and Soul Sonic Force.

The release, in 1979, of *Rapper's Delight* by the Sugar Hill Gang (Sugar Hill Records) is commonly regarded as the first rap record. It was, however, preceded by the B-side track *King Tim III (Personality Jock)* by the Fatback Band, although the Sugar Hill Gang's song is often cited as the first example of the genre to be heard by a wide audience due to its commercial success — around two million copies of the record were sold globally. The lack of commercial interest in the genre in its early years meant that the culture could develop with relative autonomy outside of the machinations of the recording industry. There was a distinct reluctance to commit rap music to vinyl from the pre-eminent performers of the era, seemingly due to the view that hip-hop was seen as an extended live and spontaneous musical form and therefore not suited to a recording. This is a relevant idea which, as will be shown later in this study, retains value as it was found in the fieldwork that many research respondents perceived hip-hop to be more artistically authentic within the live arena rather than on record. Many hip-hop performers reacted to *Rapper's Delight* by stating that they thought that a hip-hop recording would be impossible to produce. For many in this burgeoning culture, the onus was on live events, not mediated performance but, as the popularity of the genre spread, the music '... no longer indexed live events but was disseminated by way of self-contained texts ...' (Dimitriadis, 2009: 74). During the initial years of the culture's commercialisation, all of the original elements of hip-hop were present as a mediated spectacle but around 1985 hip-hop became synonymous with rap as breakdancing and graffiti were no longer seen to be conducive to mass marketing strategies. In this respect, the mid-1980s and the commercial crossover success of acts such as Run DMC and LL Cool J can be seen as key moments in the co-optation of hip-hop by the culture industries.

A shift in lyrical content, visual presentation and overall artistic outlook of a new rap sub-genre occurred in the late 1980s and is largely seen as a product of a number of combined elements—a reaction from West Coast America artists to their East Coast peers and rivals, who they often saw as too middle-class and intellectual and did not truly represent their own experiences or values, and as a reaction to the escalating gang culture and economic deprivation in the post-industrial city. It can be suggested that gangsta rap, more than any other form of hip-hop culture, revels in its own commodification as it celebrates the accrual of material gain (Krims, 2000). Gangsta rap relies largely on messages concerning the significance of territorial awareness, misogyny and the reality of living life at street level. In content and form, gangsta rap lyrics '... explore how groups and individuals negotiate their social positioning and, as artists, their own roles as cultural mediators, commercial producers, and musical personas ...' (Quinn, 2005: 12). The group N.W.A. (Niggaz With Attitude) are seen as the founders of the gangsta rap sub-genre. Their first single *Boyz-N-The Hood* tells a narrative of a day in the life of rapper Eazy E, containing liaisons with car thieves, crackhead friends and an instance of domestic violence towards his girlfriend—all of which would become regular and long-standing narrative themes within gangsta rap. Gangsta rap relies on a sense of nihilistic experience, a disillusionment with post-industrial, late twentieth century, inner-city existence. This sub-genre is significant as '... it emerged from and voiced the experiences and desires of an oppressed community in a period of economic transformation ...' (Quinn, 2005: 11). Perry suggests that the gangsta rapper successfully subverted and reconstructed stereotypes in order to reveal them as false or not metonymically sound and that '... the glamour of the high-rolling drug dealer is exploited for the sake of a counter-hegemonic space, an alternative power in the face of white supremacy and the panoptic surveillance of black bodies in ghettos ...' (2004: 104).

Critical theorists such as G. Craige Lewis (2009) see hip-hop culture in general as a negative expression of the views of the black diaspora. On closer inspection such criticisms generally only refer to gangsta rap. The shock tactics of gangsta rap has led to the music being associated with issues of youth violence and crime in popular discourse and has, according to Bennett (2001) resulted in rap being more rigorously censored than any other contemporary youth music. The scapegoating of hip-hop in the popular press, in line with Cohen's notion of moral panics (1972), has arguably allowed the perpetuation within popular discourse of the stereotyped image of black culture, and significantly black masculine culture, as aggressive, criminal and uncivilised. bell hooks asserts that '... within white supremacist capitalist patriarchy, rebel black masculinity has been idolised and punished, romanticised yet vilified ...' (1992 : 96).

Hip-hop today is a global, multi-billion dollar industry. The majority of the genre's commercially successful rappers had their origins within the gangsta sub-genre but have somewhat diluted their sound in order to cross over into the mainstream (Garofalo, 1993). Hip-hop has grown from an underground subculture from New York and has spawned multi-national organisations and artists. The graffiti and breakdancing element of hip-hop culture has been all but lost to the mainstream public sphere as a tangible form of artistic expression, replaced in importance by the elements that can easily be commodified by multinational corporations.

Perry (2004: 10) states that, despite cross cultural influences and collaborators, hip-hop culture and rap music remains a form of black American music. Four reasons are given for this claim — (1) AAVE (African American Vernacular English — often referred to as Ebonics) is the prime language used, (2) it has a direct derivation from black American oral tradition, (3) it has a direct derivation from black American musical traditions and (4) its political location in society is distinctly linked to black people, music and cultural forms. Kitwana (2005: 156) argues that the technological age in which we live helps the culture to remain a form of black expression regardless of the degree of commercialisation that occurs. Hip-hop is still very much dominated by young black artists with only a few white rappers gaining credibility and commercial success — Eminem (USA), Beastie Boys (USA), Skinnyman (UK) and Professor Green (UK) amongst them. Afrika Bambaataa (cited in Fernando Jr., 1994) states that he sees hip-hop as a colourless culture because many of the records that he played at the beginning of his career spanned both the musical and race spectrum, from jazz, to soul and R'n'B through to heavy metal and European electronic bands such as Kraftwerk.

Studies in hip-hop

Hip-hop has become a focus for research in the sociology of popular culture as well as generating a significant body of work which is aimed at a populist arena, as an aspect of fan culture. Hip-hop has become a cultural field and an industry in itself has burgeoned in this respect in recent years. Toop (1984), Fernando Jr. (1994) and Chang (1995) offer historical celebrations of hip-hop which do not fully engage with issues relating to representing images and audience reception and identity formation. Biographies of rappers are also popular and plentiful. Eminem is an example of an artist who has not only written two autobiographies (*Angry Blonde* in 2000 and *The Way I Am* in 2009) but has also had a number of books written about him (Gittins, 2001; Bozza, 2004; Nelson, 2008; Hasted, 2009; Heatley, 2012 and Westerfil, 2012).

There has been an expansion of qualitative studies of hip-hop in recent years as theorists look to examine the uses of hip-hop and rap in the lives of those who both create and consume the culture on a regular basis. Such a shift has occurred in relation to the third wave of popular music studies, namely a focus on the mundane uses of music in every day life (De Nora, 2000). In the last ten years there have emerged a number of international studies on hip-hop (Solomon, 2005; Condry, 2006; Ntarangwi, 2009). There are both theoretical and textual studies on hip-hop but there are few qualitative accounts of the interpretation of the commodified form of hip-hop culture for consumers in the UK. This study, therefore, seeks to address this gap in the literature.

Qualitative studies of hip-hop

One significant British study researched white consumers of hip-hop in Northern England (Bennett, 1999c, 2001). Bennett states that the predominately white nature of his research location, Newcastle, resulted in '... a celebration of blackness in the absence of blackness ...' (2001: 99). Those who actively engaged with hip-hop and rap were subjected to a form of deflected racism from the mainstream *towny* youth. This tool of division was used by the hip-hoppers as a means of further establishing their claims to authentic cultural activity and the subversion of pejorative terminology allowed them to separate themselves from mainstream sensibilities. His research presents a clear sense of hip-hoppers as 'other' to mainstream culture and offers an interpretation of these groups as clearly distinguished from the parent culture, regardless of subsequent work by Bennett which argues against the concept of youth collectivity in support of the post-subcultural turn (Bennett, 2011). Bramwell (2015) and Webb (2007) offer valuable insights into British variants of hip-hop and the cultural activity of young people engaged in grime and trip-hop respectively. Bramwell sees both hip-hop and grime as liberatory forces that drive a sense of community and belongingness for his London based research participants. Both musical forms are central to the identity formation of his participants and help these individuals to form tightly bonded friendship groups. Webb's focus is much more on the transformation and modification of the musical form in relation to localised elements of the global flow, thereby utilising the work of David Harvey (1997).

France and the UK are the research sites in relation to hip-hop for Rupa Huq (2007). Extensive empirical evidence is offered in her work, notably from Manchester with a group of young people involved with a hip-hop project. Hip-hop is seen here as a positive influence in the lives of the young people in this study as a means of keeping out of trouble as well as being an important source of collective and individual identity. Huq criticises attempts to demonise hip-hop culture and rap music through moral panics and argues that, rather than a tool of social and ethnic division, hip-hop was seen as a means of uniting various groups. The projects that she focuses upon in her ethnographic work are seen as routes of empowerment for her respondents and also contribute to their identities. Huq's empirical evidence demonstrates the positive impact that involvement in hip-hop culture had on her research respondents and she states that this is not an aspect of the form which is reported enough. Huq utilises the concept of subculture in a cautious manner as she is fearful of the '... intellectual strait jacket ...' (2007: 24) that can potentially be placed on the researcher by utilising such a theoretical framework.

Harrison's (2009) research incorporates participant observation in the Bay Area of San Francisco and interview data sourced from local hip-hop producers is presented. Thornton's (1995) idea of subcultural capital, and its use as a means to identify group boundaries, is a key consideration in Harrison's work. He discusses the needs of the different collective groups in the field to distinguish between themselves and others with less cultural engagement and knowledge. It is in the sense of subcultural capital, that Harrison terms 'knowing what's up', that helps subculturalists in their situational assessments of one another (2009:

111). Such aspects include dress code, vernacular speech patterns and cultural knowledge. This is an important aspect that also developed in my own fieldwork as it became evident that many individuals who engaged in hip-hop and grime required markers of opposition to enable a more nuanced understanding of their own cultural practices and values.

Joseph Schloss (2009) also reinforces the value of cultural knowledge and uses the term 'foundation' to illustrate the historical appreciation of the form which was of paramount importance to the b-boys in his study. Schloss's concept of foundation can be used as a marker of subcultural acceptance and affiliation. Schloss's study focuses on the dance aspect of the culture rather than the more common academic investigations of rapping and/or DJing. Schloss does not apply subcultural theory in his work although his use of the term hip-hop community can in many ways be seen as synonymous with subculture as there are forms of collectivity, resistance and distinctive identities at play. Within Schloss's study, participant observation at hip-hop parties and interviews with b-boys, b-girls and DJs inform the findings viewing hip-hop in a very optimistic manner, as a community resource which enables many to socialise in safe environments. For Schloss, hip-hop as seen in the field is entirely different to the mediated rap imagery that pervades American television networks. Schloss does not ask his research subjects about their views and opinions on mainstream rap imagery to any great extent, therefore this is an area that needs further enquiry. In this book, the recurring images that are projected by mainstream record labels in hip-hop videos and other promotional material are discussed in detail with the research groups in order to more fully understand audience decoding of representing images.

Tiongson's (2013) ethnographic study was also undertaken in the Bay Area of San Francisco and illustrates how the concept of nation can be conceptualised within the context of hip-hop. The research focuses on Filipino DJs and how their creativity renders racial differences benign due to their utilisation of a black cultural form. Authenticity is a key concern for Tiongson but rather than centring the debate on artistic authenticity his focus is on racial authenticity for young Filipinos in the light of appropriating a black cultural form. India MacWeeney (2008) suggests that knowledge of the global cultural form allows individuals to establish a sense of authenticity and 'street cred' within their own localised spaces. Her ethnographic investigation into the identity formation of Chicano teenagers from the Northern New Mexico city of Española showed that group affiliation and cohesion centred on cultural knowledge as a means of an individual's validation by the collective. These studies show that local variants of the culture are constructed through an understanding of the global mechanisms of hip-hop. The cultural knowledge, the foundation, serves as a means of gaining acceptance into substantive elective cultural groupings. MacWeeney addresses aspects of audience interpretation in her ethnographic account, focusing on matters of taste value judgements and authenticity rather than an analysis of the ideologies and their reception present in rap music. Authenticity, for the participants in MacWeeney's research, is the fundamental aspect for group engagement in hip-hop collectives. Of note is the research subjects' reluctance to discuss what makes an individual authentic. Instead, they centre their discussion on what behaviours and attitudes leads others to being labelled as inauthentic. This was an area that I was very keen to discuss with my research respondents to see if such views would be held by groups of young people in the UK. Harrison (2009), Schloss (2009) and MacWeeney (2008) all discuss the need for the substantive groups in their respective research to differentiate themselves from others who are deemed to be not worthy of social affiliation.

International research sites on hip-hop, including Japan (Condry, 2006), Germany (Bennett, 1999b) and East Africa (Ntarangwi, 2009), have formed the basis for a small number of ethnographic participant observation studies. Although some studies do not utilise subcultural theory in their exploration of the form they are of relevance here due to the research methodologies used. Condry's work looks at hip-hop identity in the face of globalisation and argues that a vehement sense of Japanese identity is evoked in the country's rap artists as the culture developed as a grassroots response to the cultural form rather than as a result of commercial factors. He asserts that the subsequent drive by major labels to push hip-hop in the Japanese marketplace resulted in not just the massification of popular culture but also to an increased diversification of niche markets which catered for specialised fans. Condry argues that in the 1990s, popular culture became an increasingly central component of life for Japanese society in general. In his study he positions subcultures as being sufficiently able to relocate to spaces and forms of consumption that may bear relation to, but are significantly different from, this newfound mainstream reliance on forms of cultural engagement. The issue of globalisation is also addressed by Ntarangwi (2009) who argues that East African hip-hop allows a platform for social commentary for those who engage with the culture although the work presents no direct evidence from audience members to verify this assertion. Interviews with hip-hop artists are detailed yet the voices of the audience are absent, although Ntarangwi claims a number of things on their behalf. Andy Bennett (1999b) contributes to the literature with his study of a community music project based in Frankfurt-am-Main, Germany. Rap music was seen as being reworked by a number of ethnic minority groups as a mode of expression for a number of local issues. The study focuses on Turkish language rap and how it was seen to construct a doubling of marginalised identity (Toynbee, 2002). The global form was assimilated using a complex exchange which aided the articulation of peripheral identities for the individuals who created and consumed these variant and localised hip-hop forms.

Sharma (2010) and Neff (2009) both utilise in-depth interviews for their research but focus on hip-hop practitioners rather than consumers. Sharma looks at *desis*, second generation Asian immigrants in America, and how they navigate musical networks to align themselves with the underprivileged black population. The ethnographic research focus for Sharma is to consider class, racial and geographical aspects and how these impact upon the creativity of the desi population. Neff (2009) researches the role of hip-hop culture in the Mississippi Delta, an area synonymous with the Blues music of the 1920s, from the perspective of its cultural creators rather than the consumers. Subcultural theory is a key area addressed by Mair's (2008) study of desi culture in America. The focus here is on desi appropriation of hip-hop dress code and how this is used as a marker of differentiation. In-depth interviews were utilised as a means of assessing desi hip-hop identity and Mair concludes that the alignment with black culture comes from desi disenfranchisement from the wider upwardly mobile culture that pervades American cultural values.

Dimitriadis (2009) discusses the uses of hip-hop culture and rap music in a study which ran for two and a half years in an unnamed small Midwestern American city. For his research subjects, consumption of this cultural form established a sense of personal distinctiveness and ownership of place which reflected in the identity and friendship networks constructed by these young people. Dimitriadis notes that taste in rap music, and subsequent value judgements from others, was seen as very much connected to notions of place as the research respondents stated that they favoured one geographic variant of rap music over all others (i.e. West Coast, East Coast, Southern and other regions). This stress on the local is seen as the result of an anxiety of place, wherein rappers attempt to '... single themselves out in a broadly homogeneous global culture ...' (Dimitriadis, ibid.: 74). Although Dimitriadis does not use subcultural theory in his writing, it is clear that matters of autonomy, consistent distinctiveness and cultural resistance are present in these groups.

Anthony Gunter's (2010) study on black youth focuses on education, home life and 'on road' (i.e. street corner and public spaces) subcultural activity. He states that hip-hop was seen by many within his research group as a transmitter of the image of the 'badman'. This appealing character type is emulated by those who wish to be seen as possessing forms of power and respect in their local area. Gunter, however, points out that this form of social performance did not extend to criminal activity and, in fact, such behaviour was seen in a negative light. The hyper-masculinist posturing engaged in by a number of Gunter's research respondents is seen as a way of negotiating safe paths through neighbourhood life. Reference to hip-hop in Gunter's work is, however, limited as other forms of music take a more central role in the lives of the young people in his study.

Critical investigations of hip-hop culture largely focus on the aural aspect of the form, namely rap music. A notable exception to this is Nancy McDonald (2001) who undertook participant observation in London and New York in order to uncover the 'voice' of the graffiti artists that she observed and interviewed. Utilising subcultural theory she found that the secretive, male-dominated groupings involved in graffiti used the form to portray certain masculine characteristics, including territorial marking. The art form allowed them a platform to express their identities and frustrations at the disparity that they saw in society. MacDonald's study follows the general trend in writing in the field as perceiving hip-hop culture as possessing a positive impact on the lives of the individuals in the research.

Textual studies of hip-hop

The textual analysis of hip-hop discusses the culture from two approaches, first a description of the form and second a macro-theoretical stance on arguments of poverty and marginality.

Feminist analysis of hip-hop centres on the representation of gender and the perceived misogyny present in rap lyrics and imagery (Rose, 1994, 2008; Morgan, 1999; Sharpley-Whiting, 2007). Mainstream hip-hop culture is seen to reinforce and perpetuate patriarchal ideology. In *The Hip-Hop Wars*, Rose states that the existence of sexism in hip-hop music is beyond doubt and that rap music '… promotes sexist and demeaning images of black women as its bread-and-butter product …' (2008: 114). The audience's understanding of poetic fictionalities in gangsta rap is discussed by Quinn (2005: 34) wherein she assumes the reading position of the audience as one of sufficient sophistication to be able to develop an appreciation of the rappers' utilisation of metaphor and allusion. However, Quinn, in line with the majority of the work in the current literature, does not offer any evidence which is empirical in nature, thereby weakening her argument. The topic of poetic fictionalities is addressed in this study by an examination of the qualitative data and is discussed in Chapters 6 and 7.

Marxist perspectives on hip-hop are offered by Cashmore (1997), Ogbar (2007) and Asante Jr. (2008). They argue that the white ownership of mainstream rap music has aided the representation of blacks in the media as criminally minded and hyper-sexualised deviants. Such use of caricature and parody can be seen as instruments of oppression and are aspects of the '... routines of institutionalised domination ...' (Pieterse, 1995: 226). Minstrelsy was an earlier form of cultural representation which also contained such portrayals of deviancy in its characterisation of blackness (Lott, 1995; Meer, 2005; Pfeifer, 2007). This is not to suggest that mainstream rap music imagery contains what Young (1996: 55) terms aggressive imperialist visions but that white hegemony is maintained through the repetition of imagery which becomes naturalised as a result of its ubiquity (Cashmore, 1997; Asante Jr., 2008). hooks (1992) argues that the subtle nuances of media representations of blackness rarely challenge white supremacy; rather they can be seen to reinforce and reinscribe it. George (1988) argues that black artists have been directed away from communicating with their own communities by white corporations in order to accommodate the white market. In this respect, imagery and lyrics are directly affected by issues of ownership and subsequent control. The chapter on representing images in this book focuses on this area and emphasises the perspectives of those who consume rap and grime music on a regular basis.

Hip-hop is often seen as a site of cultural resistance, an aspect of diasporic experience offering a voice for those marginalised in society by economic or socio-political factors (Rose, 1994). The origins of hip-hop culture were very much from 'the streets', from the post-industrial city which '... radically altered black communal sensibilities in the late 1970s and 1980s ...' (Neal, 1999: 125). This was due to extreme poverty, an economic collapse and the destruction of openly available public spaces (Rose, ibid.: 27). Hip-hop, in its 'golden age' between 1987 and 1993, addressed the relative invisibility and marginal cultural position of black youths in America (Dyson, 2007: 64). It was a medium by which the expression of black cultural values could be transmitted and a medium through which black identity could be forged through the music's lyrical narratives. It was, according to Public Enemy's Chuck D, 'a black CNN', (Basu and Lemelle, 2006: 3) informing its audience of real events and experiences of the composers and performers of the songs. It is this aspect of authentic performance that is addressed further in this study, wherein I draw upon the markers of authenticity as espoused by the research participants in the different youth groups.

Neal states that '... hip-hop may represent the last black popular form to be wholly derived from the experiences and texts of the black urban landscape ...' (1999: 126). Differing localised variations of the culture are evident around the world as each geographical area appropriates its own version in order to say something about the populace's particular existence. The edited collection by Tony Mitchell in *Global Noise: Rap and Hip-Hop Outside the USA* (2001) demonstrates that hip-hop has become a source of identity formation for many young people around the world. These papers (by Swedenburg, Pennay, Wermuth and Urla amongst others) are written from an historical and theoretical position and link with many of the ethnographic studies in this area as they seek to unearth the local meanings of a cultural form. Musical appropriations and aural adaptations, such as UK grime are a common feature of engagement with elements of hip-hop culture as individuals use it to enable them to gain a platform for expression.

On a macro-analytical scale, Lipsitz (1994: 33) uses the concept of subculture and states that identities are constructed through hip-hop at a local level whilst also involving a global consciousness. In his work, culture is seen as a privileged site for transnational communication as hip-hop artists work through (rather than outside) existing power structures in order to determine, in Gramscian terms, a war of position. This requires the forming of a counter-hegemonic alliance as artists seek to utilise the tools available to them in this global post-colonial culture. Lipsitz claims that although rap music is controlled by centralised monopolies it still retains an expressive ability to serve '... as a conduit for ideas and images articulating subaltern sensitivities ...' (ibid.: 36). This position is also offered in the work of Rose (1994) who views rap music as a vehicle for politicised black expression. Using the notion of hidden transcripts from the writing of Scott (1990), Rose suggests that hip-hop '... uses cloaked speech and disguised cultural codes to comment on and challenge aspects of current [racial] power inequalities ...' (ibid.: 100). Although Rose does not make the connection herself, such a position implies the character of the Signifying Monkey (Gates Jr., 1988) who is an important element in the notion of a double identity in African-American oral and literary traditions. This character is a metaphorical device between perceived subservience to the dominant culture and knowing recognition of a trickster, an individual who has some degree of autonomous control over his own destiny. The Signifying Monkey possesses a command and manipulation over his masters utilising '… cunning, humour and deceit to obtain personal gain …' (Smith, 2005: 179). The roots of the trickster character within African-American life can be traced back to the times of slavery and are seen as an attempt to deal with the lack of power within the daily lives of the slave community. The Signifying Monkey is an important functioning element of the hidden transcript, wherein a dominated culture use such a figure in order to attain some sense of self-determination for themselves in an attempt to ease the burden and the suffering of their existence (Gates Jr., 1988: 51). Perry (2004) views hip-hop as a black democratic space, wherein individuals can assert a sense of their own localised identity through the utilisation of the cultural form. However, she draws a distinction between the grassroots form and the commodified, co-opted strand of hip-hop, suggesting that '… numerous talented artists with progressive values remain local, while the excessive and consumerist ones go global …' (ibid.: 197). The data from the fieldwork shows an important distinction between consumption of commodified hip-hop and localised, authentic practices.

Conclusion

This chapter has shown that at present there are few empirical academic studies on the notion of the reception of hip-hop by its audience. The aim of this book is to address this imbalance. The work of leading academics in hip-hop studies, including Krims (2000), Rose (1994, 2008), Ogbar (2007), Quinn (2005) and Perry (2004) does not offer an analysis of the day to day activities of individuals and their interaction with the culture. Those studies that do engage at an empirical level, such as Huq (2006), Harrison (2009) and Schloss (2009) discuss the varying roles of hip-hop culture in the lives of the research subjects but their work does not address the issue of audience interpretation of texts. This book privileges the reception and opinions of the audience over a purely theoretical reading. Such an approach seeks to offer an appreciation of the effects of the culture's ideologies through an analysis of the responses and perceptions from hip-hop and grime consumers.

Chapter 2

Subcultural theory

"Looking for some new meanings ... "[2]

Introduction

This chapter focuses on the central debates and perspectives within the field of subcultural theory. It takes into account the interactionist ethnographic drive of the Chicago School, the structural considerations of the CCCS and the focus on consumerism by postmodern theorists to explore the actions, values and behaviours of the research participants. The first two chapters in this book should be seen as a way to explore the key concepts and ideas which underpin the work as a whole, as well as serving as an insight for those new to the field.

Subcultural studies — an overview

The focus and meaning of the term subculture has changed over its life span within the social sciences. A number of varying positions have arisen in subcultural theory since the early studies of deviant youth by the Chicago School of the 1920s. Interactionist, functionalist, neo-Marxist and postmodernist research has been undertaken in this field in order to examine youth group collectivity and to validate the theoretical claims that each paradigm offers (Williams, 2001). Huq states that '... subcultural theory is best described as an amalgam ...' (2007: 17) as it has been rooted in a number of established academic traditions. These include Chicago School micro-sociology which has its base in American behavioural social science, the functionalist attempt to construct a framework for deviancy and structural Marxism's focus on symbolic resistance. Blackman suggests that '... the concept of subculture is a chameleon theory which possesses different and opposing definitions, from its use as a deficit model to describe 'subnormal behaviour' to its use as a concept to express resistance, vitality and consumer choice ...' (2004: 104). Many of the early studies in this field, by Anderson (1923), Thrasher (1927) and Cressey (1932) did not directly address issues of subcultural identity and definitions of the terminology. Their focus lay largely on describing the cultures of groups who were perceived as failing to follow conventional norms and societal values and there was a considerable emphasis on groups who engaged in criminal activity.

A prototype of the subculture concept is offered by Durkheim through his introduction of the term collective representations (Bell, 2010: 163). Such collective forms of representation play a crucial role in the development of identity and serve to underline aspects of variance between the collectivity and wider society. The work on deviance by Durkheim (1895/1964) proposes an understanding of delinquent groups as a normal response by ordinary people to their experience of social divisions. He states that '… to classify crime among the phenomena of normal sociology is not to say merely that it is an inevitable, although regrettable phenomenon … it is to affirm that it is a factor in public health, an integral part of all healthy societies …' (ibid.: 67). In *The Rules of Sociological Method*, Durkheim explains that criminality is a normal aspect of societal life and helps to reinforce shared values in the wider populace as, by definition, crime is an act which offends collective sentiments. These sub-groups act as forms of collective identification through which the individual may restore some of the detachment and distance felt within the wider culture. Here it could be suggested that deviant groups are making sense of their own reality and localised spaces as a reflection, and rebellion against, the anomie of the every day as experienced by individuals within the parent culture. Rules of behaviour and ways of thinking are formulated, perhaps in an informal sense, in order to establish a new culture that, although different, is not entirely and actively in opposition to mainstream modes of behaviour.

Interactionism and functionalism

The interactionist approach favoured by the Chicago School of qualitative researchers led to the detailed empirical examination of non-normative groups (Bulmer, 1984). Thomas and Znaniecki's *The Polish Peasant in Europe and America* (1918) set the methodological template for Chicago researchers as they insisted that theory should be grounded in diverse forms of empirical observation and evidence (Haenfler, 2010: 5). The main research focus for the University of Chicago's Sociology department was the idea of the individualistic agency of those under analysis. Three significant pieces of research published by the Chicago School illustrate a focus on deviant groups on the peripheries of society with Nels Anderson's *The Hobo* (1923), Frederic M. Thrasher's *The Gang: A Study of 1,313 Gangs in Chicago* (1927) and Paul G. Cressey's *The Taxi-Hall Dance: A Sociological Study in Recreation and City Life* (1932). These studies share a common theme, namely the notion of people and place as organically tied together. For Anderson, Thrasher and Cressey the city was a space that enabled people to move through it and, as a result, be transformed. The social ecology of the city was a major concern for Chicago School researchers and territories were mapped out in the city according to instances of poverty and the distribution of ethnicities (Jenks, 2005). Shaw and McKay (1942) argue that when disruption to the equilibrium of city life occurs subcultural groups emerge. Such instances include economic struggle, political unrest or periods of rapid social change. Understanding the social context of marginalised groups, their behaviours and values, was central to the working methods of the Chicago School researchers.

As an individual who had spent some time begging and working in temporary, low paid manual labour prior to his enrolment as a student, Anderson's study can be termed as insider research (MacRae, 2007). His methodology centred on participant observation, a research tool favoured by Chicago School researchers, and his study contains details of four hundrecd interviews and sixty biographies. The hobos were seen to have a number of defined spaces within the confines of the city, each site being used for different aspects of hobo life such as communal meeting areas (termed 'the stem') or for sleeping (termed 'the jungles'). Anderson describes the jungles as '… the melting pot of trampdom …' (1923: 19), where the social and racial hierarchies evident in mainstream society were absent. The hobos are described as existing within a set of unwritten, but abided by, laws of community which pulls together a set of potentially disparate individuals into shared values which do not conform to normative society. There is very little in the way of sociological analysis in *The Hobo* but the work still serves as a valuable insight into matters of fieldwork in the discipline's formative years.

Thrasher (1927) used a combination of quantitative and qualitative methods to conclude that gangs were the result of social interaction and shared identity rather than psychological aberration. He states that the result of the collective behaviour of gangs is '… the development of tradition, unreflective internal structure, *esprit de corps*, solidarity, morale, group awareness, and attachment to a local territory …' (1927: 57, italics in original text). The social disadvantage of these gang members is highlighted by Thrasher although structural issues are not fully drawn out in this work. The gang replaced normative institutions such as the family, education and religion as a source of identity formation and were initiated through casual interaction. Such an argument can also be seen in the work of another Chicago School theorist, William Foot Whyte (1943). The formation of gangs, according to Thrasher, was a means for individuals to attain and assert forms of identity and empowerment in the modern city.

Industrialisation had led to a loss of collective identity and was superseded by an emphasis on individualisation and competition. This concept draws from the dual concepts of *Gemeinschaft* (community) and *Gesellschaft* (society) developed by Tönnies (1887/1957) and it is in the sense of community that subcultures exist. Community is distinguished by emotional, close-knit bonds and stability.

In his study of taxi-dances, Cressey (1932) shifts focus away from the male-centred studies offered earlier by the Chicago School by detailing the female involvement of this phenomena. He does, however, spend considerable time describing the social circumstances of the male customers and hall owners. The term taxi-dance describes the practice of girls who are expected '... to dance with any man who may choose her and to remain with him on the dance floor for as long a time as he is willing to pay the charges ...' (Cressey, 1932: 3). Covert participant observation was used to examine a distinct social world which had identified rules of engagement along with '... its own vocabulary, its own activities and interests, its own conception of what is significant in life, and — to a certain extent — its own scheme of life ...' (ibid.: 38). The morality of the taxi-dance halls was seen as oppositional to the conventional norms and values of wider society although the capitalist exchange aspect of this subculture can be seen as a microcosm of mainstream culture.

For this group of researchers, the most important aspect of sociological investigation was an '... immersion in the first-hand experiences of concrete situations ...' (Shils, 1948: 6). The focus on an etic approach can be seen as a weakness of the methodologies of the Chicago School theorists as this approach does not fully match with the supposed presentation of the first-hand experiences of the research subjects, but privileges the interpretation of cultural forms by the researchers.

A number of the approaches of the Chicago School informed the research in this book. The strength of the Chicago School studies lie in their emphasis on ethnographic detail, ensuring that the phenomena under consideration are understood from the perspective of those who live their daily lives within the sphere of the cultures being portrayed. The method of naturalistic inquiry as promoted by the Chicago School allows for the social and cultural activities to be viewed within the natural settings in which they occur, rather than in laboratory settings or attitude surveys which are methodologically flawed for the social scientist. The prioritising of empirical research over theory can also be seen as a positive aspect of the Chicago School approach to sociological investigation. It is argued that theory must not '... anticipate, deform, or obscure the facts ...'

(Downes and Rock, 2011: 69). The Chicago School unknowingly developed the first model of subculture (Thornton, 1997) and there have been calls recently to more closely follow Chicago style methodologies in ethnographic research, as well as acknowledging the relevance of such an approach to the study of contemporary youth culture (Colosi, 2010).

Robert Merton utilised Durkheim's concept of anomie to develop his idea of social strain and subsequent deviant behaviour (Bell, 2010). Merton argued that the social structure of any society includes cultural goals, i.e. shared and culturally agreed aspirations, along with the institutionalised means of attaining those goals. Strain, dysfunctionality and alienation are experienced by individuals when social structures constrain their opportunities to realise shared values of achievement and such psychological factors can lead to deviant behaviours (Gelder, 2007). Merton states that, '... social structures *exert a definite pressure* upon certain persons in the society to engage in nonconformist rather than conformist conduct ...' (1938: 672, italics in original text). Deviant behaviour is, therefore, the outcome of blocked avenues of personal progress.

A. K. Cohen popularised the term 'subculture' in his book *Delinquent Boys* and perceived them as *cultures within cultures*, but also that there exist *subcultures within subcultures* (1955: 12). Cohen advanced the theory of deviance to a collective adaptation of subculture rather than an individualistic approach (Williams, 2011). For Cohen, subcultures correspond to the sense of anomie felt by a particular group of individuals. Cohen's emphasis is on deviance and criminality, not identity. His notion of people 'reacting to form' followed a recognition of psychogenics and owes a debt to the work of Freud and an interpretation of the imperfect mastery of the Id. He suggests that individuals react against blocked avenues to progression by negotiating, within a collective identity, a new set of rules and standards of behaviour which may be applicable and adhered to by them. In this respect, '... what people do depends upon the problems they contend with ...' (ibid.: 51). This negotiation is seen as a solution to the issues faced by those who perceive themselves as not fitting into mainstream sensibilities and a collectivity is formed '... to establish new norms, new criteria of status which define as meritorious the characteristics that they do possess, the kinds of conduct which they are capable ...' (ibid.: 66).

Cohen sourced his data from the Chicago School studies and therefore the research subjects that he discusses were male and largely working-class and an argument is forwarded that a significant part of the turn to delinquency stems from issues relating to socialisation and socio-cultural adjustment. This relates to the dominant norms and values in a culture, described as middle-class values by Cohen, and how working-class youths view structural barriers as hindering the formation of any degree of cultural (i.e. middle-class) aspiration. Cohen does not preclude those from the middle-class as also experiencing degrees of frustration although '... the problems may be different and to different problems the conceivable alternative solutions may be different ...' (ibid.: 73). The status-frustration for working-class boys can lead to the '... legitimation of aggression ...' (ibid.: 131), invoked against the sources of their frustration. The distinction between working-class and middle-class experience, a focal point to his argument of subcultural formation, is not fully drawn out in Cohen's work and a number of superficially analysed issues are raised in regards to the presence of middle-class delinquents. He admits that his work lacks any solid research with regards to middle-class delinquency and that, therefore, the suppositions offered are '... frankly a speculative toying with possibilities ...' (ibid.: 160).

One defining subcultural characteristic that Cohen incorporated in his writing was the idea of group autonomy. This aspect was defined as the '... intolerance of restraint except from the informal pressures within the group itself ...' (ibid.: 31). This self-sufficient approach to subcultural being is significant as it places importance on the division between those on the inside and those on the outside of the group. Cohen's notion of deviance has been described as a gang-into-subculture model by Blackman (2004: 107). It is clear in Cohen's presentation of subcultural groups that there is a clear distinction between those who were deemed as inside or outside of these deviant groups. There is no sliding-scale, or degrees of activity, presented in the literature, an aspect of the research on subcultures which this book seeks to address with the purist/peripheral model of engagement.

For Cloward and Ohlin (1960) there is a function to subcultural affiliation as it is seen as a solution to issues of adjustment. They note that '... deviance may be understood as an effort to resolve difficulties that sometimes result from conformity ...' (ibid.: 38). Access to potential social mobility and ultimately money is denied to those from working-class origins through a combination of cultural and structural factors. Significantly, these cultural influences are developed by a lack of opportunity and access to education. Cloward and Ohlin differ from Cohen in regards to how issues of adjustment manifest themselves in their research subjects. For Cohen, status plays a significant part in the problematic faced by working-class youth whereas the over-riding concern in the work of Cloward and Ohlin relates to money. Short and Strodtbeck (1965) consider the fact that gang delinquency was a notable social problem after World War II. The increased affluence and mobilisation within the post-war years in American society saw those who could not succeed in such a manner form subcultural identities, in keeping with the Mertonian concept of anomie. Such positions influenced aspects of my own research although my focus is on cultural engagement rather than deviancy.

Howard Becker (1963) took an interactionist perspective on deviance, looking at the relationship between jazz musicians and outsiders, known as squares, to determine subcultural identity. The squares are seen by the musicians as opposite to everything they stand for and do. Those in the musicians' subculture maintained that '... the strongest element of the colleague code is the prohibition against criticising or in any other way trying to put pressure on another musician in the actual playing situation 'on the job'. Where not even a colleague is permitted to influence the work, it is unthinkable that an outsider should be allowed to do so ...' (ibid.: 86). This clear divide between the musicians and squares is reinforced not just in the realm of musical endeavour but in other social activities where non-conformity to social norms by the musicians is seen in a positive light by their peer group. Appearance and behaviour are seen as obvious signifiers of the boundaries between these two groups of people —'... every item of dress, speech and behaviour which differs from that of the musician is taken as new evidence of the inherent insensitivity and ignorance of the square ...' (ibid.: 90). The musicians consciously self-segregated themselves, using vernacular language as one tool of separation with the squares and it is this form of collective agreement and behaviour that sustains a sense of subcultural allegiance. Becker does not label the subculture of musicians as transient, instead suggesting that they are a stable and long lasting collective.

David Matza, in line with arguments put forward by Becker, criticises the functionalist approach to subcultural theory by A. K. Cohen who '... portrays a delinquent subculture that is a reaction formation, an oppositional response to the pious legality of bourgeois existence ...' (1964/1990: 34). For Matza, the portrayal of conventional culture in the writing of functionalist writers in this area is a major criticism as they present a simplified, one-dimensional image of middle-class respectability and adherence to the law. The dichotomous separation between delinquent subcultures and conventional culture is reductive and serves to hinder a deepened understanding of the phenomena of juvenile criminality as the division is not clear but '... subtle, complex, and sometimes devious ...' (ibid.: 37). Those within the delinquent subcultures exist within certain parameters of the conventional culture which has an affect on the subculture and which the subculture, in turn, affects. In this respect, for Matza, subcultures should not be perceived as oppositional. Subcultures are encircled by mainstream culture and, therefore, can never be seen to be totally insulated and autonomous.

The notion of drift as developed by Matza relates to what he calls a soft determinism (ibid.: 27) wherein the social scientist must appreciate that the social actor is neither wholly free nor constrained by societal convention. The drift is the space between freedom and control where the delinquent exists between criminal and conventional action, engaging in both from time to time. This notion is presented as a dynamic continuum, a state of flux which allows for the formation of an autonomous subculture as set against the parameters of conventional, law-abiding behaviour. Drifters, however, are not perceived as possessing agency of action as their behaviour is framed within the laws which identify such individuals as delinquent. Underlying influences operate to initiate delinquency and Matza describes this guidance as '... gentle and not constraining. The drift may be initiated or deflected by events so numerous as to defy codification ...' (ibid.: 29). There is a transiency to Matza's drifter which links his activities to age. The floating between criminal and conventional behaviours results in only the minority becoming hardened adult criminals, whereas the majority do not transgress after a point. The identification of subcultural engagement as fleeting and related to adolescence, and the concomitant issues that come with this life stage, is common within the literature on subcultural theory. The idea of flux, of movement between criminal and conventional action, and the degrees of criminality are a significant aspect in regards to the formulation of my own purist/peripheral conceptual model. This book will argue that subcultural belonging exists within a dynamic number of rules of engagement and such substantive groups cannot simply be portrayed as a dichotomous division between insiders and outsiders.

The American functionalist theory of subculture was critically examined by Downes (1966) as a deficit model of social inadequacy. Further, Downes states that A. K. Cohen's examination of subcultures was limited as he was '... avowedly more concerned with the process by which a subculture is created than with the mechanisms by which it is maintained ...' (ibid.: 1). Downes' study was in the form of non-participant observation and was located in two east end districts of London, Stepney and Poplar. Downes's fieldwork data suggested that there was a lack of the structured cohesion as presented in the New York gangs by

Cloward and Ohlin and he states that '… the groups responsible for the bulk of delinquency were simply small cliques whose members committed illegal acts sometimes collectively, sometimes in pairs, sometimes individually, in some cases regularly, in others only rarely …' (ibid.: 199). The affiliation of these groups was not centralised around deviancy and group sizes were small, the average being between four and five members. Again, severe deprivation of access to the legitimate opportunity structure is given as a cause of the formation of the sub- and contra- cultures. Downes is critical of the use of the term subculture in the work of Cohen and Cloward and Ohlin as the term '… is too readily applied as a blanket term to any set of sub-group norms, values and beliefs that deviate from an 'ideal-type' dominant middle-class normative system …' (ibid.: 255). His main issue is not with the validity of the term subculture per se, but with its application to groups who do not demonstrate clear counter-norms, values and beliefs as the basis for the violation of the law. In this respect, Downes's calls for a more precise use of the term subculture within the social sciences rather than as a catch-all term for gangs of youths.

British cultural studies and the
Centre for Contemporary Cultural Studies

British subcultural investigation of the 1970s centred on the writings of the Birmingham Centre for Contemporary Cultural Studies (CCCS) and in this section I move on to consider their methodologies and findings before discussing some of the criticisms of this approach from the literature. The theories developed by this group of writers were initially outlined by Phil Cohen (1972/1990) and then elaborated further in *Resistance through rituals* (Hall and Jefferson, 1975). The notion of resistance was central to the examination of subcultural groups for the CCCS. In marked contrast to the earlier structural functionalist theory of Cohen which was based on deviance, the CCCS centred their analysis on a complex Marxism (Hall, 1980) which emphasised issues of social class and ideology. The CCCS' contribution has been seen as a high point in the study of youth groups centred on popular music (Hesmondhalgh, 2005: 22), although the approach focused predominantly on youth style rather than music (Bennett, 2009: 256). The CCCS utilised five areas of analysis: style, resistance, bricolage, homology and hegemony (Blackman, 2005: 112-113).

The work of British sociologist Phil Cohen (1972/1980) is seen as the first cultural studies approach to subcultures (Storey, 1996: 117) wherein he identified subcultural 'signifying practices'. His work was a move away from the idea of an inextricable link between subcultures and deviance. This work is very much rooted in the analysis of working-class culture and its responses to the dramatic changes that were going on in the 1960s. For Cohen, youths who sought subcultural affiliation engaged in '... an attempt to retrieve some of the socially cohesive elements destroyed in their parent culture ...' (1980: 83). The problem faced by working-class youth in this period was the contradiction between traditional working-class puritanism and the new focus on hedonistic consumption. This ideological issue was paired with a problem at an economic level which offered these individuals an opportunity to be a part of the '... socially upwardly mobile élite or as part of the new lumpen proletariat ...' (ibid.: 83). It is these contradictions, which remain hidden and unresolved in the parent culture, which subcultures seek to express and resolve *magically* (ibid.: 82). Cohen, using an Althusserian interpretation of Lacan's notion of 'the imaginary' and Levi-Strauss' concept of 'myth', argued that the real and unconscious force of ideology led to the attempted resolution of social contradictions through '... multiple narratives of bricolage in the form of style, symbols and ritual ...' (Blackman, 2005: 5). The twin ideas of 'imaginary relations' and 'magical solutions' see subcultures as a way of symbolically recreating new forms of solidarity within a community that feels ostracised from the parent culture.

Resistance through rituals (1975) is a collection of diverse essays which details the areas of focus for the CCCS and includes a number of ethnographic and textual studies of subcultures. The Cultural Studies approach was to read youth subcultural style as a text, to interpret each subculture through its creation of meaning. Subcultures, in this work, belong to the working-class as a result of the experience of subordination and are sites of temporary resistance against a symbolic class war. These groups were seen as a means of winning space and as a form of collective defiance. Jefferson (1975) argues that the appropriation of an upper-class style of dress by Teddy Boys articulates, at a symbolic level, '... an attempt to defend ... a constantly threatened space and a declining status ...' (ibid.: 81). This subculture had a strong and determined group-mindedness which was read partly as a way to address the destruction of the socially binding force of extended kinship networks in post-war Britain. This notion draws on the work of Downes (1966) and Cohen (1972) and asserts that this strong sense of collectivity, and concomitant subcultural characteristics such as territoriality and sensitivity to insults, results in the meaningful phenomenon of a defence of their space, often through the use of physical violence. Indeed, many of the

Teddy Boys' attacks on others, such as ethnic minorities, are seen as a defence of status and as a means to reclaim some sense of empowerment.

Hebdige (1975) focuses on the manner in which the mods' style expropriated consumer commodities in order to rework their meanings into expressions of subcultural rather than dominant values. The very essence of mod was style and Hebdige is clear that this group were not passive in their consumption. For the mod to project style '... it became necessary first to appropriate the commodity, then to redefine its use and value and finally to relocate its meaning within a totally different context ...' (ibid.: 93). Aspects of the parent culture such as scooters, medically diagnosed drugs and negatively perceived character traits (i.e. laziness and vanity) were inverted by the mods in order to affirm a sense of opposition to mainstream culture that was subversive rather than obviously confrontational. In this respect, mods portrayed themselves as upwardly mobile in terms of dress code. They were seen as an aspirational group in this respect. Skinheads on the other hand, as with the Teddy Boys in Jefferson's work, were seen by Clarke (1975) as an attempt to reclaim a sense of collectivity that centred on masculine working-class values. The impoverished social and economic position of the working-class was perceived to be worsening through the second half of the 1960s and this resulted in '... an intensified 'Us-Them' consciousness among the lower working class young ...' (1975: 99). The oppression felt by this group culminated in a form of group solidarity which was essentially defensive but with tendencies towards aggression to scapegoated others.

Although Paul Willis does not use subcultural theory in *Learning to Labour* (1977) and *Profane Culture* (1978) his methodological approach is significant. Ethnography, for Willis, '... shows subjectivity as an active moment in its own form of production — not as a whispered bourgeois apology for a belief in individual sensibility ...' (1978: 170). The experiences of his research subjects are therefore presented in a non-minimised manner and without recourse to the passive reflexivity of social structure and conditions. Willis' preference for counter-culture over subculture has greater political connotations (Blackman and France, 2001: 182). In his study, Willis (1972) argues that subculture is a construct which is exclusive, overly mechanistic and lacking rigour. He advances a sense of agency for his research participants that is arguably lacking in other work from the CCCS. Willis argues that each social class faces different problems—for the working-classes this can be seen to be oppression, whilst the middle-classes suffer from alienation (Willis, 1977: 1). This structural, class based focus allows for a discussion of the different responses that the bikers and hippies had to their preferred forms of popular music. The working-class bikers favoured the use of fast paced singles which they danced to whereas the hippies had a preference for progressive rock which, it is argued by Willis, demonstrates a desire for deferred gratification as this music was seen as rhythmically complex and therefore required high levels of concentration during the listening process. Willis' account suggests that the working-class use of music in this case is on a physical level compared to the middle-class hippies' more cerebral approach. There is value to Willis' work here, despite his earlier rejection of subcultural theory. His findings on the variations in listening patterns and forms of different social groups is of note and was one area that I took into my own research to more fully evaluate socio-economic affects on cultural practices.

Blackman (2005: 112-113) outlines the five areas of analysis that were utilised by the CCCS: style, resistance, bricolage, homology and hegemony.

First, for consideration of the term 'style', a semiotic analysis approach is used to reveal the meanings behind the implementation of certain forms of dress and the spectacle of subcultural groups. Hebdige used the work of Barthes (1972) to draw upon the idea of semiotic readings of subcultural items, including hair, clothes and ritualistic manners of being in order to '... uncover the latent meanings of an everyday life which, to all intents and purposes, was 'perfectly natural' ...' (1979: 9). The connotative examples used include safety pins and tubes of Vaseline, each of which he suggests possess potential meanings other than and beyond itself. Hebdige's use of the idea of myth, of the invisible, coded and culturally embedded meaning structures that are seen to be naturalised and normalised by the dominant ideology, are discussed in depth and these concepts are linked with the work of Gramsci and the notion of hegemony. Hebdige saw the subcultural activity of the Teddy Boys of the 1950s, the mods of the 1960s and the punks of the 1970s as a means by which working-class youths could renegotiate their own space and identity, rejecting the norms of the parent culture which they were seen to be responding to. For Hebdige, the stylistic aspects of subcultures were used as a tool to define themselves against the mainstream as they appropriated everyday household objects and subverted their meaning in order to suit their own needs and tastes. This bastardisation of household objects, such as safety pins, was seen by Hebdige as a means by which the spectacular subculture could express itself, as a system of communication (ibid.: 104).

Second, the notion of resistance comes from the work of Louis Althusser (1971) and refers to the activity occurring in a site or space which holds the potential to create, recreate or which possessed a sense of relative autonomy.

The CCCS reading of subcultures saw them as sites of resistance to mainstream culture and can be considered as oppositional to a perception of the values of the culture which it rejects. Subcultures are defined as being opposite and resistant to parents, teachers, police, 'respectable' youth, adult working-class and middle-class cultures (Hebdige, 1979: 73) who may be seen as components of the mainstream. However, the form of opposition taken up by subcultures is problematic and has, in many writings, been overly simplified (Muggleton, 2000). It has been argued that only when subcultures have a specified political intent do they become singularly oppositional (Brake, 1985: 7). The work of the CCCS has been described as exaggerating the political nature of subcultures (Huq, 2006) although their focus is in terms of symbolic politics. In this respect, then, we must view subcultures as fragmented and differential aspects of mainstream sensibilities and activities.

Third, Levi-Strauss (1966) wrote on bricolage and homology which relates to an understanding of value, meaning and internal order. Bricolage is the reordering of objects and their meaning and is used symbolically in order to express an idea counteracting the parent culture, for example, the use of safety pins by punks. This allows subcultures to establish their own unique sense of identity and spectacular sense of style in order to emphasise their difference to the parent culture. John Clarke's essay *Style* defines the concept of bricolage in *Resistance through rituals* as a means of re-ordering particular objects through the discourse of fashion. He states that '... when the bricoleur re-locates the significant object in a different position within that discourse, using the same overall repertoire of signs, or when the object is placed within a different total ensemble, a new discourse is constituted, a different message conveyed ...' (1975: 177). Subculturalists, therefore, produce new culture through their investment of new meaning (Williams, 2011: 74).

Fourth, the first application of the term homology to subcultures came in the work on hippies and biker culture by Paul Willis (1978). Homology can be seen as '... the symbolic fit between the values and lifestyles of a group ...' (Hebdige, 1979: 113). Subcultural homologies '... may arise from the 'discovery' of a valued cultural commodity or may be stimulated by commodities directed at a subcultural market ...' (Brown, 2007: 68). Willis argues that the values bestowed on a motorcycle — freedom, power and risk — are homologous with the core perspectives of biker culture. Epstein (1998) proposes three main operating platforms for subcultural expression, namely the level of basic historical ideas, the level of values and the level of material expression. All three aspects are studied by a social scientist to encapsulate the parameters of a subculture, the social space in which it exists, and the meaning of style (Hebdige, 1979).

Fifth, Gramsci's (1971: 13) idea of hegemony features heavily in the writing of the CCCS. The term refers to the management of social consent by the dominant classes. Gramsci uses two terms, social hegemony and state domination to explain how the élite maintain their domination over the masses. Social hegemony refers to 'spontaneous' consent given by the general population to the ideas of the dominant classes. Values and ideas are naturalised and are historical inasmuch as they are founded and reinforced by the position of the ruling classes in terms of production. In this respect, mass media images and constructs can be seen to reinforce dominant values.

Subcultural instances, according to Hebdige, occur when a solution to a particular set of circumstances is needed (1979: 81), usually in relation to the parent culture. In *Subculture: The meaning of style*, Hebdige once again focuses on a semiotic rather than empirical methodology to uncover the meanings and values behind subcultural activity. Whereas groups such as teds, skins and mods were perceived as being hostile towards ethnic minorities the punks were portrayed as being more obviously open to the influence of black cultural forms. Hebdige states that '... although apparently separate and autonomous, punk and the black British subcultures with which reggae is associated were connected at a deep structural level ...' (ibid.: 29). In this respect, Hebdige highlights the previously ignored aspect of race relations as a key factor in subcultural identity. Hebdige calls for a reassessment of the history of British youth subcultures since the 1950s, taking into account the varying responses to the presence of black immigrant cultures. The work of John Clarke and Tony Jefferson in *Resistance through rituals* is criticised by Hebdige for omitting a full discussion of the influence of black cultural forms on white youth subcultures. The paradoxical nature of magically recovering a sense of white working-class distinction through the utilisation of black culture, dress and argot is noted by Hebdige who claims that in black West Indian culture the skinheads saw '... a culture armoured against contaminating influences, protected against the more frontal assaults of the dominant ideology, denied access to the 'good life' by the colour of its skin ...' (ibid.: 57).

There is an overplaying of the role of style in the work of Hebdige. He argues that the commercialisation of the visually spectacular aspects of subcultural identity can be seen as a death knell for subcultures. Hebdige offers the example of punk style being used in advertising campaigns for Zandra Rhodes wherein '...

the accompanying article ended with an aphorism — 'To shock is chic' — which presaged the subculture's imminent demise ...' (ibid.: 96). The proclaimed death of punk here is undoubtedly premature as substantive groups have identified themselves with this label from the 1970s to the current time, albeit in different variant forms to those described by Hebdige. It can be argued that the importing of visual subcultural aesthetics into mainstream culture does not necessitate the eradication of subcultural being. The work of the American Ned Polsky (1971) is significant here as the Beats in his research were very much concerned with remaining invisible to the parent culture of the squares and this is an aspect that Hebdige fails to take into account. The visual punk style of the late 1970s was more spectacular and arguably more confrontational than subsequent punk forms such as new wave and straightedge. Along with this, bands such as The Sex Pistols, The Buzzcocks and The Clash achieved record sales that meant they crossed over into the mainstream, thereby further increasing public awareness of the subcultural form. Rather than signalling the passing of this cultural form as a meaningful expression of youth subcultural resistance, the increasing mainstream awareness and popularity of the style and music of punk resulted in the divergence of the subcultural form into an array of articulated identities (Wood, 2006).

There have been a number of critiques centred on the investigative style, methods and subsequent subcultural theory of the Centre for Contemporary Cultural Studies (Clarke, 1981; Thornton, 1995 and Muggleton, 2000). These problems have been summed up as three inter-linking headings — *omissions, structural overdetermination* and *methodological problems* (Huq, 2006: 10).

First, *omissions* relates to the sets of young people excluded from the varying studies. The subcultures discussed in the work of the CCCS were almost exclusively male, white, heterosexual and working-class. There is a marginalising of female subcultural involvement in *Resistance through rituals* but there is at least an attempt to incorporate such an investigation in the book, unlike many other previous works in this area. McRobbie and Garber (1975) discuss the invisibility of girls in subcultures, proposing that they are much more likely to congregate with friends in private, personal spaces such as bedrooms and are unlikely to find affiliation in subcultural activity. This notion has been attacked by, amongst others, Wulff who states that in her own ethnographic work there was no significant variations in behaviours between boys and girls as '... boys also stuck together in their bedrooms for hours on end, while the girls were 'muckin' around' on the street corner often waiting for the boys to appear, since the street corner was a meeting place for *both* girls and boys ...' (1995: 5, italics in original text). The emphasis on youth in the work of the CCCS fails to fully address the longevity of many subcultural forms (Hodkinson and Bennett, 2012). The transience of subcultural affiliation is overstated in *Resistance through rituals* and the privileging of youth does not allow the CCCS to investigate the phenomenon in a deeper manner. To counter this, the opening lines in *Resistance through rituals* make it quite clear that the subject of the volume is quite specifically youth cultures.

Second, issues of *structural overdetermination* suggest that ethnography is used by the CCCS to confirm and validate the researchers' political agendas. This position has been addressed by Gary Clarke (1981/1997) who states that an observable youth subculture is seen as the starting point from which a backwards analysis is undertaken '... to uncover the class situation and detect the specific set of contradictions which produced corresponding styles ...' (1997: 176). The dynamism, temporality and flux present in subcultures are therefore absent from the writings of the CCCS and, as Huq claims, '... analytical rigidity breeds inconsistencies ...' (ibid.: 14). The multifarious nature of subcultural existence is, however, addressed in *Resistance through rituals* in its leading theoretical paper. Subcultures '... can be loosely or tightly bounded. Some subcultures are merely loosely-defined strands or 'milieux' within the parent culture: they possess no distinctive 'world' of their own. Others develop a clear, coherent identity and structure ...' (Clarke et al., 1975: 14).

Third, *methodological problems* relate to the priority given towards secondary source material but also, in the ethnographic studies undertaken by the CCCS, leads to a number of avenues of investigation being unexplored. Huq (2006: 16) argues that areas of potential criticism towards the research subjects, i.e. their homophobia, sexism and *Paki-bashing* practices, are skimmed over or read as heroic working-class responses to societal upheaval. There is a tendency in the work of the CCCS to neglect the 'osmotic' interaction between subcultures and other social forms (Weinzerl and Muggleton, 2003: 7). This term suggests that the defining space between subcultures and mainstream culture is less rigid than previously considered. A criticism of Hebdige's (1979) work on style is the reliance on a semiotic approach as there is no empirical research presented from the field. It is argued that the lack of data in the work of the CCCS results in work which is little more than '... abstracted discussions about youth subcultural phenomena ...' (Williams, 2011: 31). There is no clear demonstration of an appreciation by the Birmingham School of how the individuals under investigation made sense of their own experiences as the theorists rely heavily on secondary sources of data rather than an interpretation of their own empiricism. A focus which privileges the reading of culture as a text, and thereby a reliance on semiotic analysis of the spectacular aspects of subcultural being, limits the space for the voices of those involved in the cultures within the CCCS examination. Such an approach must ensure that the groups under analysis do not end up '... being reduced to the specifics of certain spectacular practices ...' (Hodkinson, 2012: 571). This is an often overstated criticism of the CCCS as some of the chapters do include empirical work. Both Corrigan and Willis present detailed primary empirical evidence which goes some way to negate such criticism. The majority of the essays in *Resistance through rituals* do rely heavily on secondary source material and in this respect the work lacks a detailed and first-hand examination of subcultural research subjects, yet the different approaches taken in the study result in a rich and varied work. As discussed, Willis (1978) details the value of ethnographic work in *Profane Culture*, and this work offers extensive empirical evidence which goes some way to counteract claims that there is a failing in this respect in the body of work produced by the CCCS.

Little space is given in the CCCS account of youth culture to the actual function of popular music as a cultural resource (Bennett, 2000: 47). The teds, mods, skinheads and punks in the literature are all engaged in music centred subcultures yet there is a tendency in this body of work to limit the analysis of how the musical artefacts are used and read by these youth groups. The emphasis is largely on the visual stylistic aspects of each subculture rather than on a full examination of how each group centres their activities around music. Paul Willis (1978) is the only CCCS theorist of note at this time to discuss the social meaning of popular music with any degree of focus. The emphasis in his work is on the class-based variations between the biker and hippie subcultures and he therefore offers a structural analysis. The semiotic position taken by the CCCS privileges an analysis of the visual aspects of the subculture as identified by the theorists whilst failing to fully address the incorporation of popular music into the daily lives of those under investigation.

The work of the CCCS established cultural studies as an academic discipline and allowed for an analysis of substantive youth groups which did not over-emphasise aspects of deviance. The criticisms of *Resistance through rituals* are just in the sense that there are clear gaps in the work yet there are no claims by any of the contributing authors to do anything other than what is presented. The cumulative nature of social science does not seem to have been taken into account by a number of the theorists who criticise this work and rather than seeing it as a valued addition to the literature on post-war youth cultures that can be built upon in future research, their preference is to diminish its validity by focusing on what is absent from the text, rather than what is present.

The post-subcultural turn

The discourse and search for a viable analytical framework in youth culture research has been labelled the 'post-subcultural turn' (Bennett, 2011: 493). Post-subcultural theorists question the idea of identifiably distinct and consistent subcultures, suggesting that young people's identities are increasingly fluid and often overlap. Postmodern theories of youth culture incorporate approaches linked to consumerism and a fluidity of cultural identity frameworks (Bennett, 1999a; Muggleton, 2000). Postmodern subcultural theory '... seeks to move away from models of social constraint and places greater emphasis on agency in the search for individual meaning in subcultural practice ...' (Blackman, 2005: 8). The postmodern idea of culturally fluid identities is in contrast to the seeming irrelevance of homogeneity, fixity and demarcation of subcultural being as evidenced in the work of the CCCS (Muggleton, 2000: 128). This has led Hodkinson (2007: 15) to label such theoretical positions as anti-subcultural.

Weinzierl and Muggleton (2003) trace the first use of the term 'post-subculture' to the work of Chambers in 1987, though they make the point that the use of the phrase in the works of Polhemus (1996) and Muggleton (1997) is much more widely known. Within current sociological debates, the actual terminology of this area is coming under increasing scrutiny. In writings on post-subcultural theory, including the work of Bennett (2000), Chaney (2004) and Blackman (2004) there are arguments surrounding the importance, relevance and subsequent difficulties of utilising the term subculture as opposed to tribes (Clarke, 1981), stratified taste cultures (Stahl, 2003), neo-tribes (Maffesoli, 1996), temporary substream networks (Weinzierl, 2000), scenes (Straw, 1991) and collective lifestyle statements (Chaney, 2004). There have been calls to rethink the terminology in this area, not to simply repudiate it (Carrington and Wilson, 2004), and a realignment of how these phenomena appear to reflexively negotiate rather than directly mirror the structural experience of social class. Williams (2011) claims that within the field of youth cultural theory, the constant attempts to replace the term subculture with alternative terminology ignores the multiple layers of analytic concepts which may be usefully incorporated in order to more fully understand the diversity of contemporary youth groups.

Marchart (2003: 83) uses the phrase the heroic years of subcultural studies when referring to the studies that looked at the micro-political aspects of cultural life, following the works of Gramsci, Foucault and DeCerteau amongst others. He calls for a return to the inclusion of macro-political investigation in the field of cultural studies, although he notes that this should be restricted to the theoretical level. The heroic years have passed and, in its place, today's discourse centres more on post-subcultural analysis. This approach defines itself as explicitly postmodern and aligns itself with postmodern sensibilities including fragmentation, dispersion and empty simulation, following the writing of Baudrillard (1994). Steve Redhead (1997) proposed a move from the use of the term subculture to that of clubculture. He suggests that youth subcultures, if they ever existed, have been surpassed by loose, globally based youth formations grounded in the media/market niches of contemporary dance music. Subcultural style could no longer be understood as a form of resistance for working-class youth as it was asserted that a number of identifiable visual styles were being amended, amalgamated and reinvented by those involved with rave culture, in line with the pick-and-mix sensibilities of postmodern culture. This newly found disconnection between style and musical tastes was, for Redhead, confirmation of the irrelevance of the CCCS interpretation of spectacular subcultural being. Young people's cultural practices were '... now seen as agentic and affirmative, not as 'magical' or impotent ...' (Williams, 2011: 32). Redhead contends that subculture theory is outdated although this does not necessarily mean that subcultures themselves no longer exist. The fragmentation of the audience makes subcultural theory hard to sustain and those groups that can be labelled as subcultural are '... frequently bounded in market niches of the contemporary global music industry — techno, bhangra, gangsta rap, ambient, jungle — even when they 'originally' came from the 'streets' ...' (1997.: 103).

David Muggleton's essay *The Post-subculturalist* (1997) relies on a theoretical reading of youth groups to conclude that subcultures were a phenomenon of the past. Subcultural choice is a key factor as post-subculturalists '... no longer have any sense of subcultural 'authenticity', where inception is rooted in particular sociotemporal contexts and tied to underlying structural relations ...' (ibid.: 180). The 1980s and 1990s are seen as a time of fragmentation of the social, where youth culture revolves around the reordering of style through hybridisation and revivalism and there is a fluid nature to subcultural identity which is made possible by the postmodern condition. A huge array of spectacular styles co-exist at any one time and Muggleton claims that individuals freely exchange one form of subcultural identity for another as and when it is seen fit to do so. For the post-subculturalists, as the boundaries of collective identity dissolve, so to does the relevance of subculture as a workable concept as there no longer exists a clear sense of opposition and resistance to the mainstream culture in postmodernity. Muggleton's work is seen by the author himself as largely conjectural (ibid.: 167) and he finishes the essay by asserting the need for empirical evidence to support the theoretical positions offered, an approach whereby '... the subjective meanings and perceptions of the subculturalists themselves constitute the first, privileged level of analysis ...' (ibid.: 183). Such empiricism is presented in his book *Inside Subculture* (2000). In his later work, Muggleton argues that subcultures still exist, albeit in postmodern form. The structural constraints of class, gender and ethnicity no longer play a significant part in the formation of youth identity, instead Muggleton asserts that '... there are no rules, there is no authenticity, no ideological commitment, merely a stylistic game to be played ...' (ibid.: 47). The emphasis on the surface quality of style, consumer choice and the resultant fluid nature of post-subcultural identity formation gives the individuals under investigation a sense of agency denied to them by analysis which leans too heavily on a consideration of structural constraints.

Steven Miles (2000) uses the work of Angela McRobbie (1993) to illustrate his point that subcultures have become commodified and are, therefore, a component of the culture to which they should seemingly be opposed. He states that '... the process of commodification appears to have undermined this analysis in the sense that the oppositional force constituted by young people has arguably been incorporated into the dominant order ...' (ibid.: 6). The issue may not be to focus on the power structures within the experiences of youth subcultures per se, but more importantly on how the individuals that make up 'youth' themselves perceive a negotiated place, a social space for themselves within that network of relationships that exist in larger society as a whole. Miles suggests that '... the notion of *lifestyles* is now potentially far more useful than that of youth subcultures ...' (2000: 7, italics in original text). The term 'lifestyle' presents problems inasmuch as it connotes a level of permanency throughout the life course of an individual, thereby disregarding the supposition that adolescence contains degrees of transience.

In youth culture studies, according to Geoff Stahl, there has been an over dependence on the notion of style. He suggests that it '... overemphasises a symbolic response to exclusion ...' (2003: 28). Utilising a postmodernist perspective, Stahl proposes that mainstream society has seen an encroachment of the visual (ibid.: 29) which results in a displacement of referents and an erasing of any potentially radical politics. This is echoed in the work of Chaney (2004) who states that the term subculture is now a redundant one due to the recent changes in contemporary culture which have altered the profile and characteristics of the parent culture to which subcultures are so often defined against. Chaney sketches out his conceptualisation of contemporaneous society's relationship to the culture industries by suggesting that:

Culture has become more important;

Culture has become less stratified;

There has been a shift towards multiculturalism;

There have been shifts from ways of life to lifestyles.

This argument of post-subcultural writing attempts to illustrate mainstream shifts which eradicate the potential opposition of subcultures as seen in the work of the CCCS. It is maintained that the changing nature of mainstream tastes, seemingly placing cultural engagement in a more centralised position, limits the spaces available in which subcultures can manoeuvre. For Chaney, identity through cultural consumption is significant for those who previously were seen to be outside of substantive group affiliation in earlier studies. The previous scholarly over-reliance on structural considerations is also addressed by Chaney who agrees with Bennett (2000) that there no longer exist obstacles to cultural engagement from structural forms. A significant area of contention for postmodern theorists in this area centres on the fact that academic discourse on subcultures in the 1970s utilised class as the main focus for analysis. Subcultures were seen as the naturally occurring collective solution to experienced problems. Both Muggleton (2000) and MacDonald (2001), amongst others, question this approach, suggesting that the social scientist should concentrate on the individual and their explanations of subcultural activity as opposed to attempting to relate such activity as being inherently and unquestionably linked to wider economic and social factors, a meta-narrative in Marxist terminology. The focus on the individual as opposed to the group has led to a rejection in postmodern subcultural writing towards the idea of collectivity (Blackman, 2005).

Bennett (1999a) uses the work of Michel Maffesoli to suggest that the term 'subculture' is no longer relevant in its application to the study of youth groups and that the idea of the *tribus*, often referred to as neo-tribes, should be used instead. The term subculture, for Bennett, has become problematic insomuch as its use has become increasingly contradictory. He suggests that perspectives of youth culture '... overestimate the coherence and fixity of youth groups ...' (ibid.: 605).

It is claimed that modern youth culture groups are, therefore, seen as temporary and fluid and a new label from which investigations can take place is a necessity. Notions of fixity, for Bennett, are associated with structural Marxism which he argues is no longer a relevant analytical paradigm. The neo-tribal approach to the study of youth culture argues for an understanding of '... how and why young people are brought together in collective affiliations ... neo-tribal theory allows for the function of taste, aesthetics and affectivity as primary drivers for participation in forms of collective youth cultural activity ...' (Bennett, 2011: 495). Maffesoli claims that societal groups today exist to serve the needs of the individuals involved in them and that the '... sole *raison d'etre* is a preoccupation with the collective self ...' (1996: 43, italics in original text). Secure forms of identity have been lost and, in their place, a sense of dis-individuation occurs according to Maffesoli in *The Time of the Tribes*. Collectivity allows individual identity to be subordinate to a group who favour appearance and form (ibid.: 98) and are, therefore, an aesthetic form of sociality (Sweetman, 2004: 86). However, Maffesoli's examples of neo-tribes are those groups who have a few drinks, who sit in cafés or simply spend time chatting with friends (ibid.: 25). Such instances do not describe marginalised subcultures but, on the contrary, explain the particular circumstances, views and habits of mainstream, non-subcultural existence. Bennett's concept of neo-tribes centring their collectivity on aspects of taste and aesthetics are important for my own study as it was found in the field, as will be demonstrated throughout the chapters that follow, that little significance was given to the notion of aesthetics for many in the research groups as they favoured acceptance into a group via cultural knowledge. Some in the focus groups, notably the purists, vociferously rejected the idea of dress code or other forms of aestheticism being a relevant marker of subcultural affiliation as such things were perceived as being commodified elements and, therefore, of little significance.

Blackman (2005: 12) offers a criticism of Bennett's attempts to incorporate the term neo-tribes into academic discourse. The term relates to the temporary and fluid nature of a contemporary consumer society and Blackman contests that this term, more than many others, brings with it an association of fixity. The term tribe, for Hesmondhalgh, also holds such connotations and therefore fails to acknowledge the more temporal nature of many subculturalists and their allegiances (2005: 24). The search for new terminology in this area (termed the *rhetoric of newness* by Gelder, 2005) is seen as a response to the centrality of class to structural Marxism. Throughout the studies using postmodern leanings there is a utopian idea of contemporary society, one in which people possess an array of choices with no hurdles to overcome before partaking in them. This does seem somewhat naïve and again it is relevant to note that few of these studies incorporate empirical data into their findings. Williams states that a major weakness of the post-subcultural position is '... that of certain scholars' unwillingness to empirically link ... identities and performances to larger socio-cultural structures that come to appear rather permanent in their effects ...' (2011: 37).

Bennett's use of the term neo-tribes, which has been described as '... less a question of belonging to a gang, a family or a community than of switching from one group to another ...' (Maffesoli, 1996: 76) avoids any idea of structural constraint on individuals and their situations. Neo-tribalism surpasses the principle of individuation by incorporating a supposition that individuals possess free reign in their decision making processes and subsequent fluidity of affiliation and identity. Both Blackman (2005) and Hesmondhalgh (2005) object to Bennett's positioning of consumerism at the forefront of the neo-tribal experience, suggesting that structural factors clearly block young people's access to consumer goods. In Bennett's response (2005) to this criticism, he uses hip-hop as one example of how obstacles of class have been overcome by youth culture, although his defence is weakened by the fact that he is attempting to relate the origins of hip-hop in the early 1970s to contemporaneous issues of the study of youth culture. Hesmondhalgh argues that Bennett is correct in his view that the CCCS '... might have overestimated the boundedness and permanence of the group identities they were studying, but simply to offer instability and temporariness as alternatives does not get us very far ...' (ibid.: 24). Bennett does not fully discuss the constitution of group boundaries and therefore this presentation of youth groups positions can be seen as too polarised. The replacement term 'tribes' holds many of the connotations of fixity and longevity that Bennett suggests are no longer a relevant aspect of youth cultural groups and that his postmodern analysis seeks to avoid.

Postmodern ideas of identity through style do not take into account the complexities of contemporary subcultures and ignore the possibility of structural factors and how they may impinge on an individual's access to consumables. Also, this notion of style links with Hebdige's notion of spectacular subcultures, those groups who through their visual appearance can be easily identified by the social scientist. Polsky, however, in his earlier study of the Beats, declares that an aim of this group was to remain inconspicuous to the outsider, that they did not'… flaunt their physical presence before the public gaze …' (1971: 150). For Polsky, to simply observe the most obvious signs of subcultural exhibitionism is to ignore the depths of the phenomenon and he states that such an approach renders the social scientist as little more than a 'tourist' (ibid.: 151). A knowing distance can be placed between a subculture and mainstream artefacts (Wood, 2006). In this respect, we must be aware that subcultures do not, and indeed cannot, exist in a vacuum. They are responses to the class contradictions and this involves the contestation of identity and the ownership of space.

The notion of style, however, is seen by post-subcultural theorists to be an increasingly significant component of general cultural identity and is no longer merely the domain of subculturalists. As discussed, this argument is put forward by Chaney (2004) but his writing is open to criticism as his work maintains a distance from those groupings that he suggests are no longer to be identified as once they were. There are no interviews with subcultural members and no real tangible examples or any form of empirical evidence offered. The postmodernist stance taken in this writing supposes that the parent culture has invested time and effort into areas of cultural life that were previously solely the domain of subcultural groups. The argument fails in the respect that Chaney does not establish a fully fleshed out argument, he merely observes one phenomenon; that non-subcultural groups are now engaged in cultural thoughts and processes, and reports another; that subcultures are now no longer as identifiable and distinct as a consequence. Although one could suggest that it is clear that the parent culture is now investing energy into matters of cultural consumption, an alternative view is that this, in fact, increases subcultural resistance to the normative values as represented by this supposed shift in the cultural concerns of the mainstream. Chaney does not counter the possibility that a shift within the parent culture may determine, and possibly force, a shift in subcultural values and identity formation. There may well be a fight for cultural space but this is a fight that has not yet eroded subcultural activity. As mainstream culture expands and alters, then arguably so do the symbolic creative activities of the subculturalists (Willis, 1990). Chaney's assumption seems to be that for a once marginalised culture to crossover into the mainstream there must be a knowing acceptance amongst the subcultural group that the game is up and, consequently, such subcultural activities and affiliations must cease to exist. A subculture cannot, after all, be seen to be resistant if its messages are willingly accepted into popular discourse. Co-optation into mainstream sensibilities does not confirm a negligible value to the oppositional stance taken by the subculture. This form of opposition, in fact, becomes more embedded and separate from mainstream taste in response to the mass commodified variant of the culture. In this respect, a cultural form can exist within both the mainstream and subcultural underground. The aural generic forms may be similar but the symbolic meanings and variances between the two remain.

The notion of the 'spectacle' aspect of contemporary musical subcultures is taken up by Keith Kahn-Harris in his discussion of the global Extreme Metal scene. He addresses the notion of subcultures that fall under the radar of mainstream visibility and recognition and he asks the question is spectacular practice that occurs unobserved still spectacular practice? (2004: 110) He argues that the CCCS definition of spectacle concerns public awareness of the subculture and its practices, thereby offering the position that the more marginal a group is in terms of the pubic conscious the less likely it is that it may rightfully be termed as subcultural in line with the thinking of the CCCS. Kahn-Harris proposes that the Extreme Metal scene does not fit into the subcultural paradigm as it cannot be considered sufficiently spectacular, yet it does not comfortably sit within a post-subcultural framework as there appears to be no obvious fluidity or transience in group membership or levels of commitment. Scenic infrastructures are utilised to avoid spectacular exposure (ibid.: 117), an aspect which is seen as a threat to the scene's long-term survival. The subcultures' response to problems posed to them by their material and social class position is to remain obscure, underground and out of the view of mainstream popular culture as opposed to the original CCCS evaluation of a subcultural experience of a fleeting moment in the limelight. It is the defence of a metaphysical territorial space which perhaps distinguishes contemporaneous subcultural existence from their historical peers. The increased plethora of media platforms which exist today perhaps make this invisibility more difficult for subcultures to maintain, and yet it is this space which allows a complete sense of autonomy which is essential to subcultural being (Hodkinson, 2002).

These structural factors clearly undermine Bennett's position whilst Shildrick and MacDonald state that once one accepts that '… social divisions still shape youth cultural identities, the postmodern tendency to celebrate the fragmented, fleeting and free-floating nature of contemporary youth culture becomes difficult to sustain …' (2006: 126). Class divisions can often determine which aspects of the culture individuals actively engage with. The postmodern analysis of youth culture '… obscures the effect that difference (structural or otherwise) and differential access to power have on producing meaningful contexts (and contexts of meaning) for cultural activity ...' (Stahl, 2003: 30). This is a fundamental aspect of the post-subcultural turn that needed investigating in the field. In Chapter 3, I discuss the findings with regards to socio-economic constraints experienced by the research participants and the research suggests that structural constraints, in this instance socio-economic class and gender, still affect cultural participation.

The notion of scene has been viewed in popular music studies as a replacement term for subculture. The term was introduced into academic discourse by Will Straw (1991). Scenes are '... kept in motion by a series of gigs, club nights, fairs and similar events where fans converge, communicate, and reinforce their sense of belonging to a particular scene ...' (Peterson and Bennett, 2004: 11). For Hesmondhalgh (2005: 23), scene is a less tightly bound concept than subculture and it is argued that it is a useful concept in the correct context, where the focus is more on place and space. In such spaces, differential forms of cultural activity can be observed and reported (Measham and Moore, 2009). The geographical concentration of the idea of scene can be seen to homogenise the individuals involved and obscures the idea of both individuality and collectivity. This concept is inextricably linked to the fluidity of identity which is central to the postmodern perspective. The use of the term scene infers a sense that people come and go (Haenfler, 2010: 130) and also carries with it connotations of a set geographical position and, therefore, is problematic when considering the global connections evident in contemporary cultural forms (Lipsitz, 1994). The longevity of engagement and fixed cultural identity for a number of the research respondents in this study makes it difficult to fully apply the term scene to these individuals as will be discussed later. The cultural practices of many of the respondents occurred in private spaces rather than in a manner identified by theorists who utilise the term scene. The denial of public space, therefore, has resulted in increasingly segregated and privatised cultural practices (Robinson, 2009), thereby affecting the collective spaces available to subcultural practitioners and impacting upon a notion of scene.

There is no return, for Hesmondhalgh (ibid.), to the term subculture in the study of popular music although it does retain some residual value in the sociology of youth. He asserts that the study of popular music privileges youth in its work and that this approach has '... become an obstacle to a more fully developed understanding of music and society ...' (2005: 21). The research for this study, however, identified young adults who retained an active engagement in hip-hop culture. The concept of subculture maintains a valuable position in the study of popular music for research that shifts from a central focus on youth as music tastes are no longer as staunchly dictated by age as once they were (Osgerby, 2008; Hodkinson and Bennett, 2012). This approach allows for an assessment of the transience of identity as evoked by the postmodernist theorists as opposed to notions of longevity and fixity present in the work of the CCCS.

Post-subcultural theorists state that identities are considered as being unique through the purchasing of consumer goods (Miles, 2000: 5). This is echoed in the work of Muggleton (2000) who states that there is an emphasis on surface qualities within contemporaneous youth identity formation. The post-subcultural position implies a degree of postmodern dandyism (Callinicos, 1989) wherein youth are portrayed as being capable of '... little more than high street consumption ...' (Bennett, 2011: 498). There is still a notion of a politics of style in the work of Muggleton (2000) and Miles (2000) and it is argued that consumerism stabilises the lives of those individuals who partake in identity through the 'supermarket of styles' available in postmodern society (Polhemus, 1997). MacDonald et al. (2000), Hollands (2002) and Blackman (2004) criticise this focus on individuality and consumption as a means to understand the social as proponents of the postmodern approach demonstrate a reluctance to integrate social structure into their analysis. Redhead's (1997) supposition that subcultures are free-floating signifiers utilised to enhance differentiation of individual experience, thereby declaring an end to authentic subcultural experience, is not developed through supporting empirical evidence. Blackman contends that '... empirical reality supports the view that youth culture is more socially complex, group orientated, diversified and meaningful than Redhead allows. The new emphasis on the individual and pleasure fails to give young people rights, agency or critically recognise the structures and institutions that seek to impose marginal status on the young ...' (2005: 10). For Shildrick and MacDonald, postmodern ideas of fragmentation and individuation pose the danger of '... producing a distorted and incomplete portrayal of contemporary youth culture ...' (ibid.: 128). As will be discussed in further detail later in this book, the postmodern view on youth groups retains a degree of value in relation to the sliding-scale variations in subcultural engagement which were evident in the field. Both the structural approach of the CCCS and the fluidity of identity forms and emphasis on consumerism as argued in the post-subcultural turn were found to be relevant to the varying forms of hip-hop subcultures in the research.

The return of subculture

As seen in the earlier section on hip-hop ethnographies, a number of researchers are retaining subculture as an academically applicable concept. There have been recent attempts to assess, revise and realign subcultural theory in light of the post-subcultural turn. Theorists such as Hodkinson (2002), Blackman (2005), Wood (2006), Wilson (2006) and Williams (2011) offer critical re-readings of the CCCS position and evaluate a number of the aspects of the postmodern perspective on youth culture, notably the fragmentation of cultural forms, the transience of collective youth identities and the denial of structural constraints on cultural engagement. Williams states that a major weakness of the post-subcultural position is '… that of certain scholars' unwillingness to empirically link … identities and performances to larger socio-cultural structures that come to appear rather permanent in their effects …' (2011: 37).

Sarah Thornton's (1995) ethnographic study of heterosexual nightclubs and raves invokes the empiricism of the Chicago School (Williams, 2011: 33). Thornton appropriates the concept of cultural capital (Bourdieu, 1986) in order to further an understanding of the hierarchical nature of contemporary subcultures in line with musical preference and cultural knowledge. The extension of the work of Bourdieu in Thornton's writing relates to the concept of subcultural capital. This abstract notion confers status on its owner and can be objicified in the form of fashionable haircuts and extensive and organised record collections and in the possession of cultural knowledge. The hierarchical and elitist nature evident in the groups that Thornton discusses raises A. K. Cohen's (1955) notion of subcultures within subcultures. This is a significant aspect of cultural identity as evinced in the fieldwork for my own study, though there was arguably less elitist aggression in the intentions of my research participants. Thornton states that '… journalists and photographers do not invent subcultures, but shape them, mark their core and reify their borders …' (1995: 160). From the fieldwork, Thornton argues that once an artefact such as a previously obscure dance record crosses over into mainstream culture it is viewed in a negative manner by the underground clubbers, hence their relationship with the mass media reinforces their own sense of subcultural elitism and perception of self in relation to the mainstream. This is an interesting point and one that I was keen to assess in my own work in light of the contested nature of the distinctions between mainstream and underground hip-hop.

The reformulation of subcultural theory offered by Paul Hodkinson (2002) is framed around four indicators of subcultural substance which are consistent distinctiveness, identity, commitment and autonomy. His insider research on the goth subculture combines what he sees as the useful aspects of both the Birmingham and Chicago School approaches, whilst also severing subculture's '… automatic link with resistance, problem-solving, class conflict and spontaneity …' (ibid.: 29). The cumulative nature of the four indicators increases the appropriateness and academic applicability of subculture as well as recognising the relevance of terms such as neo-tribes as a means to describe affiliations which are transient and relatively superficial. There is a complexity to contemporary substantive groups which is reflected in this approach, coupled with a rejection of the portrayal of youth groups as essentialised, homogeneous and reductive. Hodkinson asserts that subcultures are distinctive and distinguishable from more fluid elective collectives but adds that '… it remains important to recognise that even the most substantive of subcultures will retain elements of diversity, that some individuals will adopt elements of their values without any particular commitment, and that even the most committed participants are not somehow isolated from other interests or priorities …' (ibid.: 33). Hodkinson argues that some of the characteristics described by postmodern theorists are present in a number of identifiable groups yet the term subculture retains academic validity for the goths in his study, and he suggests that the term can be applied to other substantive collectives. This reformulation of theory suggests that the application of the term subculture '… does not rest upon spontaneous expression of shared structural contradictions and need not involve any form of symbolic or direct 'resistance' …' (ibid.: 196), rather his research subjects sought distinction from others and a sense of community. In this manner, he moves away from the overly structural approach of the CCCS. I utilise Hodkinson's framework for subcultural substance to assess the cultural engagement of the five research groups in Chapter 3. Each of these elements should be regarded as contributory features which, in combination with the others, assess the usefulness and academic value of retaining the term subculture. Rather than perceiving fluidity and substance as dichotomous binary oppositions it is important to note that these concepts are matters of degree.

The Toronto rave scene is the setting for Brian Wilson's (2006) ethnographic investigation of substantive youth groups. He argues that subcultural theory retains relevance in exploring rave culture as there is a significant degree of resistance in the cultural practices of ravers. His research subjects were largely middle-class and were seen to be reliant on mass-mediated forms of culture. This work, along with the writing of Thornton and Hodkinson, reframes subcultural theory by limiting the emphasis on socio-economic structural constraints as in the earlier work of the CCCS. Wilson states that '... binaries such as micro-macro, agency-structure, and social action-social systems ... are inherently insensitive to the nuanced and multifaceted aspects of social life and its micro and macro levels ...' (ibid.: 130). Wilson argues for an understanding of such elements as not simply dichotomous but as a form of continuum, a perspective taken up in my own analysis of the purist/peripheral hip-hop groups in the field. Wilson argues that the term subculture retains value in light of postmodern analysis of rave culture as such work fails to take into account the social processes that continue to define all subcultural groups (ibid.: 171). As an example of the structural aspects which affected the behaviour of Wilson's research participants, the subculturalists in his study reacted against the gender and racial segregation seen in mainstream clubs as their rave experience centred on inclusivity.

The concept of subculture is applied by Wood (2006) in his work on straightedge culture as it has explanatory potential with regards to a group's frame of reference, or group standards (Cohen, 1955: 65). The group standards become embedded in the subcultural texts and ideals and are transmitted beyond the means of the culture's originators. In this manner, subcultural identity evolves as each new member is affected by the pre-existing frame of reference. Wood states that in order for an individual to belong to this subculture they must abide by the rules of abstinence from alcohol, drugs and casual sex, thereby contradicting Sweetman's (2004) assumption that contemporaneous forms of youth culture have low levels of group cohesion and identity. Straightedge youth also often get an 'X' (or several Xs) tattooed upon their person in order to clearly project a stamp of allegiance to their subculture, thereby making them spectacular and denying the notion of transience through the use of a permanent marker of identity. Such markers help reinforce insider/outsider distinctions between straightedge and mainstream sensibilities. The spectacular specifics of this subculture are emblematic of its participants' cultural and political resistance whilst further entrenching a sense of communality.

Wood uses the notion of subcultural schism, an often overlooked phenomenon, to compartmentalise the varying divisions that exist under the broader term of straightedge. Schism is '... the division of a social group into two or more relatively distinct and opposed factions ...' (ibid.: 130). This allows for varying articulations of subcultural values between collectives and can be seen as signalling evolving cultural systems. It is argued that schism initially '… stems from the individual's sense of unarticulated or persisting discontent …' (ibid.: 140) but is sustained by intra-subcultural interaction with others who also share the same sense of frustration that their needs are no longer being fulfilled by the subcultural group. As resulting cliques are formed with their own sense of shared norms and values, and as the members of these new cliques begin to ostracise themselves from the other group, a modified version of the original subcultural frame of reference is formed. This is a useful concept as it allows for an appreciation of subcultural variance and similarity as well as being a potential source of evaluating localised appropriations of global subcultural collectives.

Williams (2011) and Haenfler (2010) also examine straightedge culture, utilising subcultural theory in their explorations of the form. Williams states that the popular discourse on straightedge internet forums centre on the values and ethics of the culture and help to validate those who are, and those who are not, sufficiently straightedge. Such activities, along with attendance at live shows or reading straightedge fanzines, enable members to solidify their frame of reference in relation to their everyday lives. This further assists them in '… moments of micro-oriented resistance …' (Williams, ibid.: 101). Haenfler (2010) focuses on the drug and alcohol free aspect of straightedge in order to demonstrate subcultural theory's relevance to contemporary youth groups. The DIY ethos of straightedge concerts links to the notion of autonomy, a key element of Hodkinson's (2002) framework for subcultural substance that is utilised in this study. Haenfler contends that the collective resistance evident in subcultural writing is evinced in the straightedge community. Subculturalists engage in the political in a personal sense, establishing an individual sense of resistance to dominant norms and values such as patriarchy and the dominance of drugs and alcohol in society.

For Wood, Williams and Haenfler, the clear sense of political and cultural resistance in straightedge practices allows participants to identify true subculturalists from a *scenester* or *poseur*, that individual who '… wears the trappings of a subculture but who others perceive to fail to live out or truly believe in the subculture's ideals …' (Haenfler, ibid.: 36). This bifurcation, between subculturalists and 'others', is a recurring aspect in the literature of subcultural theory. In order to assess the validity of this separation I took these ideas into the field to examine the relationship between the subcultural member and 'others'. As will be discussed in detail in Chapter 4, it was found that there were clear degrees of cultural activity at play which leads to the assertion that a simple 'insider/outsider' dichotomy does not fully explain the complex subcultural relationships and the hierarchical structures from the field. Williams (2011) amends the bifurcation offered by stating that rather than seeing these distinctive forms as dichotomous, it is more useful to regard them not as two types of subcultural forms but to see them as '... two poles between which all subcultural phenomena may be located on a continuum ...' (: 35). This idea of a continuum was used in my own work and is presented in Chapter 4.

Hollands (2002) states that '... despite the fact that subcultural theory cannot be applied *carte blanche* to youth today, it is invariably the case that the perspective has been too easily dismissed and stereotyped ...' (: 155). Postmodern theorists tend to inaccurately perceive the work of the CCCS as conceptually rigid despite the assertion in *Resistance through rituals* that a wide range of cultural potentialities exist within the framework of subcultural theory. Postmodern theorists focus their attention on loosely-defined milieux whilst rendering the existence of groups with clear and coherent identities and structure as impossible in contemporary society. When applied to loosely-bounded collectives it can be argued that some of the perspectives and terminology offered by post-subcultural theorists retain some residual value and applicability.

Conclusion

As has been shown, the term subculture is today under academic scrutiny within the literature. Thornton, Hodkinson and Wilson offer criticisms of subcultural theory as practiced by the earlier theorists, but attempt to address, refine and reformulate the theoretical parameters of the concept. For these writers there are undoubted problems with the traditional model of subcultural analysis, as there are with the methodologies employed and the findings of post-subculture theorists. However, rather than simply repudiate the terminology these writers aim to renegotiate the boundaries of the term subculture and to place limits on its usage and meaning. The alternate terms offered by post-subcultural theorists are, however, of some value in describing the cultural activities of those whose engagement is undoubtedly ephemeral and lacking in substance. Subculture is still a valid term in academic discourse as it offers an opportunity to distinguish between those who display a sense of commitment and longevity to a particular set of distinctive norms and values which are in contrast to conventional, mainstream culture.

Competing terms such as lifestyle, neo-tribes and scenes all have something to offer the social scientist in certain contexts. The literature has been used to inform the study's research methodologies in a number of ways. As a result, a grounded theory of subcultural engagement was allowed to develop. The emphasis in this study is on the research participants rather than a focus on particular aspects of spectacular experience which are seen to obscure the motivations, identities and cultural understandings that lie underneath (Hodkinson, 2011: 558). I have argued that the literature can put forward an essentialised portrayal of subcultural groups. In the subsequent chapters, the development of the purist/ peripheral model seeks to move beyond the simple dichotomous representation between subculture and mainstream. It focuses attention on an appreciation of the dynamic and contested nature of the substantive groups presented in this study, along with a reappraisal of Cohen's (1955) idea of subcultures within subcultures. Hesmondhalgh (2005) is correct to call for a move away from an over privileging of youth in studies of popular music consumption, but such a theoretical shift can be seen to ignore the relevance of popular music in the lives of key cultural practitioners. Subculture as a concept can be applied to young adults and should not be restricted to studies of youth, although it retains relevance in the study of the latter group. This book, therefore, offers an examination of hip-hop culture and grime music use by individuals who can be categorised as youth and young adults. It was found in the fieldwork that seemingly opposing paradigms in the literature remain relevant in consideration of the varying positions and activities of the youth groups in the research. Rather than see structural and post-subcultural analysis as conflicting, the fieldwork allowed for an opportunity to examine each perspective in relation to the youth groups under investigation to assess their validity.

The alternate terms offered by post-subcultural theorists are of some value in describing the cultural activities of those whose engagement is undoubtedly ephemeral and relatively lacking in substance. By considering the work of Hollands (2002), I aim to explore the idea that the varying paradigms present in the literature on subculture can be utilised to explain varying levels of cultural engagement. This study draws on the fieldwork data to assess the different forms of subcultural identity and activity in evidence. I reflect on how both structural and postmodern perspectives can be applied to, and are seen to hold relevance for, the different purist and peripheral forms of hip-hop engagement for the young people in the study.

Chapter 3

Hip-hop subcultural substance

"It's bigger than all these fake-ass records ..."[3]

Introduction

The aim of this chapter is to utilise Hodkinson's (2002) framework of subcultural substance to examine the degree of applicability that the term subculture retains for describing substantive youth groups and their cultural activities. As the previous chapter demonstrated, the term subculture has in recent years come under increasing academic scrutiny but it is argued in this chapter that the term retains validity in the face of the challenges to its use posited by scholars who choose to utilise a postmodern perspective in their analysis. This position is informed from the findings from the field rather than from a purely theoretical perspective which can be seen as a major weakness of a number of studies on subcultural theory which omit the voices of those under investigation.

I will begin by introducing the focus group participants from the qualitative research before outlining their initial involvement with hip-hop culture. The chapter will then establish Hodkinson's four indicators of subcultural substance as a means to assess the subcultural validity of the groups examined. Each of the factors pertaining to subcultural substance — consistent distinctiveness, identity, commitment and autonomy—will be discussed in further detail and these sections will contain the opinions of respondents from the focus groups in order to further an understanding of the groups. The terminology and positions developed here will enable a further discussion of agency in hip-hop in the chapter that immediately follows.

It was found in the field that there existed a complex relationship between different research respondents and hip-hop culture which could not easily be homogenised. The chapter will use the data from the field to highlight varying levels of subcultural engagement which suggests that both the classical structuralist and the postmodern approach to youth groups retain academic value as each paradigm holds relevance when applied to different groups engaged in hip-hop culture. The groups are labelled as either purist or peripheral, a distinction which I will develop further in the chapter that follows.

Subcultural identity in five focus groups

The focus group interviews for this study were spread across a wide geographical area of South East England. The research sites were Rochester, Canterbury and Ashford, all in Kent, along with Brighton in East Sussex and Lewisham, South London. The Rochester, Brighton and Lewisham group interviews were undertaken at educational institutions to which each member was affiliated, whilst the Ashford and Canterbury discussions occurred in a number of places, ranging from coffee shops, pubs and, on three occasions, in the home of two of the Canterbury participants. Each meeting lasted roughly an hour and every group met on six occasions, apart from the Brighton and Ashford groups where the meetings numbered five.

When directly quoting the focus group participants in this book, aliases have been used in order to allow the participants full anonymity. The gender of names has not been altered. The focus group participants were:-

The purists:

Canterbury: Catherine, Simon, Andy, Luke and Chris;

Lewisham: Ash, Jemal, Isaac, Emmanuel, Dave;

Ashford: Josh, Rachel, Adam, Trevor and Matt.

The peripherals:

Rochester: Zac, Jon, Dan, Sarah and Loul

Brighton: Kate, Rob, Paul, Alice and Tony.

The Canterbury group

In Canterbury, Catherine, Simon, Andy, Luke and Chris were 'purists' and we met six times over an eighteen month period although I often still see some of this group in social situations after becoming friends with them. We met through Simon who was at the time an employee of a Further Education college that I had contacted and he became aware of my research through a colleague. He was informed that a researcher was aiming to talk to young people about their involvement in hip-hop culture and he emailed me directly to ask if I would be interested in talking to his group of friends, all of whom had been hip-hop fans for many years. When I was informed of the age of his peer group my initial reaction was to look elsewhere as the intention was to investigate youth responses to, and uses of, hip-hop culture. However, studies on music subcultures can often be hindered by the temporal boundaries of age placed onto the study of youth (Hesmondhalgh, 2005: 21), thereby neglecting an area that is rich in sociological value. With this in mind, it was felt that this group would serve as illustrative of the longevity of subcultural activity. On three occasions with the Canterbury group, Simon and Catherine's home served as the meeting place. This further developed my own knowledge of their practices and values as I was allowed the opportunity to undertake participant observation at a number of gatherings and parties.

Luke was the only black member of this group (the rest were white, all research subjects in this group were British) and he was also the oldest at thirty-eight years-old when the focus group meetings began. Catherine was the youngest at twenty-six and her boyfriend, Simon, was thirty-one. Andy was twenty-none and Chris was thirty-two. Simon and Chris were members of a local hip-hop DJ collective and they had, on various occasions, DJed in support of a number of established hip-hop acts. This group acknowledged the fact that they were middle-class although they were at pains to point out that they had all come from working-class backgrounds. Luke in particular was very vocal about his teenage years living in South London.

It was with the Canterbury set that I established the strongest connection, most likely due to our similar ages and interests. As will be demonstrated, they were very knowledgeable on a range of rap and hip-hop related topics and they engaged well in my research as they saw it as a means to discuss and to reflect on their own experiences in an area of their life that they were extremely passionate about. They were the group who embraced the research and unlike some of the other focus groups never once sought to assess my own cultural knowledge. Discussions with this group were vibrant and enjoyable for all. There was a relaxed feeling in the interviews and, unlike in many similar situations, when I pressed the record button on my dictaphone nobody froze — they were all desperate to have their opinions heard which often made it tricky for me in conducting the interviews as there was a tendency for them all to talk over one another.

This group dressed casually but not necessarily in a manner that could be described as overtly 'hip-hop'.

The Lewisham group

Every member of this group was black except for Dave who was Caucasian. All of the respondents were British citizens. They all reported that they considered themselves to be from the working-class and lived in local authority accommodation in the surrounding areas. They travelled by public transport to

college as none of them owned any form of vehicle. All of the group were students
on a Music Production course. At the outset of the focus group interviews Ash,
at sixteen years-old, was the youngest of the group whilst Dave was the oldest
(nineteen). All of the other respondents in this group were eighteen years-old
when the focus group meetings began. The dress code of the educational provider
allowed the respondents to wear their own clothes to college. All of the members
of this group dressed in recognisable hip-hop clothing including low slung jeans,
hi-top trainers and baseball caps. Branded sweaters and trainers (mostly Adidas
or Nike) were worn and it was noticeable that the same items of clothing were
worn on almost every occasion that we met. This suggests that either these
visual markers were so strong for them that they wanted to present themselves
in this manner every time we met or that, due to their relative levels of income,
they were not in an economic position to possess more clothes of a similar style.

The meetings with this group took place in one of the classrooms where
their Music Production course was taught. The room had desks laid out in four
rows facing a large whiteboard which dominated the far end of the room. For
the focus group meetings, the furniture was rearranged so that we could all sit
around two desks pushed together at the back of the room. Posters were on three
of the four walls, mostly concerning the different arms of the music industry.
For example, one poster illustrated in diagrammatical format the structure and
workings of the major record labels and their subsidiaries. All of the members
of this group were engaged in hip-hop and grime production and performance
both inside and outside of college.

The members of the Lewisham group were the most sceptical about this
project and in the first two meetings were very reluctant to offer anything in the
way of personal opinion and were especially reticent to answer questions about
their cultural activities outside of the college. They were clearly suspicious of
my intentions and it took one of them to overhear a conversation I had with
their course leader before they relaxed. They heard us talking about artists such
as Dizzee Rascal and Wiley and how they had crossed over to mainstream
acceptability — it seemed that just this small amount of knowledge was enough
for the group to be convinced that I wasn't an undercover police officer! They
were very open about the fact that they had heard the conversation and from
that point on the relationship I had with them was much more open and honest.
However, when they were informed by the course leader that I had interviewed
established rap artists and that I had more lined up they constantly asked me to
pass on their mix tapes or *SoundCloud* URLs as a means for their music to be

discovered. This group were prone to testing my own knowledge, particularly in the first two sessions, where they would ask me whether I knew the work of a particular artist or not. Some I had heard of, others I had not, so I responded honestly and once the interview was over I used the internet to research some of the names mentioned only to find no trace of them, thereby suggesting that this group were making names up to see if they could trick me into pretending to know more about the culture than I did.

The Ashford group

This group solely consisted of white members, all of whom were born and bred in Ashford. They termed themselves as British working-class although one or two members raised doubts about this class labelling. Josh and Adam tended to view themselves in the lower middle-class due to their disposable income which enabled them to purchase computers and numerous software packages that allowed them to create their own beats.

Rachel, the only girl in the group, was a very dominant vocal force in the discussions. She was the person who had introduced me to the rest of the members of this group on our first meeting. My initial contact with Rachel was through a member of staff at a college of further education where she was enrolled as a student. This gatekeeper put me in contact with Rachel via her *myspace* page. This internet site was used to promote her creativity as a rapper. She seemed interested in the study and we agreed to meet outside of the college environment. All of our meetings took place in a coffee shop in Ashford town centre.

The Ashford group had members between eighteen and twenty-three years-old. This was the only group across the five that had a discernible spokesperson. The rest of the group were very deferential to Rachel's responses and clearly valued her opinion. As with the Lewisham group, there were clear markers of hip-hop dress code in evidence with all members of the group although their style of dress would fluctuate somewhat from meeting to meeting. Baseball caps and hip-hop oriented sweaters were usually worn although on occasion one or two of the group would turn up in non hip-hop specific attire. All of the members of this group, with the exception of Matt, were engaged in creative aspects of hip-hop culture in either a production or performance aspect.

After our first meeting I asked whether a more suitable venue for our meetings could be found as I realised that the background noise in the coffee shop would render it difficult for me to listen back to the focus group recordings on my dictaphone but they seemed to enjoy that first meeting and insisted that all subsequent discussions take place there.

The Rochester group

In all, three participants in the group were not British and all of these were from the Rochester group. Lou was from Nigeria, Zac from Ghana and Dan was South African. All three of these participants were black. Both Jon and Sarah were white British. Each member of this group was a student at a fee-paying school in Rochester studying A-Levels in a variety of subjects. Lou, Zac and Dan were boarders at the school whilst Jon and Sarah were day students. The five members of this group ranged from sixteen years-old (Sarah and Lou) to nineteen (Zac). The other two were both eighteen at the beginning of the focus group stage of my research. As a result of their private education and their parents' occupations, these individuals can be seen to belong to the middle-class.

The meetings with this group took place in a number of classrooms at the school during the students' lunch breaks. There was no uniform at this school and so every member was free to express their identity through the clothes they wore. Lou, Zac and Dan wore recognisable hip-hop dress code with low slung jeans commonplace. Jon and Sarah were a little more conservative in their appearance although Jon's short bleached blonde hair was more than a little reminiscent of his cultural hero Eminem. Lou and Dan often wore jewellery which was akin to rap performers within the sub-genre of gangsta, namely thick necklaces, expensive watches and diamond studded earrings.

Only Sarah in this group had not entertained the idea of performing. Lou, Zac and Dan had paid money to enter a recording studio to record a demo a few months before our first meeting (though none were satisfied with the outcome and all agreed that they were unlikely to spend more money on this venture in the foreseeable future) whilst Jon professed to occasionally performing other people's raps at parties and social events. The members of this group who did perform admitted that they had little creative input into their routines and simply mimicked the vocal styles and lyrics of their favourite performers. This was a very relaxed group and each meeting was positive with a strong relationship between myself and the members of the group. The meetings were scheduled for an hour each with this group and there were a couple of occasions where we overran due to losing track of time as our conversations intensified. This was the group that seemed most reflective of their own cultural practices and would often refer back to comments made in previous meetings or points of discussion which highlighted their cognitive engagement with the process.

The Brighton group

As with the Ashford group, all of the participants in Brighton were white. Their institution was a co-educational Grammar school on the outskirts of the city. The school had a strict uniform regime in place which meant that no obvious symbolic visual signifiers of hip-hop culture were employed by this group during our meetings.

The members of this group were A-Level students in their final year of Sixth Form. All were eighteen years-old at the start of the focus group process except Kate who was seventeen. The meetings were conducted during lunch breaks in a classroom within the Media Studies department. None of this group admitted to creating or performing rap music.

It became clear from an early stage in this work that each group characterised variations of hip-hop centred subcultures. Our discussions concerned many topic areas, including a life history of each participant's involvement with hip-hop and grime music, as well as conversations on the imagery and messages of the culture, their own personal involvement in a local scene as well as talking about consumption patterns. For those members of the focus groups who produced their own hip-hop and grime music, a considerable amount of time in the sessions was used to develop an understanding of their participation and how it impacted upon their cultural involvement.

In the following passages, where the same question was asked of different groups, I have on a number of occasions included the responses in continual prose form, somewhat in the form of a conversation. The letter after each name indicates which geographical location the participant is from and therefore, although it may seem as if one respondent is following on from a point made by another, this is not always the case.

Initial cultural involvement

Stratton (1997: 181) argues for a move away from the CCCS position of a politicised notion of youth subcultures towards a more socio-cultural analysis and this will be the position mainly taken within this book. Cultural formation, according to Wyn and White, is '... an active process, one which involves young people themselves choosing and deciding aspects of their own identity and future ...' (1997: 76). The emphasis on agency in recent studies on subcultures is significant and allows for a move away from the structural determinism of the neo-Marxist CCCS approach although, as will be discussed later, there was evidence from the field that structural considerations still impacted upon the forms of subcultural activity that were engaged in.

David Moore's ethnographic study of skinheads found that the participants in his work viewed their engagement with the culture as temporary, a passing phase (1994: 19). A number of studies also discuss the transient aspects of youth subcultures (Muggleton, 2000) yet the initial engagement with a subculture rarely features in writings in the field. Although what follows is only a mere sketch of subcultural attraction it is hoped that such an approach can be accommodated into subsequent studies in the field in order to develop an enhanced understanding. There has been a tendency to conceive of subcultural engagement as an organic move or one which is a 'magical solution' to a presented problem although one criticism that can be levelled at writings on subcultural identity is that the focus tends to be on an already fully-formed group rather than various stages which may lead to subcultural engagement.

The following extracts centre on initial engagement with a cultural form which may, in some cases, lead to subcultural affiliation.

> *TD:* How do you actively get involved in a subculture today?
>
> *Zac (R):* For me, it was through hanging out with people who I felt were similar to me, you know? It's not like I saw hip-hop kids and wanted to be one of the crowd. It's just that it was my crowd, like. It just kind of happened. It wasn't, like, a conscious plan or anything. You just get on with the people who share the same approach on music and that, don't you?
>
> *Catherine (C):* Unless you meet like-minded people that like similar music to you then it's actually quite hard to find out about things that aren't in the popular mainstream and, like, I know personally that most of the music I've discovered and love has come from other people's saying or playing something to me.

Catherine's claim that it is often difficult to access music beyond the mainstream was a commonly held belief amongst most of the focus group members. Some of the participants, notably in the Lewisham and Ashford groups, claimed to possess a degree of subcultural capital in this respect as they used platforms such as YouTube and pirate radio stations to engage with aspects of the culture that they saw as more genuine than commercialised forms of rap music. There is, however, still an important role that a 'significant other' plays in a member's subcultural identification even though the majority of research participants here claimed to have had more autonomy in their decision making process on first encountering the culture. The data from the fieldwork indicates that individuals claimed that they were attracted to the hip-hop subculture initially through a personal interest or engagement with rap music. They vociferously and actively played down the importance of influential peers when recounting their first contact with the music or images that they had experienced. Zac's comments above illustrate this. This may be read as a somewhat romanticised recounting of their initiation into hip-hop tastes. During the interview process, many of the research subjects discussed the pivotal roles people played in their introduction to the musical output of the culture (as stated by Catherine above) although they still maintained a level of personal autonomy when initialising their subcultural allegiance. There is, therefore, a slight contradiction here with regards to influential others. The following excerpts are illustrative of this point:

TD: Can you remember when you first heard hip-hop and what was it that made you like it?

Simon (C):   I was into a lot of dance music in the late 1980s and a lot of acts started having raps in their music. I liked that and a mate of mine gave me some of the Daisy Age hip-hop stuff which was well cool. You know, stuff like De La Soul and A Tribe Called Quest and that. I liked the happiness and the funkiness of all that. I remember seeing the video for 'Can I Kick It?' on the telly and thinking it was really cool. A load of my friends were into the more gangsta type of rap and it just didn't appeal to me for some reason. I've been into other types of music whose appeal has, like, come and gone, but rap was always there.

Dan (R):   I was on holiday when I first heard Eminem. It was on the radio or something and I just thought it was so different to all the other stuff the station was playing. It made me, like, want to listen to more stuff of his and that's when I just, like, fell for hip-hop.

Lou (R):   Back home in Nigeria, rap music was kinda big about five or six years ago and that's when I first got into it. I heard a few

things on the radio and on the TV and it just felt, like, real
or something. It was just interesting to me and so me and a
friend started to discover things and look into it more.

Kate (B):   I think I only really became aware of rap in a big way a couple
of years back. We didn't have satellite TV at home until only
recently and that's when I could channel hop and see stuff
that's not on normal telly. There was just a lot of cool stuff
on some of the music channels. It wasn't really something a
lot of my friends were into so I just kind of got into it on my
own.

Isaac (L):   The first artist I heard was Tupac. I was kind of with my uncle
and he was a big fan of him and so I started kind of listening
to him and got into him. I started getting into him loads.

When asked about their personal biographies in relation to hip-hop culture,
the majority of participants in all five focus groups talked about the attractiveness
of the music first before involving themselves with similarly minded individuals
and any form of collectivity. The quotes above illustrate the fact that there was
a self-perception of independence to initial cultural exposure and many of the
respondents went to great lengths to ensure that I was aware of this fact and
that this would be reported accurately. The extracts from both Simon and Kate
demonstrate the distancing of their tastes from that of their friends in some ways.
They both make the point that their friends were either not into hip-hop or were
fans of alternate hip-hop sub-genres. In discussing the initial impressions of
hip-hop music, this distancing of others can be interpreted as a means to confirm
the agency of a selection of cultural taste made by these individuals — a sense of
identity via initial isolationism and separation. The influence of significant others
such as Isaac's uncle, Lou's friend and Simon's mate can be seen as somewhat
minimal from the perceptions of these respondents. The participants felt that
their engagement with collectives originated from a sense of individual choice.
Such ideas aided a projection of subcultural authenticity and agency.

For these individuals, their activity with the culture cannot be satisfactorily
determined from a theorised position although what is clear is that they
were attracted to the music first and so subcultural allegiance cannot be said
in this case to be a perceived as a magical solution to socio-economic issues
(Cohen, 1972). There was a degree of opposition to popular taste values which
the research subjects saw as being of a lower artistic value than their music

of choice. The definition of mainstream as an abstract term used to signal differential tastes and values can be seen in this instant. It should be made clear that the individuals within the focus groups did not see their involvement with hip-hop as a matter of conscious choice and they certainly did not view their engagement with the subculture as transient or fluid, thereby opposing the perspective of many postmodern subcultural theorists. The Canterbury group in particular showed that some members of a subculture can continue active and enthusiastic engagement well into their 30s. Also, it is worth noting that for the majority of focus group respondents, their initial contact with rap music came through mediated, mainstream platforms such as radio and music video channels. Irrespective of a potential later favouring for underground hip-hop, for the majority of the participants within this study their first contact with the culture was via the output of major label artists. In line with Thornton's (1995) work on club cultures, it was found that for the individuals in this study the mass media was not initially seen as a form of opposition as it would become for some. As will be discussed in more detail later, as subculturalists develop their own forms of subcultural knowledge the importance and initial influence of the mass media is somewhat denied although niche forms of media are still used on a regular basis.

Four indicators of subcultural substance

Hodkinson (2002) reformulates subcultural theory in his study on goth culture. He offers four categories by which subcultural substance can be ascribed to a group. These four components give the subculture a sense of unity and solidarity of identity irrespective of such matters as geographical location or prior personal knowledge between individuals who saw themselves as belonging to and identifying with this subculture. The remainder of this chapter will deal with this theoretical revision of subculture theory and will apply Hodkinson's criteria to those engaged in hip-hop culture within the focus groups and the wider ethnographic findings. The four indicators of a group possessing subcultural substance are:

Consistent distinctiveness

Identity

Commitment

Autonomy   (Hodkinson, 2002: 30)

A sense of collective and shared identity is considered to be the most significant of the four subcultural indicators. I will argue here that the very nature of hip-hop in its commodified form often results in the fragmentation of the audience as opposed to it being used as a unifying cultural form, arguably the culture's original intentions. The geographical divide was only one factor that separated these groups, along with ethnicity, age, class and perception of self in terms of subcultural belonging. Every member in each focus group expressed their interest in hip-hop culture at the outset, although as time went by it was obvious that there was a significant discrepancy in the amount of time each individual devoted to their subcultural activities and the form of the culture they most readily engaged with. This is not to suggest that the term subculture is redundant for those individuals in the group who largely consumed mainstream, commercialised aspects of hip-hop culture as there were elements of identity and agency that they received from the cultural form. This discussion will be elaborated further in Chapter 4.

Consistent distinctiveness

There is a distinction between the shared tastes and values of subcultural groups and others. Hodkinson (2002) suggests that within the goth subculture, visual appearance was a key determinant in allowing acceptance for individuals within the group and their further recognition and status. However, we must be aware that there is no absolute sense of such ideals, that such matters will vary from group to group and from place to place. Such markers of subcultural belonging should be seen in relative terms and each subcultural grouping should be seen as an individual unit with ideals and tastes specific to that group.

One aspect of subcultural distinctiveness relates to an outward expression of style wherein clothes, make-up and hair are used as active signifiers of subcultural belonging and identification and can be seen as indicators of subcultural affiliation. This sense of subcultural style is a means of communication which signifies ideological values and aspirations (Hebdige, 1979: 100). Hip-hop dress code and the notion of unspectacular style is discussed further in Chapter 4 as a means to distinguish between the purist and the peripheral groups, yet here the focus is on the research subjects' responses and experiences to visual appearance and its meaning and consequences, a position that Hebdige (ibid.) fails to consider. A shared sense of style can be seen to be a defining aspect of subcultural identity, yet this also needs to allow for some degree of individuality, within set stylistic boundaries, so that members can stand out within the group.

TD: Can you tell if somebody is into hip-hop by what they wear?

Zac (R):	Yeah, sure. Hip-hop has its own look, its own way of moving, its own way of talking. What someone wears may give you a clue but it's more than that, too. Like, you see someone walking, wearing their cap in a certain way and you can label them hip-hop but a lot of people are getting into the look and aren't really in the know about the scene, you know what I mean? I think a lot of people are getting into having their jeans slung low, lots of different groups. I see rock kids hanging out with their jeans real low. They ain't hip-hop. That's a hip-hop look and they stole it. But you can tell when someone wears their jeans like that if they're proper hip-hop or not.
Rachel (A):	I see a lot of people wearing what they think is hip-hop gear but that don't necessarily make 'em hip-hop, you know? Like me, sometimes I'll wear stuff like Nike high-tops and hoodies, caps and whatever that says 'hip-hop' a lot more than the way I'm dressed today. Depends where I'm going and what I'm doing. But, you know what, I can wear pretty much whatever I like to a hip-hop show and nobody cares but once I went to a gig to see Fall Out Boy and was, like, dressed a bit 'ghetto' and people were staring at me like I didn't belong. I think hip-hop is a bit more accepting whereas, like, rock can be snobby, like.
Adam (A):	She (referring to Rachel) has got her own style and she don't give a fuck and that's very hip-hop, you know? People will look and think you are into something by the way you dress but hip-hop is about knowing what you know, not about what clothes you got on or what you showing. People will find you out if you're fake. It's easy to spot people that dress up special for a show or club. They look too shiny, too new, you know? It happens a lot, these safe little kids acting all grimey and gangsta but, really, they ain't.
TD:	How can you tell?
Adam (A):	You can just tell. Like, if you're watching kids at a show or club and they're mouthing the words and getting 'em all wrong, that's a pretty good sign, you know? They try too hard to

impress. Some people will just try too hard. They just seem
a little, like, desperate.

A number of the research respondents alluded to an ability to distinguish
between 'true subcultural members' and those who they saw as 'outsiders'.
However, they could not verbalise the criteria for such a distinction to a
perceived outsider such as myself because this is something that they felt came
with subcultural belonging and understanding as a form of cultural competence.
This abstract cognitive quality is of interest because this notion is slightly against
the grain of other writers in this field who, in most part, tend to take it upon
themselves to differentiate between pure and part-time subcultural membership
and how this may manifest itself (for example Moore, 1994; Muggleton,
2000). The research participants in the focus group sessions felt an inability
to express what may be termed their 'identity framework' and perhaps denied
me the opportunity to demarcate or place a value judgement on their culture.
In this respect, they were laying some form of claim to their own subculture
by restricting the knowledge and opinion of an individual perceived to be an
outsider, unworthy of such foresight.

Muggleton (2000) suggests that contemporary subcultural identity can
be seen to be more transient and fluid than previous generations may have
experienced which results in a less solid foundation for individuals to profess and
display their subcultural affiliations. Throughout the fieldwork it was found that
members of what may be called the hip-hop community see no real problems
with appearances being fluid. The majority of respondents made it clear that
subcultural belonging in this context was more about a set of shared ideals,
values and knowledge than outward displays of identity. For both Muggleton
(ibid.) and Hodkinson (2002: 46) some confusion as to their own definitions
of where such boundaries occur is evident. Their studies detail punk, mod and
goth subcultures primarily, all of whom seem resistant to those that they perceive
to be weekend subculturalists. Adam's comments above suggest that individual
style and a 'don't give a fuck' attitude are, in some ways, more important than
wearing a particular brand of trainers or appropriating a pair of jeans in such a
manner that can be visibly defined as hip-hop. Rachel's comments are interesting
in two ways. First, she suggests that the hip-hop community allow her to present
herself in a number of ways without any perceived form of prejudice towards
her. She also goes on to claim that an individual wearing hip-hop style clothing
does not automatically qualify for subcultural acceptance from others. In this

respect, the visually spectacular aspect of subcultures is less evident for those centred on hip-hop culture. This does not, however, mean that this weakens any aspect of consistent distinctiveness that can be ascribed to these groups as their rejection of the increasingly widespread commodified elements of hip-hop are exactly what maintains their distinction. These groups could be interpreted, as a result of their values, to reject the malleable nature of identity through consumer choice and the supermarket of styles emphasised in postmodern writing on youth cultures.

The notion of distinctiveness should not simply be limited to visual aspects of subcultural activity. Schloss' (2009) concept of foundation can be utilised here as many in the focus groups perceived cultural knowledge to be of more significance than spectacular style. The majority of individuals within the focus groups saw themselves to be very different to mainstream popular music tastes which were simply often referred to as 'shit' by many of the interview participants. However, members of both the Rochester and Brighton groups admitted to listening to mainstream 'chart music' occasionally. The divide between 'underground' and 'mainstream' helps the subcultural member to reaffirm their sense of difference and also enhances their identity within their peer group although for many in the research this dichotomous distinction of underground and mainstream, as will be shown, was problematic. For the respondents, their affiliation to hip-hop was due to its apparent authenticity and its seeming refusal to bow to commercial pressures.

Josh (A): Mate, I've been listening to rap since them lot [referring to mainstream culture] was into the Spice Girls.

Josh's comment bears a striking resemblance to many proclamations in hip-hop lyrics that lay claim to a degree of authenticity from a personal, biographical detail of exactly when they became engaged with rap music. The issue of authenticity in hip-hop culture is addressed in greater depth in Chapter 7 although there is relevance here in terms of the connection between the authentic and a sense of distinctiveness from conventional culture. In the extract above, Josh is using a time frame of personal involvement whilst using mainstream sensibilities and tastes as a point of reference and opposition. Although such comments of 'otherness' attributed to mainstream sensibilities were frequent in the focus group interviews, it was often difficult for the respondents to pinpoint their exact feelings towards mainstream culture that went beyond the obvious and superficial. Also, the focus group respondents failed to find a definition for the mainstream that they could agree upon. For some research subjects, although hip-hop acts were present in mainstream pop culture, they still retained autonomy and distinction from the perceived mass produced and commodified musical forms that constituted the sales charts.

Commercial success has often conceived in terms of 'selling out' (Garofalo, 1993), a term which has come under scrutiny in writings on subculture. Hebdige (1979: 96) discusses how subcultural signifiers become 'codified', 'comprehensible' and 'frozen' the moment they are translated from private, small spaces into mass produced and commodified forms. Brake (1980: 155) suggests that capitalist cultural forms do not merely contain oppressive aspects for subcultures, but can also possess liberating elements. Youths can often find, in the commodified forms of popular music, a medium which may be used as a means to express their ideals, values and subsequent distinctiveness. The manner in which subcultural spaces are negotiated and worked do not necessarily run counter to heavily marketed musical forms. The young people spoken to during this research felt that whatever sub-genre of hip-hop they consumed they perceived their musical consumption as having a level of opposition to what they saw as the values of the mainstream. Rap music presented a set of ideas and values that the focus groups believed were different to an idea of 'pop' music and in this respect they suggested a conformity to Hodkinson's notion of consistent distinctiveness in subcultures.

TD: How different to mainstream pop music is rap?
Josh (A):   It's a completely different world. Like, pop music is made for
             money whereas what I listen to, I suppose, has been made
             because people feel the need to make it. Does that make
             sense? Like, the MCs that I listen to seem to be doing it for
             more than just the money or the fame. What I listen to is the
             truth, not watered down bollocks what most people listen to.

Josh's comments were indicative of the feelings towards mainstream culture that many of the focus group respondents held. Those research subjects who had more 'underground' musical tastes regularly sought to belittle the creative ability of mainstream acts and the cultural knowledge of those who consumed mainstream forms of music. Their choice of music and culture is distant from the mainstream in terms of artistic integrity and perceived values and it is this perceived distance which is crucial to an appreciation of hip-hop subculture. The preferred artists of the majority of the research subjects were seen to possess a level of authenticity and vibrancy that was perceived as lacking from other, more mainstream, acts.

TD: How do you feel when a rap artist 'crosses over' into the charts and becomes successful? Does that have an affect on you as a fan?

Rob (B): Personally I like it when a rapper I like becomes big or sells lots of records. It kind of feels like they're getting the credit for years of hard work. I think as long as they don't totally alter their sound then I don't think it's necessarily the artist changing but maybe it's the audience who are changing. You know, they can maybe accept an artist after a while or something.

The same question elicited a different response from the Lewisham group, however:

Dave (L): When an artist that you love suddenly becomes popular then you have to say 'fair play' to them. Maybe all the graft has paid off for them. But, you know what, I can't think of one recent rapper that I know who has become popular and hasn't changed their sound. That really annoys me. When you listen to an MC grow up and follow their career and you finally think you've found someone that's the truth then they, like, just like change overnight. Then you realise they were faking it all along.

TD: Can you think of any specific examples?

Dave (L): Kanye West, Dizzee Rascal, Chipmunk, Wiley … erm … I suppose to a degree 2Pac but, to be fair, he was dead and then they started messing around with his sound, eh?

TD: And in what ways have these artists changed, do you think?

Isaac (L): Dunno, really. I just think you lose interest or whatever in them if you think that, like, they're after selling themselves out. I mean, fair enough that they're trying to make money and that but there are other ways of doing it. See, for me,

someone like Skepta has got to where he is without changing
too much and that is what he deserves credit for, you know?
He's different, though, as when people try to become popular
they dilute whatever they're doing ... ...

Dave (L): Yes, yes. Dilute — love it. That's exactly the right word, that.

The findings from the fieldwork suggest that a form of subcultural
distinctiveness can exist within the confines of a mass mediated and commodified
cultural form. Thornton (1995), Hodkinson (2002) and Muggleton (2000)
discuss subcultural music consumption and its relative distance to the pop music
sales chart. This is in line with Hebdige (1979), Brake (1985) and Chambers
(1986) who focused on groups such as mods, skinheads, rockers, Rastafarians
and similar groups. These studies present an analysis of youth groups who
attempt to inhabit spaces that were knowingly distant from how they viewed
mainstream sensibilities. However, rap music is a cultural form that has been
mass marketed for some years and yet the research participants, for the most
part, still maintain an exclusion from a personal construction of their idea
of the mainstream and, therefore, construct their own form of subcultural
substance according to Hodkinson's schema (2002). The Ashford, Lewisham
and Canterbury groups in particular discussed their desire to maintain their
sense of collective distinction away from mainstream cultural hip-hop products
through their preference for underground DJs and rappers. The comments below
highlight the significance for these groups in this respect:

Adam (A): I think that what the mainstream offers is not true hip-hop,
it's sort of like the opposite of what underground means, you
know? So, the hip-hop I listen to and try to make sort of
says something that's true rather than glamourising things
for no real reason. I suppose it makes money — like, a lot
of money—but if you're really into making things then
that shouldn't come into it. For me, that's why I listen to
underground stuff because it's made for the music and not
for the money.

Luke (C): The reason why I sort of belong to and hang round with the
friends that I do is because we kind of share the same sort
of ... erm, values. The same sort of values in hip-hop, like.
I would say that the mainstream stuff no longer represents

> hip-hop to me. It's not so much the sounds or the beats or
> the vocals, it's more about the message. Money, bitches, guns
> ... all that.
>
> *Catherine (C):* That's for kids.
>
> *Andy (C):* That's harsh. It's not for kids as such. It's ... I don't know ...
> I suppose I'd say it's for people who don't really get hip-hop,
> you know? So, like, we all know about the origins of hip-
> hop and we all know where it came from which is why we
> probably prefer the underground as it's not tainted by ... erm
> ... commercialism and that.
>
> *Catherine (C):* And I suppose that's why if people listen to mainstream rap
> they aren't really going to fit in with us as there'd be a clash
> of personalities and we can't be doing with that.

The post-subcultural perspective states that cultural artefacts are becoming increasingly important for all members of society which erodes a clear sense of subcultural identity (Chaney, 2004). As the data from the field demonstrates, this is not the case as a number of the research participants in this study, notably in the 'purist' groups, maintained a distance and distinction from conventional culture by eschewing the forms of hip-hop culture and rap music that crossed over into the mainstream. In this respect, cultural commodities may well be seen as more important in general but the research participants reacted to this by placing greater emphasis on underground hip-hop, thereby positioning themselves further from the concerns of mainstream tastes. Hodkinson's (2002) reformulation of subcultural theory emphasises the spectacular nature of his research participants and how they used this as a means to identify goth from outsider. Such aspects were absent for hip-hop purists, although the peripherals did signal subcultural belonging to others via this means and this is elaborated upon in the next chapter to further draw out the distinctions between purists and peripherals. There were still clear aspects of consistent distinctiveness for the purists, although this centred on cultural knowledge rather than visual style. The relative consistency of the purist and peripheral positions were seen to be enforced and maintained by the substantive groups that the research participants affiliated themselves to, as illustrated by Catherine's comments above.

Identity

Subcultural affiliation conveys a clear set of ideals and tastes and the notion of belonging to a clearly defined group who share similar values and forms of identity is central to the work of Hodkinson (2002). He states that the key focus of identity is on '… the extent to which participants hold a perception that they are involved in a distinct cultural grouping and share feelings of identity with one another …' (ibid.: 31). The goth subculture evinces togetherness and unity, irrespective of geographical distance between its members. Willis (1978: 111) recounts a similar shared feeling of belongingness within his ethnographic study of the hippie subculture he investigated. However, opposition and hostility towards other hip-hop subcultural groups from different geographical areas were often spoken about in the focus group meetings in my own research. Many of the participants recounted instances where hostility was felt, and violence often resulted, from *not* belonging to a particular group within the same subculture. For the Lewisham group, the idea of gangs or crews (colloquially referred to as *mandem*), based on members' geographical location (their 'ends' or 'gates') within the London area was a determining factor for this notion of division within the subculture. So strongly did they feel this divide, and the threat of possible physical violence and intimidation that came with it, that it impacted upon their movement and participation with the culture. This perceived threat of violent recrimination was also felt by most members of the other groups and many stories were told of incidents at hip-hop events where violence or potential violence and intimidation was a factor.

> *Isaac (L):*   There's stupid things going around like area codes. Like, if you're from somewhere like the Lewisham area and you go to the Bromley area then you'll probably get rushed (chased) or something. It's stupid.
>
> *Ash (L):*   Mostly, like, people when they travel they … like … if they travel in a group then, like, they'll know that they're safe but if they turn up by themselves and they get caught up with a group of people from a different area then sometimes they'll be, like, 'ah, where you from?' and they say 'yeah, I'm from this area, innit' and they might get left alone. But then sometimes people will go at them, like, 'you're not from this area, I ain't seen you around here' then they'll say 'what phone you got?'

blah blah blah. If you try talking bad to them then they'll just
beat you up.

Isaac (L):   Just because of your area code.

This feeling of physical threat has echoes of groups such as the Teddy Boys in the 1950s who were seen to use violence to defend their sense of space from other teds (Jefferson, 1975: 82). Here, we can see that the protection of a designated space stemmed from the importance of group-mindedness — collectivity being a major part of their sense of personal identification. Territoriality can be seen as '... a symbolic process of magically appropriating, owning and controlling the material environment in which you live, but which in real, economic and political terms is owned and controlled by 'outsiders' ...' (Robins and Cohen, 1978: 73). This notion of territorial policing by crews ensured that, for these respondents at least, their participation with the culture became an increasingly private activity, consisting of sites of consumption such as the internet and specialist television channels in the safety of their own homes. This was not the case for all of the research subjects, yet few of the respondents suggested that they regularly inhabited environments that were easily identifiable as hip-hop or grime spaces such as clubs or concerts, an area developed later in this book. Perhaps as a result of the average ages of the individuals within this study this was a stage that they were yet to reach although it should be noted that such spaces are rare. Most provincial towns with a nightclub rarely have hip-hop or grime nights and although specialist clubs do exist in London and elsewhere, the perceived or experienced threat of physical harm limited their participation with the subculture in this manner. Similar ethnographic findings are evident in the work of Gunter (2010). In his study, a number of focus group respondents claimed that they felt certain geographical areas were out of bounds to them as they did not know sufficient numbers of people that lived there to feel safe.

The assertion of a place as 'safe' can lead to an increased attachment between the individual and that space. This connection can, in return, lead to the desire to police the territory in order to keep it safe. Gidley (2007: 153) studied the movement patterns of youths in London and found that working-class youths, the socio-economic group to which every member of the Lewisham group belonged, tended to have smaller areas that they would occupy in their leisure time. This limited sense of movement and geography resulted in two things: exclusion from the freedom of the city and a strong sense of attachment and belonging to the local. Neighbourhood nationalism (Back, 1996) is a concern for

the members of these focus groups insomuch as they will not venture to parts
of London that they perceive to be dangerous to them. These findings are in
line with Gidley's (ibid.) research as members of his focus group named parts of
London that they would not go to for fear of gang retribution as locals looked to
protect their territories. This territoriality increases a sense of localised identity
although it also denies a sense of communality as described by Hodkinson (ibid.).

Willis' (1978) study of working-class motorbike culture and middle-class
hippies centres on locations of activity including pubs, clubs and houses.
Muggleton (2000) gives examples of pubs and specialist shops where subcultural
activity and presence exists. These sites strengthened the shared identity needed
for a cohesive subculture. However, as the fieldwork for this study unfolded it
became clear that the groups under investigation found barriers to such a full
participation. It could be argued that the messages present within some forms of
hip-hop may help to promote such anti-social territoriality. Hip-hop artists often
align their own sense of identification with a defined geographical space, posse or
crew and this may reinforce and perpetuate such behaviour in the wider culture
(Rose, 1994). The majority of narratives told by the research participants in the
focus groups that contained hostility tended towards hypothetical situations
rather than actual historical instances. It may be suggested that their belief was
based on ideals of what a night out would possibly consist of rather than an
actuality. Perhaps the isolated consumption patterns of the research participants
and their lack of disposable income, the increasing centrality of the internet
in contemporaneous media consumption and their geographical location
placed restrictions upon them. Both Hodkinson (2002) and Willis (1978) give
examples of two very different subcultural groups, goths and hippies respectively,
who state an affinity with others of the same subculture from different areas.
However, the research participants in this study rarely mentioned such factors
when retelling their personal experiences of such interaction.

The Canterbury group included individuals who had been members of the
hip-hop community for some years and they were the group most likely to
inhabit spaces such as hip-hop clubs and concerts. They felt that although such
clubs had a reputation as hostile places, they had never seen or been involved
in intimidating behaviour of any kind. There were also disagreements within
the Ashford group as to whether such instances happened regularly within the
culture.

Trevor (A): It happens a lot. I know a lot of people that have had trouble at clubs and gigs, especially in London. You go to Brixton or somewhere and there's going to be trouble, ain't there?

Adam (A): Well I ain't never seen trouble and I've been to loads more places than you have.

Trevor (A): I'm not saying it happens all the time but I know a few people who have had groups come up to them if they get separated from their mates. That place in Stratford we went to, there was all kinds of shit going on there.

Adam (A): Okay, but it ain't like it happens all the time.

TD: When you say 'trouble', what exactly do you mean?

Adam (A): People who are from different areas have got problems with new people on their patch, you know? Like, they'll try and stare you down if they don't know you but if you're with a group of mates you generally don't get into grief. I think people think there's going to be stuff going on so they're looking out for it, you know? I mean, if you go to a place that's got a reputation then you're going to be watching your back all the time. Don't mean there's going to be any hassle.

The defence of identified geographical spaces was an obvious concern for many of the research subjects. These participants, however, did not admit to engaging in an active policing of their own designated borders but were aware that this was a practice that could affect them. The goths and hippies of previous studies perhaps felt a unity due to their distance from the mainstream; that their physical appearance and beliefs set them apart from the majority and that it was such factors that linked individuals within the same subculture. Contemporary hip-hop culture does not exist as much on the peripheries of mainstream culture. This, therefore, could be a reason for such divisions. Also, over the course of its life, hip-hop has spawned many sub-genres and such musical variants were found to signal difference between subcultural members. The schism evident in the field may also bear some relation to this seeming lack of unity as there were some research participants, notably in the Brighton group, who were not in a wider group.

Although such perceptions of group disparity existed, self identification within subcultural boundaries is an important factor to address. The respondents in this study found difficulties in placing a label on themselves unless it fitted in with the expectations of the rest of the wider group that were present during our conversations. The following extracts illustrate these points clearly.

TD:	Would you term yourself as belonging to the hip-hop subculture? For instance, do you call yourself a b-boy or something similar?
Rob (B):	Yeah, I suppose other people would call me a b-boy. You can't tell today, like, but I usually go out with clothes that people can understand me from, you know? I can look at goths and emos and chavs and you can work out a little bit about them and who they are. I think it's fair to say that people can look at me in my trainers and hoodies and work me out.
TD:	So, would you call yourself a b-boy, then?
Rob (B):	Erm, yeah. I suppose. Can't think of a better term right now.
TD:	How easy is it to label people as hip-hop fans?
Isaac (L):	There's hip-hop heads, b-boys and that. I think a b-boy is probably more about the dancing side, you know? Like, they'll be the ones on street corners or in parks popping and breaking like it's fucking New York or something. I don't do all that.
TD:	How would you label yourself, then?
Isaac (L):	I'm just a guy that's well into my rap and grime, like. Don't know. I ain't ever heard anyone telling me I'm this or I'm that and I don't go round thinking 'I should be saying this, or doing that' just because of some label that I can't get around. You know, I suppose I am a hip-hop fan but that don't mean I like all hip-hop which is what's weird about when people say they love some music or other. Hip-hop is too big to like it all.
Trevor (A):	I'm a hip-hop head, but not 100%. You say, like, I'm into this and I'm into that and other people do see you like that. I mean, when you meet someone you're making a judgement right away, right? I'm into all sorts, though, not just my hip-hop. I like drum 'n' bass and grime. Hip-hop's a big part of my life but it ain't the only thing.
Matt (A):	People will see Trevor, or Rachel, and on some days … erm, like, most days, you could probably work out what music

they listen to and who they are, what they think about and
stuff. Don't mean we have to agree with them, like.

TD: Why would you not agree with them?

Matt (A): I'm not sure many people want labels on them, do they?

Simon (C): I sort of connect with rap music and so it's a big part of what
makes me me. I suppose I do dress in a certain way that people
could guess what I was into but I don't know. You just kind
of wear what you want as opposed to wearing something that
screams 'hip-hop' at other people. There's not really a uniform
or anything like that, you know? Thing is, though, everyone
that I know that's into hip-hop dresses in a similar way but
none of them call themselves b-boys or whatever. There's a
local club night that's a hip-hop night and they advertise the
night as for 'b-boys and b-girls' and I go with a load of mates
but none of us would call ourselves b-boys. Not one. I think
when you put a label on someone like that you limit what
they can do, think or whatever.

The above extracts draw out a number of significant points. First, there is a
rejection of subcultural self-labelling. Distinctions are made between rap sub-
genres and the cultural responsibility that labelling oneself brings. Muggleton
(2000: 63) discusses the notion of label-rejection, an aspect of subcultural studies
which has also been seen in previous writings in this area, such as Polsky (1971).
The general consensus seemed to be that any idea of labelling brought with it
a restriction of possibilities. The following extract taken from a conversation
with the Ashford group draws a little more from the hip-hop subculturalist's
perception of their personal affiliation with one particular musical style and
culture:

Josh (A): Thing is, hip-hop allows you to be into other stuff. I can listen
to Bloc Party and other stuff and no hip-hop head is gonna
tell me it's wrong or what have you. That's the difference
between me and some of my mates. I can listen to Slipknot
or some indie stuff but they ain't listening to rap music. The
hip-hop community ain't looking down on me just because
I'm listening to other things because that's where it all started
from, ain't it? Hip-hop is a mash-up. Samples come from all

over, not just rap music so to be a really good producer they're
looking all over popular music. That's why we can be free to
listen to other things. Some of my mates are well into their
drum 'n' bass and their mates would laugh at them if they
thought they listened to other stuff. Not me, though.

The data suggests the hybridity of styles that formed pioneering hip-hop
could be one determinant as to the seeming fluid nature of the subculture as
perceived by its own members. Simply because it is hip-hop, a genre born of a
combination of many musical and cultural styles, an allowance in this instance
is made for its members to have a more relaxed attitude in terms of their own
musical consumption and subsequent identity. It is clear that hip-hop is the
central focus in terms of musical activity for all of the research participants
yet spectacular style, such as dress code and hairstyles, did not constitute their
main modes of communication. As will be discussed further in Chapter 4, the
purists largely dismissed aspects of spectacular style and this marker of identity
separates the research participants in this study. Hebdige (1979), Brake (1985),
Hodkinson (2002) and Muggleton (2000) all use visual characteristics to
determine the subcultural affiliation of its members, particularly with regards
to the classification of those seen to be committed to the group and those
individuals who are seen as part-time or weekend subculturalists. It was found
that aspects of identity for the research participants were more complex than
has been presented in previous studies. Shared tastes and experiences helped to
form and reinforce identity frameworks amongst the research participants, but
this shared sense of identification did not extend to larger communal networks.

The Rochester focus group were a mix of nationalities and ethnicities, all
with a shared connection through hip-hop culture. They were forthright in
their belief that it was hip-hop that had enabled them to befriend one another
so quickly. At the time of our discussions, the African contingent of this group
were all boarders at their fee-paying school and had enrolled only a few months
prior to our first meeting. They agreed that their shared passion for the music
enabled them to be understood and accepted more readily amongst their peer
group. The extract that follows suggests an internal struggle within the group
to establish a sense of empowerment and hierarchical group structure through
taste. This group would regularly argue amongst themselves over which artist
they preferred and they would belittle the choices of the others within the

group. Such hidden hierarchies (Brill, 2007: 112) help individuals distinguish their tastes from others.

Lou (R): Well, he's (indicating towards Zac) into Ludacris while we're (pointing at himself and Jon) more into Lil' Wayne. Like, Ludacris is okay but he's a little bit immature, you know? He talks about, like, not big boys' things (laughs). I think that's more what kids listen to, you know? Lil' Wayne's more about reality. You know, mature stuff and things like that.

Zac (R): I like Lil' Wayne, yeah he's cool but, Ludacris has got more concepts than him.

Sarah (R): Ludacris? I like him but ...

Lou (R): You know why I think Lil' Wayne tops the charts? Because of his own mix-tapes. (nods of agreement from the others).

Zac (R): No, but on those songs he doesn't have good enough hooks.

Lou (R): No, he may not have good hooks but he'll kill the song for you. Hooks don't make the song good, man ...

Zac (R): Like 'Lollipop' has got a good chorus, I'll give him that and 'Fireman' is probably his ... that's his best ever song so far and ...

Lou (R): How many Lil' Wayne songs have you listened to, huh?

Zac (R): Obviously quite a lot. You hear it everywhere, man. I listen to him right now as much as ...

Lou (R): You (referring to Zac) are like, um, think that um ... rap music is listened to by gangsters and black people and stuff like that. You know, you're meant to talk about mature stuff, you know, as we get older and stuff. Ludacris jumping around and stuff — who has time for that?

Zac (R): Ludacris has been ... has ... (the others in the group talk and laugh over Zac, ignoring what is being said).

This is just one of many examples from the fieldwork where this group found differences in their appreciation of hip-hop culture. The main point of difference seems to centre on the notion of authenticity more than any aspect of vocal or musical performance. The idea that Lil' Wayne is more worthy due to his relatively more mature lyrical content and visual representation compared to Ludacris reflects the ages and interests of this group. Lou's view is that there should be a stage reached by the listener when he has outgrown certain formats of the genre, formats which may be seen to be child-like. This labelling of oneself as more authentic can be seen as a standard hip-hop trait, but can also be seen as a means of gaining dominance within a group setting. In this example one or more of the research participants vie for dominance to demonstrate the possession of more subcultural knowledge.

Simon Frith (1978) and Mike Brake (1985) state that, for most subcultures, music plays a background role to subcultural affiliation although Brake does name the Northern Soul groups as different in this respect (ibid.: 156). For the majority of my focus group interviewees they saw rap, and to a lesser extent grime, as a central part of their day to day experiences and a key determinant in the formation of friendship groups. Visual aspects of the culture, those that may be termed as spectacular style, are significant but play a comparatively minor role compared with involvement in, consumption of and knowledge about hip-hop music. There was an anti-consumerist approach found in the Canterbury, Ashford and Lewisham focus groups who shunned mainstream artists for more "street level" acts who were perceived as possessing a greater degree of authenticity.

Hodkinson (2002) argues that the use of qualitative data allows for a greater degree of attention to the opinions of those actively engaged in substantive groups and aspects of personal identity are more likely to be explored as a result. Such findings on identity from the fieldwork suggest that the ephemeral nature of contemporary youth collectives, as proposed by postmodern writers such as Muggleton (2000), Chaney (2004) and Bennett (2005), cannot be applied to the research subjects in this study. Here, the notion of identity was often contested for a number of reasons. Territoriality and intra-group hierarchical position were significant in this respect and were key elements of challenges within and between subcultural groups. The reinforcement of forms of identity was achieved through these means. It was found from the fieldwork that the focus groups perceived their hip-hop and grime identity to be a positive aspect of their life. Despite the persistent rejection of labels, the research participants accepted that they were involved in a distinct cultural grouping.

Commitment

From within the fieldwork the level of activity within the research participant groups can be seen beyond the realms of simply labelling oneself as belonging to the hip-hop subculture. The data suggests that the forms of activity and the length of time spent immersed in hip-hop culture may be seen to have some bearing on the perceptions of others within the subculture.

TD:	How do you consume hip-hop music and culture?
Isaac (L):	Mostly on the internet. I use Limewire or Myspace to check things out, see who's good and that. YouTube is good, too, but I prefer limewire and myspace because it's music based so you don't get carried away with the image thing.
TD:	How many hours a day do you think you spend listening to rap music or thinking about it?
Isaac (L):	Every single second, man.
Dave (L):	I can honestly say that I think about it more than anything else. Music is so important to me that pretty much everything I do centres on it. Like, I'm walking down the street and I'm thinking of some lyrics and rhymes or I'm at home and there's always something on that's hip-hop whether that's, like, an album or I'm on the 'net looking for stuff. If I'm reading, it'll be a hip-hop magazine or something. When I go out, it's usually to hang out at someone's flat listening to hip-hop or chatting shit about it.
Emmanuel (L):	See, maybe I'm different but I think I don't spend as much time worrying about hip-hop compared to these guys. I've got other things going on like my football and studying and that so, you know, maybe it's that I've got more things going on. If I just did hip-hop and grime in my head all day long then I'd get nothing else done. These guys (referring to the others in the group) make more music [than me] so I guess that's why it's in their heads all day. Seriously, man, it's hard to get this lot to chat about anything else that ain't rapping and stuff.

Dave's comments illustrate his commitment to creativity as well as consumption. He gives the example of undertaking a mundane activity ('walking down the street') which allows him an opportunity to consider his own rap lyrics. Both Dave and Isaac make it clear that they consider their involvement with hip-hop and grime culture to be totally immersive. Emmanuel's assertion that he is less committed than other research participants does not devalue his contribution to the Lewisham set but it does reinforce both the variations in cultural engagement between individuals and the all encompassing nature of the culture in relation to the identities and activities of a number in this focus group.

>   *TD:*   Can you work out someone's level of commitment simply by
>   what they're wearing?
>
>   *Rachel (A):* I don't think you can put your finger on just one thing that
>   makes someone look like they don't belong, but you can just
>   tell. With hip-hop, though, if you can show a love for the
>   music then you'll be accepted into the scene. It ain't about
>   having loads of money and all the latest designer gear, it's
>   about being comfortable in yourself without having to prove
>   anything to other people. I'm not really worried about what
>   people have got on more than I am that they're there for the
>   right reasons.
>
>   *Ash (L):*   You can just tell. I mean, I can't say how. Can't explain to you.
>   I just know. We just know. For instance, say someone tries
>   talking to me and they don't know what they're talking about.
>   They'll look pretty bad. They're just fronting or something.
>   I love hip-hop but can't stand people who just say they do.
>   They don't deserve to call themselves hip-hop. If you go to a
>   big show, some shit like 50 Cent or Eminem, and you telling
>   me all those people at that place gonna know what they're
>   talking about?

Here, the research respondents are critical of commitment if it is only linked to disposable income to display a sense of the spectacular. The knowledge of hip-hop and grime comes with subcultural longevity, the ability to 'know what you're talking about' in Ash's words, which demonstrates subcultural substance (Hodkinson, 2002). The assumption is that the immediacy of the purchase of a cultural commodity is of significantly less worth than the attainment of knowledge accrued over a number of years. In this respect, the idea of commitment correlates to a sense of subcultural activity and longevity. This can be seen as an illustration of cultural activity leading to solidarity, as well as marked divisions within the youth groups. The separation between purist and peripheral subcultural actors is developed in the following chapter and stems from the qualitative data. Whereas previous studies in this field (including Moore, 1994 and Muggleton, 2000) arguably homogenise the subcultures under investigation through a simple dichotomous presentation of individuals as either 'in' or 'out' in terms of subcultural acceptance, the purist/peripheral model presents a sliding-scale of subcultural agency to develop more detail of the complexities present in the groups within this study.

Hodkinson states that '... subcultures are liable to account for a considerable proportion of free time, friendship patterns, shopping routes, collections of commodities, going-out habits and even internet use ...' (2002: 31). The excerpts from the focus group meetings presented in this study clearly demonstrate the importance of such factors to the groups. Vinyl record buying may have, in previous years, been seen as a marker of subcultural commitment but this aspect has been eroded somewhat by relatively accessible free and/or illegal downloads from the internet. Of the five focus groups, only the Canterbury collective engaged in searching out and buying rare, often canonical, records. Record collecting is often seen as an '... accentuated, and more committed, form of popular music fandom ...' (Shuker, 2004: 316) and the Canterbury members who engaged in this activity can therefore claim to possess a form of subcultural commitment. Record collecting can be seen to be a demonstration of the '... obscurantist interest in the marginal ...' (Straw, 1997: 11) which links to the separation of purist and peripheral cultural practitioner as further developed in the following chapter. The fieldwork respondents who engaged in record collection aimed their activities towards the latest underground hip-hop releases as well as rare funk and soul records from which they could sample drums and breaks. They openly suggested that this could have been due to their age.

> *Chris (C):*   I collect a lot of vinyl. A lot. I suppose I grew up with my mum and dad's record collection and started getting into the feel of actually holding the music, like. It's a bit different these days with the MP3s and all that. I know a lot of DJs who play from their laptops or whatever but I just don't think you can beat the sound of vinyl, can you? I mean, it's where hip-hop came from. Digital is a little bit too clean for me.
>
> *Simon (C):*   Probably because we DJ we want different things from music. I need to be able to handle it and see it. I need a reference point for my beat juggling and I use sticky labels on my vinyl so I know that I'm no good at juggling on digital decks.
>
> *Chris (C):*   We still go out a lot together to go record shopping but we have to go up to London these days as all the local record

shops have closed down [around here]. There are a fair few
decent websites that sell rare records but there's nothing that
can beat that feeling of unearthing a fucking gem in a rack of
records.

Simon (C):   We must have spent thousands of pounds on digging for
records over the years. That's a bit scary.

For both Chris and Simon it is clear that the ownership of particular
records sustains their own sense of subcultural identity. A key feature here is
that these individuals do not merely consume these recordings but use them
in the framework of their own cultural practices. The commitment to vinyl
demonstrated by Chris and Simon can be seen as an attempt to keep older
hip-hop related activities from becoming obsolete. These individuals, in effect,
are preservers of the cultural tradition (Shuker, ibid.: 316). Shopping routes
have been altered in order to sustain a collective activity and these respondents
have committed to their subcultural being by spending a significant amount of
money, time and effort in following this leisure interest.

From the fieldwork it can be seen that the possession of musical artefacts
was still regarded highly by members of all of the groups in this study, yet the
formats and the means of ownership have changed in recent years. Subcultural
identity is still to be gained by those with access to new musical material, notably
those tracks or albums that have been leaked onto the internet prior to the
record company's official release date. The internet has changed the listening
patterns of many young people. It was found that status is ascribed to those
in the group who have managed to download the latest track or album before
others within the group. The music is then often duplicated onto compact disc
and distributed amongst the group. The internet offers a democratic liberatory
potential for those engaged in the consumption of music (Huq, 2006: 162). A
number of studies have discussed internet usage yet they have centred on virtual
subcultural communities (Hodkinson, 2002; Bennett, 2004; Gelder, 2007) and
have largely ignored the day to day use of the internet by youth groups as a means
to access music. Laughey suggests that the idea of peer group exchange of musical
products '… could be interpreted as analogous to promenade performances of
demonstration in early youth music cultures …' (2006: 136). In this way, then,
the possession and distribution of musical artefacts can be seen as a marker of
subcultural identity. This is a variable form of commitment when compared to

the potential hours spent sourcing rare vinyl in a record shop yet the attainment of music, through whatever means, maintains a level of prime importance.

Adorno (1976) proposes a categorisation of musical listeners. He defines the *culture consumer* as '... a copious, sometimes a voracious listener, well-informed, a collector of records. He respects music as a cultural asset, often as something a man must know for the sake of his own social standing ...' (ibid.: 6). This definition can be applied to Simon and Chris, as the extract above illustrates. However, this also highlights the fact that some within the field have moved beyond passive consumption to active production. Hodkinson (2002: 31) argues that subcultural involvement dominates the lifestyles and practices of members and this was demonstrated in the fieldwork for this study.

Autonomy

The idea of autonomy, for Hodkinson (2002), relates to the organisation of subcultural events and activities with a clear focus on commerce. The Brighton and Rochester groups were predominantly mainstream consumers of hip-hop and grime and therefore, to some degree, lacked autonomy. Individuals from the other groups, however, possessed a degree of agency in creating their own forms of music and cultural surroundings. The levels of autonomy informs us of something of the culture, insomuch as it relies on its participants to perpetuate the niche underground scene in order to potentially feed the mainstream at a later date. Rarely did many of the research respondents go to highly organised and publicised events with established acts, yet some did attend and occasionally organise smaller events featuring unsigned rappers and less well known DJs from the surrounding area. Local acts such as ShyChlo, Tengo Collective DJs, MC Apex, DJ Tactical, Re-Fried DJs and Brizzie regularly played at both house parties and small club nights during the fieldwork data collection. Parties were often organised to showcase their own talents or those of friends or associates. The Ashford group in particular engaged in this form of activity quite regularly. The perceived threat of physical violence and intimidation, as discussed earlier, played a part in the organisation of events in 'safe' places, along with the sense of ownership that was acquired from arranging their own events.

> Rachel (A): If you go to a big show then you can't really do what you want, you know? We set out parties and get people that we know involved. That way we don't have to pay loads to enjoy the music. Then it's ours, you know?

There is a grassroots level of activity that flourishes today, as found from my own participant observations at hip-hop parties and events. Many in the focus groups participated in such events and these were more relevant to their every day lived subcultural experiences than the mass mediated form. In the previous section on identity I discussed how hip-hop could be viewed as a fragmented and divided culture yet this is only really within the macro scale of analysis. When one takes a closer look at smaller events, as I did through grounded research, a picture emerges which places subcultural autonomy at its heart. The creative process that research participants within the focus groups engaged in is a factor rarely studied and yet it is arguably a focal point for assessing the degree of a subculture's autonomy.

It is significant that the majority of focus group participants who were engaged in actively producing cultural artefacts centred their activities on music. Aspects of breakdancing and graffiti writing, considered as staples of the original elements of hip-hop culture, were absent from the lives of these research participants. Simon and Chris from the Canterbury group were part of the Tengo DJ collective and regularly played at events and parties organised by themselves, friends or event promoters. They often sold CDs of their mixes at these events in order to make money and to increase awareness of their abilities in the hope of securing future bookings. Simon also played a number of shows under the name DJ Readybreak during the fieldwork. Rachel from the Ashford group, in her guise as ShyChlo, performed regularly as both a solo artist and as the rapper in the band ShyChlo and the Boys. ShyChlo had a number of CDs and self-printed t-shirts that were available to buy at her gigs and from the band's website. These instances of cultural autonomy for commercial gain were rare in the focus groups as many of the respondents preferred to organise parties and events that did not aim to make money. Where house parties were organised, people would collectively source DJ equipment, speakers and records for the night. Guests were invited to bring their own records along and, if they wished, to take turns behind the decks. Such events were regularly organised by the Canterbury group who saw their communal party experience as very much in keeping with the original ethos of the hip-hop movement where the emphasis was on solidarity and non-elitism. The autonomy in this example does not stem from a leaning towards commerce but to the sustaining of hip-hop culture as a collective force in the face of the mass mediated focus on individualism and a capitalist drive.

Gender and social class constraints

This section moves away from a discussion of subcultural substance and centres on issues relating to perceived social constraints to cultural activity. As discussed in the literature chapter, the post-subcultural turn suggests that structural considerations such as age, gender, ethnicity and social class no longer significantly impact upon an individual's cultural engagement. Such an approach is offered as a criticism of CCCS methodologies which were seen as too reliant on an analysis of structure rather than the agentic capabilities of those being studied. Data from the research participants brings this perspective into question because these social factors were significant with regards to their own cultural participation. The focus group data, coupled with information gathered from participant observation in the field, show that both gender and socio-economic position were an important influence on participants' cultural engagement.

On gender, Kahn-Harris (2004: 117) states that there is a tendency for female involvement in youth culture to be constructed around the consumption of mass mediated texts. My own ethnographic work found that there is a degree of truth in this as the more obscure and marginalised a space, for example smaller concerts, club nights or the personal spaces of hip-hop groups, there would be a comparatively low level of female involvement. It was found from the number of concerts attended during the participant observation component of the fieldwork that hip-hop events with a more mainstream appeal, such as Jay-Z at Hyde Park in both 2008 and 2010, along with other similarly sized shows, had a female presence although smaller shows were significantly dominated by males in the audience. This is not to suggest that females do not actively engage with the cultural form as it was found in the research that they played a significant part in hip-hop subcultures, both in terms of consumption and production. The research subjects, although mostly males, included female participants whose comments were given equal status within the focus group conversations. It is evident from the research findings that females who engage with hip-hop culture do so with the same degree of passion, fervour and subcultural affiliation as their male counterparts. Female participation was found to be at a lower rate than males, but they are far from absent. McRobbie and Garber (1975) suggested an invisibility of girls in youth subcultures which was not the case in the research for this study, while for many male research participants their cultural practice took place in their private sphere. This places these respondents in a position akin to the females in McRobbie and Garber's work as they felt public space was often denied to them. This results in a subcultural form which is somewhat removed from aspects of promenade and spectacular display evident in earlier studies (Hebdige, 1979; Blackman, 1995).

Rachel, from the Ashford group, stated on several occasions that as a female rapper she believed she had to prove herself more than her male counterparts. She raised awareness of the relative lack of females engaged at what was termed the grassroots level, namely at small club nights and similar hip-hop gatherings. As an accomplished freestyler, Rachel felt that the hostility which was often present between herself and male rappers stemmed from the rarity of a female performer as opposed to any sense of innate misogyny:

Rachel (A): See, on stage is a whole other world 'cos they're [male freestyle opponents] seeing me and just playing to the crowd with their chatter. I know enough of these guys to know that what they're saying on stage ain't necessarily what they think of me off stage but they're just playing to what the people want to hear, like kind of what the people expect to hear from an MC dissing a female. When I give it back to them (laughs) then maybe they think twice about pulling them tricks next time.

TD: So, the crowds you play in front of are very much male dominated?

Rachel (A): Mostly, yeah. You go to these little grassroots places and you have to ask yourself where the females are at as it can be fairly … erm, sort of empty of girls. Move that stage to a big festival, though, and you'll see thousands of girls.

TD: Why do you think that is? Are girls sort of excluded from these grassroots places?

Rachel (A): Definitely not. If you go to these places you'll see girls mixing it with the boys but, I don't know, there just seems more men that go out than girls to the smaller places. I think that maybe my experiences are different as I am putting myself out there by getting up on stage so maybe when the men are calling me out that's 'cos I'm on stage rather than in there [the club] in the first place, see?

TD: And how many female rappers are there in a similar position to you?

Rachel (A): Not enough, that's for sure. So, like, with the local circuit [in Kent] I can't name you one other girl freestyler but up London there are a few about.

Grassroots activity in hip-hop culture in terms of active engagement in the night time economy was found to be lacking in female involvement, both at a creative and a participatory level. This disproportionate gender bias was not seen to be a result of conscious discrimination. As has been stated, there were occasions in the ethnographic research, notably at large scale concerts, where relatively large groups of females were in attendance. It was found from the focus group research that many of the female participants, regardless of their passion for the culture, favoured subcultural engagement in private spaces as they perceived environments such as clubs and smaller hip-hop shows to be oriented around masculine behaviour. They restricted their cultural engagement as a result of their perceptions of gender.

The data from the fieldwork suggests the existence of social class barriers to participation in the wider hip-hop culture for many in the focus groups. The agentic and creative activities engaged in by the research subjects are largely based on their relative socio-economic position. The findings of this study bring into question the previously described post-subcultural position as many of the less economically privileged members of the focus groups were seen to be bound by their class positioning. The Lewisham respondents in particular perceived their identity as being defined by their locality, socio-economic grouping and, in some cases, by their ethnic backgrounds.

One extensive discussion with the Lewisham group centred on the Jay-Z concert in Hyde Park in the summer of 2008 and how none of them could afford to participate in this event. They all agreed that, had they enough disposable income, they would attend the show but as ticket prices were beyond their means they felt that this denied them access to *their* culture.

Jemal (L): If you're going to start playing big places like that and charging them prices then there's no way you'll be playing to just a hip-hop crowd. It's a shame, like, ain't it? And he'll know, man, he'll know. There'll be all types of people there, some trying to just, like, catch sight of Beyoncé or whatever.

The size of this concert, and Jay-Z's commercial success in general, was interpreted by most of the research subjects as a move away from an authentic hip-hop experience. Jemal's comments highlight the perception that the increased cost of concert tickets was freezing out true hip-hop fans. This results in 'all types of people' attending, a number of who have no real or long lasting interest in hip-hop culture. There was a pattern of thought which suggested that the mass commodification of hip-hop had somehow taken away the sense of enclosed identity and autonomy felt by the hip-hop community. The research subjects made it clear that they felt full participation with hip-hop culture was denied them due to the expense of concert tickets, CDs and the technical equipment needed to produce their own musical tracks. Although it is true that such obstacles did not prevent them from partaking in the culture in alternate ways, it was clear that these participants felt that forms of cultural exclusion due to structural constraints hindered their full engagement with hip-hop in its varying forms.

Hollands' (2002) ethnographic study of dance culture concludes that there is a social class distinction between the mainstream and the 'hip'/'proper' club scenes. He states that the working-class are more inclined to consume mainstream music and night-time locations whereas middle-class youth will engage in music and activities which can be seen to be exclusive, with a superior shared taste. The fieldwork in this study found that a number of the middle-class participants, specifically from the Canterbury group, tended to have a greater appreciation for the technical intricacies of turntablism, usually as a result of their own practical engagement with the activity. Very few of the working-class members in the focus groups had an interest in this aspect of the culture, instead their focus centred on the vocal performance aspect. These distinctions of cultural engagement as a result of social class can be seen to suggest that avenues of participation are blocked for the working-class who cannot realistically afford records, turntables and a mixer, whereas the use of their own voice has no economic barrier. Access to their particular participation is therefore hindered by socio-economic restraints although some of the working-class research subjects had access to such equipment through the educational courses they were enrolled on. In this instance the patterns of consumption and access to certain tools of creativity are affected by social class position. This is not to suggest that all of the middle-class research subjects engaged in the same forms of cultural activity. The Rochester group showed no real interest in turntablism and so the claim here is not that socio-economic status influences preferred forms of cultural activity but that it can impact upon opportunities to explore and develop an appreciation for forms that are perceived as inaccessible. This reaffirms the previously mentioned assertions by Shildrick and MacDonald (2006) and Stahl (2003) that social divisions shape cultural identities and forms of engagement.

Conclusion

This chapter has illustrated that subcultural substance is evident in contemporary groups centred on hip-hop and grime culture and that, as a result, the term subculture still retains undoubted academic validity. The comparative levels of consistent distinctiveness, identity, commitment and autonomy in the cultural expression of this study's research subjects manifests itself in various ways, enabling the demarcation of subcultural participation developed in the next chapter. The use of Hodkinson's framework to explore the field supports the idea that some of the groups studied were resistant to mainstream culture, despite this term being ambiguous and in many respects difficult to determine exactly what was meant by the mainstream. What was clear, however, was the fact that the concept of the mainstream was used as a term of abstraction, thereby reducing the cultural engagement of others to being of no value or significance. This term serves as a marker of separation and therefore adds to the subcultural capital of the participants in the field. The data produced from the qualitative research shows that the different youth groups engaged in varying levels of agency and cultural practice on a collective basis, an aspect which is dealt with in greater detail in the chapter that follows.

Hodkinson's concept of subcultural substance, as a means to refine the term subculture, has support from specific parts of the data in particular through the distinctiveness, identity, commitment and autonomy of the research participants. The visual spectacle of subcultures (Hebdige, 1979) is challenged by the findings in this study as some of the research subjects put less emphasis on fashion which they viewed as being linked to the commodification of hip-hop culture. Hodkinson (2002) proposed that geographical location was not a barrier to potential friendships and amicable relationships between young people from varying locales was sustained through subcultural allegiance. The findings in this study suggest that this is not the case for hip-hop and grime subcultures. There was a sense, real or perceived, of territorial policing within the culture which limited both the movement and the cultural activities of many of the research subjects. A form of neighbourhood nationalism (Back, 1996) was evident within the subcultural practices of a number within this study although differences within the groups highlight the variable forms of cultural engagement.

It was found that structural considerations did impact upon the cultural activities of the participants, significantly in variations between the working- and middle-classes and the aspects of the culture that they engaged with on a regular basis. Levels of disposable income were a key factor in denying access to material resources which made certain aspects of the culture, such as tickets for large hip-hop events or record decks, unobtainable to them. There was a relative lack of female engagement in grassroots level hip-hop activity although it was found that selected female participants in the research used hip-hop culture as a means to form strong subcultural affiliations and as a key marker for personal identity.

Chapter 4

Purists and peripherals

"I'm not trying to say that my style is better than yours ... "[4]

Introduction

This chapter is concerned with the ability of the research participants to construct their own cultural identity in an active manner. Here I present the idea of a sliding-scale of subcultural participation as an attempt to develop the idea of a continuum of subcultural engagement (Wilson, 2006). Where the previous chapter validates the continued academic use of the term subculture, the purist/peripheral model introduced here highlights distinctions of subcultural engagement and was developed from the findings from the emic research methods. The descriptive tool attempts to move away from the dichotomous, essentialised and somewhat elitist insider/outsider perspective present in writings on subculture (Moore, 1994) and also helps to further explain the varying responses to rap texts by the audience as seen in the chapters that follow. This conceptual model relates to comparative levels of subcultural affiliation, activity and identification and should be seen as a continuum of engagement. These labels, purist and peripheral, are not essentialising terms. They are utilised within the framework of a dynamic culture and are applied as a result of the empirical evidence obtained from the field. It will be shown that varying positions in the writing on subcultural theory, including structural and postmodern perspectives, can be applied to the young people in this study.

Purists and peripherals

The fieldwork demonstrated a clear division between those with an active engagement in shaping their localised hip-hop scenes and those who engaged with hip-hop culture from a distance, their activities centring on mainstream mediated consumption of the form. The division between the two groups as laid out in the rest of this chapter and in the book in general should be seen as a sliding scale between agency and relative passivity via consumption. By utilising a split audience reception framework (Riley, 2005: 301) it is hoped that a more developed understanding of the multiple and varying ways in which cultural products are read and used can be achieved. The terms purist and peripheral should be seen as tools to more fully understand degrees of cultural activity within subcultural groupings. Also, these two terms originated in the following comments from research respondents:

> *Simon (C)* :   I think there are clear distinctions in hip-hop culture between those who DJ, make beats, rap or whatever and those who just buy stuff — in that sense I guess our involvement is a little more pure to the origins of hip-hop where we change the culture as we make the culture. I suppose we're purists in that sense.
>
> *Alice (B)* :   There are loads of people who are more into rap and sort of grime culture than we are. We're on the peripheries of the real serious, kind of hardcore fans.

As highlighted in the last chapter, the peripheral groups were those from Brighton and Rochester. The research respondents, who were more actively engaged in hip-hop culture and who maintained a degree of autonomy away from mainstream commodified hip-hop images, were from Ashford, Canterbury and Lewisham and are described as purists. They demonstrated more pronounced degrees of agency and their activities and tastes were distinguished from the peripherals. The individuals labelled peripheral were open to the fact that they had little active engagement with the culture. The following excerpt comes from a focus group meeting with the Brighton group :

> *Tony (B):*   I don't make hip-hop music. I don't even try to rap along to the songs I listen to. That would sound pretty silly, I think.
>
> *TD:*   Do you know anyone who makes their own hip-hop music?
>
> *Tony (B):*   I know a few people in bands, like indie and rock, but I don't know anyone that actually makes hip-hop music or raps or what have you. I mean, why would we?
>
> *Paul (B):*   I can honestly say I don't know anyone that makes rap music. A lot of my friends are really into it but I don't have friends who write raps or create beats or stuff. I think, living here, we're a lot removed from the people who actually make it.

The Brighton group perceived themselves as within the hip-hop scene but they made frequent references throughout the qualitative data collection process to those who they saw to be more in the centre of the culture. They felt they were lacking in the experience needed to define oneself as possessing subcultural knowledge. Paul, in the above extract, offers his geographical location as a reason for his own non-immersion in the creative aspects of the culture. His perceived distance from the culture's creative epicentres determines his own form of engagement. This point is developed further by the following comment from a member of the Rochester focus group:

> *Dan (R):* My involvement in hip-hop is, like, as a buyer. I mean, I listen to rap and love it but as a culture I think maybe we're on the outside of it, you know? Not a lot happens around here for rap fans so I wouldn't say that I'm, like, really involved too much. I watch TV and listen to the radio and go see stuff on YouTube and that and that's how I get to know what's out there and what's good.

The data suggests that subcultural knowledge equals status and it is the abstract concept of status that purists have and peripherals relatively lack. Peripherals clearly possess aspects of hip-hop and grime knowledge but to a much lesser degree than the purists. In terms of hip-hop, Schloss's notion of foundation (2009: 50), as discussed previously, is of significance here. As can be seen from Dan's comments, peripherals tend to rely on mediated forms such as television to gain their foundation. The variations in level of cultural knowledge between the two groups presented here is a major factor of their demarcation and separation as will be illustrated in the following section detailing the variances in musical knowledge.

From the data it was found that the purists were perceived as significantly fewer in number than the peripherals. With regards the number of purists compared to peripherals, one member of the Ashford group commented:

> *Adam (A):* Ain't many people doing what we do, you know? Like, there's loads of people going to gigs and buying the records. It's [hip-hop] getting bigger each year, like ... but still not many people actually doing it. Hip-hop is more than just listening.

In the focus group discussions it became clear that there was a difference in self perception between the two groups. One of the Canterbury respondents suggests his purist ideals by stating:

Simon (C):   We kind of just do hip-hop all the time, you know? That sort of means that we are hip-hop as, like, we're changing it a little bit and playing around with the sounds and stuff. It's almost as if the culture changes when the people change it. But ... most people that I've spoken to at gigs, clubs or whatever are just, like, so numb to actually doing anything. They'll download the tracks or watch the telly but that's about it. That's their level, you know?

Here, Simon is alluding to the possible differences between the purist and peripheral hip-hop consumer. He makes the claim that through purist agentic action the culture is altered. This is a means of asserting ownership of the form. However, he claims that very few people seem to be actively engaged in making music ('playing around with the sounds'). He states that 'downloading' or 'watching' are essentially passive deeds through the fact the individuals who solely engage with hip-hop via these activities are, for him, 'numb to actually doing anything'. From the data we can begin to see the difference between purists and peripherals on a number of occasions in the focus group interviews. An Ashford group member said:

Adam (A):   Go into the street now and ask all the kids if they can rap and most will put their hands up. All the little kids are doing it these days but they ain't doing anything new. Like, I don't know ... they're copying someone else's flow or just spitting the lyrics they've learnt from a track. That's different to what we do. We're trying to push things on and push ourselves. Those kids out there spitting bars in the shopping centre or wherever don't have the balls to get up on stage. They're just not that into it. They're just copying and they'll be found out in the end.

This sense of 'pushing things forward' compared with 'just copying' is an important one as it illustrates the relative passivity of the peripherals from the purist perspective. The extracts above put forward the purist view that there is no desire for innovation or creativity in the peripherals — they do not 'do' the culture, they merely 'copy'. This sense of active engagement was used by both the purist and the peripheral groups to identify the differences between one another. For the purists, this sense of division was a way to enhance their own identity and as a means to affirm their sense of distinctiveness. They used their level of commitment and activity to highlight the hierarchical nature of hip-hop taste groups.

I have determined six markers of differentiation between the purists and the peripherals, derived from the fieldwork. I will develop a number of these aspects further in the sections that follow.

Purists	Peripherals
Underground tastes by choice	Mainstream tastes
Actively engaged in the culture	Relatively passive consumers of mediated
No specific requirement to display	version of the culture
subcultural dress code	External signs of cultural affiliation evident
Critical of crossover/mainstream artists	No real concept of underground artists
Knowledge of recording industry	Little industry knowledge
Creative engagement	Consumptive engagement

Although the table makes a clear division between these groups, seemingly as binary opposites, the conceptualisation of these labels should be seen as existing within a relative sliding scale. These are not absolute terms and there is no suggestion that an individual must exhibit all of these characteristics to be confirmed as either purist or peripheral. The five groups of research respondents can be positioned in either a purist or peripheral framework with little difficulty. This is not to suggest, however, that every individual engaged in hip-hop consumption falls neatly into either of these two categories. Some crossover between these two opposing forms was found during the fieldwork.

The peripheral stage in a sense could be seen as being a transient phase of subcultural being as it could lead on to the accrual of sufficient subcultural knowledge to allow for acceptance into a purist group. It would be far too simplistic, however, to suggest that this is the aim of those in the peripheral group as many in the field were content with their level of cultural commitment and the identity formed as a result, thereby potentially leading to long term subcultural engagement at this level. The peripheral stage, however, serves for some as a step towards greater subcultural engagement. As seen in Chapter 3, the research participants engaged initially with mediated, mainstream forms of hip-hop culture before, for the purists, developing more cultural knowledge and subsequent underground tastes. It is evident that one cannot be considered a purist without prior experience in gaining the accepted level of foundation which can be seen to come with peripheral engagement. For some, then, this stage is a stepping stone to purist subcultural identity. Post-subcultural ideas of superficiality and transience (Bennett, 1999a; Muggleton, 2000) can be applied to those who seemingly do not wish to engage with the culture beyond the peripheral level. Such a perspective could be applied although this group do form strong aspects of identity, and gain aspects of agency, from their cultural activities whilst also affirming the post-subcultural argument that subcultures lack depth (Redhead, 1997).

In the sections that follow I will further develop the distinctions between the perceptions and practices of the purist and peripheral groups.

Music tastes and knowledge

The musical preferences of the purists, in terms of consumption rather than in their own creative practices, were for underground artists. Acts such as Madlib, MF Doom, El-P, DJ Format and Saul Williams were seen by the purists as more authentic, genuine and artistically motivated in comparison to mainstream hip-hop artists' drive for commercial success and the material rewards that come with it. An economic incorporation by the dominant culture of cultural forms can '... empty them of their resistant content and paradoxically make them support the dominant order ...' (Blackman and France, 2001: 180). The underground nature of the musical tastes of the purist group reflects this notion of resistance to mainstream images that can be seen to back up the dominant capitalist mode.

> Simon (C):   I remember seeing the front cover to Eric B. and Rakim's *Paid in Full* and remember feeling a bit weird 'cos it seemed to be promoting ... you know, like, materialism and money and all that stuff. Made me feel weird and I think that's when I noticed a big change in hip-hop. A lot of the more mainstream stuff now just go on about money and making paper and all that. It's a shame because hip-hop used to be much more about being against stuff like that, you know, *Fight the Power* and that.

The purists would declare their musical preferences on the basis of art, not commerce, an aspect developed further in Chapter 7. In the extract above, Simon claims that what used to be seen in his perception as a form of protest, anti-establishment music has transmogrified into a form which celebrates materialism. This is where the resistance to mainstream commodified hip-hop stems from for the purists as they maintain that their culture has been altered to fit sensibilities that do not match their own. Underground artists, although still commodified in order to sell records, are perceived as retaining much of the ideas and values of hip-hop's pioneering artists, particularly in relation to politically conscious lyrics.

It was found that the purists demonstrated an extensive knowledge of hip-hop acts beyond the mainstream whilst also maintaining an interest in more popular aspects of rap. The peripherals, on the other hand, largely had no concept of acts outside of the mainstream popular music charts. None of the peripherals admitted to reading hip-hop specific magazines or using the internet to search for new acts. Their personal choices were largely controlled by the cultural gate-keepers working within mainstream broadcast networks such as the BBC, Kiss FM and a range of television music channels. The peripherals' radio listening habits did not even extend to listening to specialist programming such as Radio 1's Tim Westwood Show or the BBC's urban radio station, 1Xtra. Instead, their hip-hop choices were informed from day-time listening habits of mainstream radio stations.

TD:	How much rap music do you listen to?
Rob (B):	I'm kind of mainstream more than anything but, say, if I saw, like, a music video that I liked on MTV or something then I might go and download it but I wouldn't go out of my way to look for or download rap music ... I wouldn't go and research my own bands and that, I just choose music based on their hits, their singles.
TD:	What kind of stuff recently?
Rob (B):	Erm ... Black Eyed Peas, Eminem ... although that's not that recent ... Kanye West, 50 Cent. Mainstream rap people really ... sort of hip-hop stuff.

Rob's acceptance of the term mainstream is of significance here. He claims a populist hip-hop taste for himself, although this attitude was something of an exception for the peripherals. On several occasions during the fieldwork, the peripherals stated that their listening tastes were underground even though their preferred artists were what Harrison refers to as music industry rap (2009: 29). This is illustrated in the following exchange from the Brighton group:

Alice (B): The stuff I listen to is pretty, like, underground and edgy. Stuff like 50 Cent, Kanye West. I love all that. The mash-up Kanye did with that Daft Punk song was pretty amazing. Cutting edge, you know?

Rob (B): Kanye's interesting because he hasn't used gimmicks or anything like that to get where he is. He lets his music do the talking and that's why he's stayed true to the underground.

The peripherals had a desire to be seen as authentic hip-hop fans and they understood the need to project an idea of underground integrity, yet they were placing such labels on multi-platinum selling artists and themselves as consumers of such acts. We see here that the Brighton group were seeking to present themselves as having niche musical tastes in order to project a notion of authentic subcultural engagement and approval.

The purists had an extensive knowledge of mainstream acts even though they were clear in their assertion that they did not actively seek to consume this variant of hip-hop music. Their perception of major label rappers was that they were inauthentic due to the ownership of the artists by corporations who had no real understanding of the culture of hip-hop. However, information such as latest record releases, tour dates and which record label particular artists were signed to was known and discussed by this group. The peripherals demonstrated little understanding of the machinations of the recording industry. The symbolic creative activities in which the purists engage can be read as forms of localised resistance to the global consumer hip-hop culture. The purists were also involved in archiving the culture through their research into historical hip-hop recordings.

TD: What kind of hip-hop do you listen to?

Luke (C): I'm quite old school with my tastes. I still listen to a lot of KRS-One, De La Soul, A Tribe Called Quest — all the stuff that I was listening to when I first got into hip-hop.

TD: Do you listen to anything a little more contemporary?

Luke (C):	Sure. It's stuff like Lupe Fiasco, MF Doom, Atmosphere … you know, not exactly your middle of the road kind of stuff.
TD:	Why do you listen to those types of artists?
Luke (C):	You know, to me they're more like the original hip-hop I got into than all that chart rap. People like Kanye West, P Diddy or 50 Cent or whatever ain't saying anything to me that I want to hear. They're cogs in a machine because they're … you know, I'm not sure they have anything to say. I don't really like that vacuous aspect of how rap's turned out, you know?
TD:	How do you mean vacuous?
Luke (C):	That chart stuff is just empty, isn't it? Hip-pop. You hear it wherever you go so you can't escape it but it just seems to be lowest common denominator stuff to me.

By claiming that 'hip-pop' is vacuous, Luke is clearly implying that there is substance to his musical choices. As he makes clear, he has knowledge of mainstream rap due to its ubiquity. The notion of 'cogs in a machine' relates somewhat to Adorno's (1991) notion of standardised musical goods. The purists demonstrated a general disdain for, and rejection of, mainstream rap artists.

Adam (A):	I'm not sure what's wrong with hip-hop today. There's some of the most amazing stuff out there but nobody seems to want to know. All these big rappers on massive labels get all the promotion and so everyone just blindly goes for that. I think most people are scared to be different; they're all just following the crowd. I mean, to me that shit that gets into the charts that calls itself hip-hop is not what I'd call hip-hop.
TD:	Why is that?
Adam (A):	Hip-hop is about the live experience, it's about the moment. I don't really get all of this stuff with huge production an' that. How many of those big selling rappers can actually get up on stage and freestyle? Does P Diddy or Nelly or whoever battle? Of course they don't. And the reason why they don't is because they wouldn't know where to fucking start. They're image, that's all.

TD: So when you record one of your own tracks how do you avoid
                 production issues?
Adam (A):   Everything we do is in one take. No overdubs.

The manufactured nature of mainstream chart hip-hop was an aspect that
was mentioned by all of the purists during the fieldwork. The analogy of the
machine was used on several occasions, representing a formulaic, and conveyor
belt style of musical production. The constructed typification of 'us' and 'them'
(MacRae, 2004: 55) is evident in Adam's assertion of a homogenised other who
'blindly' consume mainstream rap music and 'follow the crowd'. Adam's assertion
that hip-hop should centre on the live, rather than the mediated, event is key to
understanding the position of the purists and their resistance to commodified
aspects of the culture. The consumption of artefacts by the purist group went
into their own cultural practices in a creative manner. For example, some purists
collected vinyl which was then used in their own turntablism whilst others
listened to albums or tracks in order to utilise ideas for lyrics or beats for their
own work.

The distinction between the purist and peripheral tastes relates to
Hodkinson's notion of consistent distinctiveness. He suggests that '... gaining
acceptance, popularity and status was often dependent upon making oneself
sufficiently compatible with the distinctive tastes of the culture ...' (2002: 30).
In this respect, the purist groups rely on their enhanced cultural knowledge of
hip-hop. This allows them to distance themselves from others but also serves
as a marker for subcultural allegiance and acceptance. Both the purists and the
peripherals utilised a sense of hierarchical positioning in regards to matters of
taste in order to demonstrate and sustain their own sense of subcultural worth.

Engagement in the culture

One key distinction between the purists and the peripherals was their relative
degrees of agency and activity in constructing their own sense of hip-hop culture.
As discussed, the peripherals based their consumption on mass mediated, major
label artists. Their cultural focus tended to be more narrow, often discussing
a limited number of rappers during the fieldwork. The purists, however, had
an extensive knowledge of hip-hop and grime artists and regularly involved
themselves in organising events and creating their own music in line with
Hodkinson's notion of autonomy. The important aspect of this participation is
that it comes from the purists' response to their concepts of mainstream hip-hop

music. All of the purist respondents in the fieldwork expressed their passion for hip-hop music while they had a general distrust of commercial, big selling artists. This dissatisfaction with commodified hip-hop manifests itself in a form of cultural resistance as they placed greater emphasis on producing and creating rather than simply consuming. Agency is evident in the purist groups through their pro-active engagement in creating music that they feel more connected to. The purists can be seen as more culturally active due to their proximity to, and affiliation with, local hip-hop cultures. Much of their cultural information came from word of mouth as they regularly engaged in conversations with others within their subcultural groupings. In this respect, purists 'do' hip-hop whilst peripherals consume it. However, the peripheral form of consumption is far from simply passive as they take forms of identity, group affiliation and relative forms of cultural knowledge from hip-hop and grime. This is what separates them from the mainstream consumer whose cultural engagement goes little further than simply listening and why the term 'relative passivity' is used here — not as an absolute term of description but as a comparison to the purists.

Although rare, public events were organised in pubs or clubs which were general live events spaces, not solely for hip-hop music. To this extent, some of the research participants' cultural activities occurred in the same public spaces as others, although usually not at the same time. The spaces used were not their property on a permanent basis but they felt that they had ownership over the place during nights when their preferred music was played. All of the focus groups were aware that other genres of music, including heavy metal, indie and emo, were more readily catered for with pubs in their local towns and areas which proactively attempted to attract such subcultural audiences into their establishments. The focus group members, however, did not seem to be well served in terms of the provision of a space which was exclusively hip-hop. A number of established pubs and clubs in each area did advertise the inclusion of hip-hop music on their promotional material but these were always in tandem with other musical genres such as house, reggae and R'n'B. As has been shown, purist tastes were very much opposed to mainstream rap music which was the staple diet of the clubs and pubs in each of the locations where the focus group interviews took place.

The purist rejects such spaces in favour of maintaining a distance from the mainstream form of the culture which peripherals engage in. Malbon defines the clubbing experience for youths as involving '... spaces in which they can express themselves and feel an affiliation with others, forging and re-forging their self- and group identities ...' (1998: 266). Due to the lack of regular hip-hop nights that were accessible to the purist focus group participants that matched their own taste values this bonding element was missing, as was any potential opportunity for wider social collectivity. The lack of opportunities to experience hip-hop culture in their own towns led most of the purists to display their subcultural affiliation within a tight network of friendship groups who usually met within their own personal spaces. The members of all of the focus groups, whether peripheral or purist, stated that the majority of their hip-hop activity existed within a framework of limited numbers. The night-time cultural activities of the peripherals did, from time to time, include attending clubs in order to assert their subcultural identities, in line with Malbon's quote. Their use of spectacular subcultural performance enabled them to be identified as different from the mainstream crowd who were also in attendance in the club. This is an example of the peripheral group laying claim to a subcultural identity that was recognisable to others.

Many of the purists who were involved in organising and promoting small scale hip-hop nights stated that they had experienced some hostility towards the genre from pub and club owners. This limited sense of the ownership of space available for hip-hop may in some way determine the importance placed on territory within the culture. Events which catered for more mainstream hip-hop sensibilities were very rarely attended by those within the Lewisham, Canterbury and Ashford groups and only sparingly by the peripheral groups. This mainly stems from the form of hip-hop which these clubs play but can also be seen to be a response to the perceived threats of violence as discussed in Chapter 3. For a number of purists in the research such factors were linked as they saw the gangsta rap sub-genre, the staple diet of such night-time environs, as synonymous with 'thuggish attitudes' (Luke, Canterbury) which centred on threatening behaviour towards others. Many of the participants in the purist focus groups were in the centre of localised hip-hop collectives and felt no urge to attend events promoted by people outside of their own friendship network. This relative rejection of mediated hip-hop culture can also be seen as a means of claiming a sense of authenticity for themselves and the artists within their local area. Active engagement with hip-hop culture for the purists largely involved the localisation of this global form and highlights their agentic capabilities.

Considerable time was spent by the purist group on practicing and improving their abilities in the artistic area of hip-hop they pursued. Although organised hip-hop gatherings were actively avoided by the Lewisham group they would occasionally gather in the open environment of parks in order to spit, or freestyle, their lyrics to each other. Of all the focus groups, this activity was unique to the Lewisham group. This is perhaps due to the age of each group. As an average, both the Ashford and Canterbury groups were a few years older than the Lewisham group. As a result, they were much more likely to have houses or flats of their own whereas the Lewisham group, with one exception, lived in their parental home. The park, therefore, acts as a form of communal space where gatherings of hip-hop and grime practitioners can take place in what they considered to be relative safety, within Watt and Stenson's sense of the '... invisible borders of youth territory ...' (1998: 250). These locations serve as area markers which possess some scope of ownership for this group and, therefore, a sense of security. Such spaces were regularly attended, at pre-arranged times, in order to discuss hip-hop and grime related views and as a forum to discuss more personal issues. The park also acted as a place for purists to demonstrate their lyrical and rhythmic vocal skills to one another, as well as serving the function of reinforcing cultural taste values within the group. There is, of course, a clear structural reason why this group should engage in such an activity in this location. The financial constraints felt by this group ensured that they could not afford expensive equipment such as record decks or laptops with music software to create their own music so they were therefore limited in their cultural activities.

The purists often concerned themselves with arranging what may be termed cultural instances in both public and private spaces. This was undertaken as a form of rejection of more formally organised events that they felt did not serve their cultural requirements.

> Rachel (A):   We want people to get up there in front of us all and show
> us what they got. Like, we throw our own parties to have fun
> but also to sort of create something fresh and a bit out there.
> So, like, the clubs that are around here that say they have
> hip-hop nights just play records — no mixing or mashing
> of tunes and nobody spitting over the top. That's what you'd
> see at a proper hip-hop night, you know?

For the purist groups, as demonstrated in the extract above, emphasis at hip-hop events should be on forms of creativity and participation for those in attendance with sufficient skill. People would be invited to DJ or MC at such events in a *laissez-faire* manner in order to demonstrate their abilities and to gain subsequent subcultural kudos. However, this potentially élitist aspect was not the prime aim of participation as there was a democratic and non-critical approach at these smaller scale parties. Individuals were encouraged to take part, regardless of ability, in order to develop their skill set and understanding of the culture.

> *Simon (C):* When we have parties at our own place it's all about showing each other what we've learnt recently in terms of skills on the decks and what we've been working on. If people want to come along and rap over what the DJ is doing then all well and good. That has happened a fair few times in the past but, to be fair, we're more into the DJing side of things. Mixing, beat juggling and all that. Making something new with the sounds we have.

Here, Simon is advocating a popular purist idea about occurrences at self-organised parties. These events enable attendees to show off skills on the decks or help others to develop their own DJ style. This was also a popular activity for the Ashford group although their focus was largely on vocal performance. The members of the Canterbury group in particular were vociferous about their musical tastes and stated that vinyl records were their preferred choice of format. The members of this group would meet regularly to play new records to one another and to exhibit their DJ skills, creating new combinations of sounds from both well-known and more recently released tracks through their well-honed turntable dexterity. These gatherings were frequent and exclusive as only those within the small friendship network were invited. There was a democratic feel to these nights as there tended to be equal amounts of time given to each member of the group on the decks, regardless of comparative performance ability. This practice ensured that the group were creating aspects of hip-hop culture that were somewhat unique to themselves in spaces that they felt ownership over. The isolation of this selective subcultural collective can be read as a rejection of spaces where less committed hip-hoppers may be present. In this way, the purists deny wider, perhaps more mainstream hip-hop culture in favour of creating their own spaces, styles and tastes. These patterns of subcultural interaction over-ride the larger culture industry of major label organisations and their marketing machinery. The purists are active in the creation of their own version of hip-hop culture, determining the parameters of taste and participation. It was evident from a range of parties, however, that although the participants voiced the opinion that various skills were nurtured during the gatherings, there remained a focus towards the end of the night on DJs who were proficiently more skilled than the majority. This shows that there remained a sense of hierarchy, although one based on a sense of meritocratic ability, at such events.

Unspectacular style: Hip-Hop dress code

The research findings in this aspect of the fieldwork were perhaps the most surprising. The traditionally recognised dress code for those within hip-hop culture includes trainers, low slung jeans and hooded tops. Baseball caps or beanie hats are also a common signifier of cultural affiliation. However, although such dress codes were in evidence within the focus groups, as detailed in the previous chapter, there was a significant deviation between groups on this issue. Those groups which have been termed purists recognised the fact that such codes existed but also made it clear that they did not perceive such a matter as a rule of involvement per se. Their view of hip-hop culture centred on the democratic nature of the experience rather than the superficial, materialist commodity fetishism that they perceived as the inauthentic nature of many hip-hoppers. The Lewisham, Canterbury and Ashford groups all took the opinion that visual appearance was not as important as behaviour, intentions and values in their day to day existences, although it should be noted that their visual style often tended towards recognisable hip-hop traits such as hoodies and hi-top trainers. The following exchange comes from a focus group interview with the Lewisham participants.

TD: Do you think that what you wear is an important indicator to who you are?

Jemal (L):   What you wear ain't all that important, like. You see them boys walking around town with, like, all the latest clothes on and that. Don't mean they're real hip-hop, you know? Like, I can go into a shop and buy any clothes I want to, like, show myself off as something but don't mean I'm it. Hip-hop and grime, like, they're more like about what you know. I mean, what do these people know?

Ash (L):   There's a lot of poor kids in my neighbourhood and they, like, might literally steal or save up to buy things that they might

think is what hip-hop gangsters wear or whatever. It don't
matter what you wear or how you walk, like. Them kids just
don't know what's what, do they?

The visual spectacle of subcultures has been emphasised by Hebdige
(1979), amongst others, although it seems that in many respects the hip-hop
culture as conceived and lived by the purists expects no such external signifiers
of differentiation. The fact that material cultural artefacts such as fashion
sensibilities are being resisted by the purists illustrates their subcultural agency
to actively construct their own identity framework within their own parameters.

These findings are in contrast to a number of studies on youth subcultures
which focus on the visually spectacular aspects of identity. Moore illustrates
the importance of style for the group of skinheads he was studying by stating
that '... the visual component of style is the centre of a skinhead's cultural world
...' (1994: 36) whilst Förnas et al. detail the importance to youths of '... the
impression one makes on others ...' (1995: 48) through visual appearance. Such
quotes can certainly be aligned with the position of the peripherals in terms
of spectacular style. All focus group members stated that they were aware of
hip-hop ways of dress yet it was only the peripherals who stated that it was
a requirement for acceptance in hip-hop friendship groups. They felt that an
outward projection of cultural values through style was a factor that identified
individuals as subcultural and is, in essence, a way to '... demarcate themselves
from perceived outsiders ...' (Wood, 2006: 114). An example of such a viewpoint
is illustrated in the following extract:

Lou (R):   See, when you dress hip-hop then others, like, will be able to
tell what you're into and what you like. I want to tell people
who I am and my clothes say that loudly for me.

Zac (R):   So, say you're at a party and you get chatting to some girl and,
of course, you're going to want to know about her so what
she wears is important 'cos if it ain't hip-hop I ain't chatting
to her. Like, your clothes and that say who you are, for sure.

Sarah (R):   Yeah. I love the hip-hop look and if people are wearing it
when I'm out then I know that they're likely good people that
I can talk to and hang with as we will have common ground.
There's a style to hip-hop clothes, though, and people have
to wear these clothes with a certain sense of what's right and

	wrong or … so, I think … erm … it isn't just about buying the clothes it's about knowing how to wear them
TD:	What do you mean by that?
Sarah (R):	Like, this is the way to spot a faker because they may have all the gear but, I don't know why, it just won't sit right on them. Buy the clothes, sure, but wear them right, you know?
TD:	So, just because someone is wearing what you would call the right clothes they could still be faking?
Sarah (R):	Sure. But the clothes is the thing that counts.

In contrast to the peripheral position, the purists were less emphatic in their determination that dress code was a significant factor in subcultural affiliation. The notion of subcultural mundanity, as detailed by Keith Kahn-Harris, is a way in which members of certain scenic groups can '… attend successfully to the multiple spaces within which they are involved …' (2004: 113). Hip-hop culture undoubtedly has an identifiable dress code and it is not the suggestion here that such visual signifiers are not considered or utilised by the purists. However, they do not insist on strict adherence to spectacular style in order to justify cultural affiliation. The hip-hop purists view their cultural behaviour as democratic and accepting of others who demonstrate sufficient levels of knowledge and cultural competence. Their perception of dress code is simply as an extension of the commodified variant of the culture that they constantly attempt to distance themselves from. The purists sought to emphasise that cultural knowledge was valued more than cultural style.

A summary of the differences between the purist and peripheral positions in terms of the spectacular nature of the subculture can be considered effectively by detailing the means through which these groups view their position in relation to those who they may term as 'other' to themselves, i.e. non-subculturalists. The peripherals can be termed as *outward looking* as generally their activities were focused on their presentation of self to others. Their view that visual style, as a tool of separation, aided their own sense of identification illustrates this point. Not only did forms of spectacular style help them in forming friendship groups but it also ensured that outsiders were detached from this group. The purists can be termed *inward looking* in this respect as they tended to disregard the values and opinions of those outside of their subcultural group. This resulted in the opinion that the presentation of self through dress was not necessary to demonstrate subcultural substance. Indeed, markers of subcultural affiliation for this group relied upon intangible aspects such as knowledge of the culture rather than materialistic components of style.

Agency and youth culture

In this section I will explore the terms agency and youth culture in light of the findings from the research. Agency refers to the ability of individuals to operate, through their own active will, regardless of wider social structures which may otherwise limit the choices they possess. Agents are both creative and proactive in their subcultural expressions (Wilson, 2006: 130). Giddens states that there is a form of consciousness to this agency, that the actors '... maintain a continuing 'theoretical understanding' of the grounds of their activity ...' (1984: 5). Agency can be seen as a form of autonomous self-construction (Richards, 1998: 36) and it was found in the field that the research participants often shape their own sense of hip-hop and grime culture in accordance with the notion of agency. Some are actively engaged in responding to, and consciously resisting, mainstream images and messages to which they feel a disconnection whereby they place greater emphasis on production rather than consumption. The research respondents in this study who perceived that they were more active within the culture in comparison with others identified themselves as engaged in a struggle against what they termed as a mass, passive audience who regularly consume hip-hop culture and were more likely to be influenced by the values of mainstream culture. In this respect, those who take forms of subcultural identity from hip-hop and grime perceive themselves as possessing agentic capabilities as they actively respond to a number of choices. Butler (1990: 195) proposes that agency relates to a subject who has a stable existence prior to the cultural field that it negotiates and can be seen as the capacity for reflexive mediation. The data has shown that the research participants made what they considered to be active decisions to engage with hip-hop culture and were constantly assessing their own and others forms of engagement.

Structuration theory, developed by Giddens (1976), attempts to avoid the extremes of objectivism and subjectivism. Objectivism refers to an emphasis on structure, whereby agents are seen to be '... playthings or puppets of reified social systems ...' (Stones, 2005: 14). Subjectivism on the other hand places the agent in an entirely autonomous position. The partial autonomy of agents is a notion of Structuration theory that has relevance for the research subjects within this study as this notion suggests that the actions of individuals are at times controlled by culture and sometimes by practical interests (Rubinstein,

2001: 14). Agency, then, '... refers not to the intentions people have in doing things but to their capability of doing those things in the first place ...' (Giddens, 1984: 9). As has been shown, agentic action was evident in the research with regards to the construction of meaningful cultural identities for the research subjects. However, it was clear that the research participants were not entirely free to construct and develop their own identities as structural considerations remained a significant part in the process. Miles (2000) discusses the complex and dynamic two-way relationship between structure and agency and notes that the young people in his research used consumption in a constructive manner. This backs up Willis' (1990) assertion that such groups should not be labelled as *mere dupes*, though equally they could not be termed as *pure agents* in any real sense (Miles, ibid.: 142). The purist/peripheral model attempts to describe the variations in degrees of agency evident in the field as a dynamic continuum, thereby addressing the insensitivity toward the nuanced and multifaceted aspects of social life that binaries such as structure/agency present. The chapter highlights the creative engagement in hip-hop, not simply the consumption patterns of the research subjects. In this manner, there exists a range of ways in which research participants perform their identities and a number of markers for acceptance to certain levels of cultural engagement and group approval.

Wallace and Kovatcheva make an analytical distinction between the terms youth culture and youth subcultures. The former is '... an element of media-conveyed culture of consumption ...' (1988: 154), whereas the latter possesses a defined sense of stylistic specificity. Within the fieldwork the distinctions within hip-hop and grime culture were apparent for the research participants. It was found that certain research participants rely on the idea of agency and self-determination in qualifying their own sense of self. It can be argued that agency helps distinguish between the relatively passive consumption of rap music enjoyed by a significant number of the hip-hop audience, compared to the assertive, active and creative participation engaged in by other respondents. As has been illustrated, the purist and peripheral groups demonstrated degrees of subcultural substance to be justifiably labelled as subcultural, therefore discussion of passive consumption in this study largely relates to those who the research subjects saw as mainstream consumers. However, the purists would often label those who are termed in the study as peripherals as being less active in their consumption and interpretation of hip-hop and grime.

Use of the term passive here is as a relational concept, separating those individuals who partake in culturally creative activities with those whose cultural engagement is more centred on the consumption of mass-mediated products. In this sense, the dichotomous variables 'active' and 'passive' should not be considered as absolute states. Those that are active in the culture go beyond a mere declaration of fandom and attempt to shape their own localised cultural practices. This often arose as an active rejection of the cultural form as represented by corporate record companies as the youth groups placed greater emphasis on creative engagement over cultural consumption. The more creatively active members in the focus groups for this study tended to largely discredit the mainstream output of hip-hop culture, preferring instead to focus on their own symbolic creativity at what might be termed 'street level' or within the underground.

The culturally less creative research participants, however, negotiate their own understanding and pursuit of hip-hop culture through mediated aspects delivered to their homes via satellite broadcasters and the internet. This is not to deny forms of agency to the latter group. The more active cultural practitioners involve themselves with creating music and gaining cultural competence through, amongst other things, archiving rap and hip-hop recordings. The relatively passive hip-hop consumers are engaged in the culture and take identity from it and, therefore, should once again not be seen as mere cultural dupes (Hall, 1981). They are gaining a sense of agency from the material consumed although that agency is defined by the mainstream, corporate aspects of the culture. As Gidley states '... the products of the global cultural industries are never consumed in a purely passive way ...' (2007: 149). Therefore, those individuals defined as peripheral should not be conceived as 'normative drones'. The claim here is that there is an identifiable variance in the degree of activity and agency between the two conceptual groups of peripherals and purists. Paul Willis informs us that there is no longer, if there ever was, such a thing as a 'mass', passive audience. He states that '... young people are all the time expressing or attempting to express something about their actual or potential *cultural significance* ...' (1990: 1, italics in original text). One criticism of Willis' work, however, is the tendency to homogenise the youth group that he is studying as he fails to fully develop the notion of what might be termed degrees of agency.

Subcultural élitism

Dunja Brill, discussing Sarah Thornton's (1995) appropriation of Bourdieu's concept of stratification via aesthetic attitudes, states that behind the rhetoric of equality and inclusiveness '... lurks a thinly veiled elitism which serves to reaffirm binary oppositions between 'alternative' and 'straight', 'radical' and 'conformist' and most importantly between 'mainstream' and 'subculture' ...' (2007: 112). As a result of the data obtained in the research, both purist and peripheral groups can arguably be assessed as possessing forms of elitism. The peripherals see themselves as better (i.e. possessing more subcultural knowledge and status) than mainstream hip-hop consumers who do not engage with what they see as more meaningful and committed cultural activities and identities, whereas the purists see themselves as superior in taste and subcultural knowledge to the peripherals and mainstream consumers. There is an undoubted exclusivity to subcultural participation at the purist level and it is through the accumulation of subcultural knowledge, and subsequent acceptance into the group, that this is achieved. Although, as has been shown, there was a democratic air to purist cultural events, such practices occurred within tightly bound network groups wherein individuals had to meet certain levels of approval in order to fully participate. Such exclusionary strategies were incorporated to ensure that their engagement was not tainted by those who they perceived as beneath their own level of commitment, engagement and knowledge. The inward looking nature of the purists does not illustrate an aggressive or confrontational manner in terms of accrual of status within the subcultural environs.

The purist/peripheral model highlights the elitist structures evinced from the fieldwork in terms of subcultural groupings. It is clear that for a purist group to accept a new member a certain level of knowledge needs to be demonstrated by that individual. The divisions between purist and peripheral sensibilities show a marked contrast in values and ideals, aspects which are expanded upon in the chapters that follow on responses to mediated texts. However, it was difficult to ascertain exactly what an individual needed to demonstrate in order to gain acceptance into either a peripheral or purist group. The members of these groups were clearly selective and yet their criteria were neither obvious nor willingly discussed. It could be suggested that this was due to their reluctance to allow a seeming outsider knowledge of such an area or because such stipulations varied from case to case. During the fieldwork, the research subjects found it difficult to verbalise their opinions on this matter. Although purists and peripherals may well have integrated in day to day activities such as the workplace or college, their social activities were significantly different to diminish their chances of mixing in a social context.

Conclusion

The purist/peripheral divide is a developing theory of description which uses abstract terms which are informed by an holistic understanding of the ethnographic fieldwork in the study's wider research. This chapter has further developed Hodkinson's notion of subcultural substance (2002) and applied it to the focus groups to illustrate the range of agentic positions in contemporary subcultures. The model adds to the discourse of substantive, collective groups which differs from previous work on subcultures which homogenised the insider/outsider dichotomy for ease of description and analysis. This study does not ask for a return to the conceptualisation of subcultures as theorised by the CCCS but seeks to contribute to the discourse of the sociological concept. Structural constraints retain a prominent position in the study of cultural groups but aspects of subcultures being magical solutions to class issues were not clearly in evidence within the field. Contemporary subcultures are not specifically centred on class resistance to cultural hegemony, a position of the Birmingham School, nor are they as transient and fluid as writers from the postmodern tradition would have it. There is a clear sense of agentic resistance at play as displayed by certain youth groups within the fieldwork. The active engagement and re-appropriation of the culture by the purists demonstrates forms of cultural opposition to the dominant hegemonic culture. This engagement is on a sliding scale of agency between the purists and the peripherals who demonstrate varying degrees of subcultural substance in their cultural practices. The data clearly demonstrates the modes of identification and differentiation between the purist and peripheral groups.

The scepticism of the purist groups towards organisations aiming to make a profit from rap music establishes a distance between what are perceived as authentic, street level artists and the wider, commodified culture. It is in this form of commercial resistance that increased subcultural substance can be seen. The purists construct their own hip-hop or grime culture around themselves. They are reliant on record companies to provide them with new material to buy, mix, sample, reference and suchlike. Yet there is a sense of autonomy and control about these groups which is lacking from the relatively passive consumption of the Rochester and Brighton sets. The agentic and resistive manner in which the purists engage with hip-hop and grime culture establishes a heightened sense of subcultural identity. The peripheral groups can be termed subcultural as they form collective identities around hip-hop culture, thereby displaying a sense of distinctiveness. Although their consumption revolves around more mainstream product than the purists they still possess degrees of agency which means they should not be termed cultural dupes. The differences between the purists and peripherals illustrate the complexity of a contested, dynamic cultural form. The peripherals' sense of spectacular style aligns them with many earlier studies on subcultures, whilst the rejection of such matters by the purists can be seen as a response to the ever widening importance of cultural style to mainstream society (Chaney, 2004). Purists, as exemplified by the Canterbury and Ashford research subjects, demonstrate instances of subcultural longevity that is absent from many studies in the area of youth cultures.

Chapter 5

Grime music

"I've changed from back in the days ... "[5]

Introduction

The focus on grime music in this book developed from the grounded theory approach incorporated in the research and was driven by the interests of a number of the research respondents. At the outset of this work I had anticipated more data would be produced on young people's responses to UK hip-hop. However, most of the research subjects stated that they had only selective interest in this geographical variant of rap. Artists such as Skinnyman, Professor Green and Roots Manuva were not used as reference points during the interviews. Most of the focus group respondents claimed that they preferred American rap as it was more authentic. UK rap was, in their eyes, home-grown simulacra (Briggs and Cobley, 1999: 349). When the conversation of UK hip-hop artists came up, only the Canterbury and Lewisham groups had any extensive knowledge yet none of the focus group members in any of the locations preferred UK artists to their American counterparts. UK hip-hop was perceived as too derivative of the original generic template from the USA and there was a common feeling of disconnection with the music as a result. Grime music, however, was seen to be an authentic British form of cultural expression.

Few ethnographic or qualitative studies of grime culture exist in the literature; those that do take a genealogical approach to the music and focus more on its creation than its reception. de Jong and Schuilenburg (2006), Bennett and Stratton (2010) and Jones (2012) all focus on describing the cultural form as an example of the articulation of British voices within a localised variant of hip-hop. These studies briefly discuss the form of grime and its construction from a production context but not its consumption and the audience's interpretation. Although relatively little has been written to date on grime culture, it was clear at the *It Ain't Where You're From, It's Where You're At* international hip-hop conference hosted by Cambridge University in 2016 that a number of researchers were working in this area and that more academic engagement with this field was forthcoming.

In this chapter I begin by discussing the origins of grime music before detailing some of the genre's key codes and conventions. I then use the data from the research to discuss the research respondents' creative engagement with the culture, the various sites of consumption utilised, and then a discussion of the visual components of grime as evidenced in music videos and how the audience interpret such imagery. As grime was predominantly discussed with the Lewisham group I only use comments from those participants in this chapter.

The origins of grime

Although grime music has clear links to hip-hop, the origins and vibrancy of grime cannot simply be understood as a mere re-appropriation of American rap music—its musical properties are rooted in the traditions of the African diaspora (Charles, 2016). Grime music is notably faster than hip-hop, yet the vocal delivery is akin to that of rapping, mixing a style which is also reminiscent of Jamaican toasting. Grime started in London with young men and women from the inner-city rapping over computer generated beats which owe a debt from a range of influences including UK garage, jungle, dub reggae and Jamaican dancehall. Bow, in East London, is seen as the birthplace of grime and 2002 often cited as its year of inception. In its early days, grime was also known as Eskibeat and sublow and it is EZ from Kiss FM who is credited with first using the term grime. Wiley is widely regarded as the figurehead of the movement at this time but his origins, much like grime's, begin with UK garage as he first had a hit in the UK charts as a member of the garage collective Pay As U Go whose track *Champagne Dance* entered the charts in 2001. Subsequent Wiley tracks including *Eskimo*, *Igloo* and *Ice Rink* used low end basslines (around 40Hz) which would become staples of the grime sound along with the use of half time, down tempo beats which reflected the sub-genre's more pessimistic, darker lyrical themes and aural tones which differentiated this new genre from the UK garage scene which it developed from. The recurring theme of ice in the titles of Wiley's early tracks highlights a move away from the up-tempo aural characteristics of garage to an increasingly colder, more negative sound.

The emergence of the grime scene has coincided with a decrease in the price of production technologies as well as the increase in networks of inexpensive distribution (i.e. internet sites such as Myspace or SoundCloud as well as YouTube). The immediacy of such internet sites, with instant access to new tracks as they are uploaded by the artists, was seen as an attractive aspect of grime music consumption by those in the research as they viewed this platform as being against the preferred and standard practices of the recording industry, thereby highlighting grime's enhanced connection to the streets more so than the corporate machinery. This key area of concern, that grime artists were somehow using unconventional distribution practices that went against the interests of traditional record label marketing strategies, was voiced by the focus group respondents and reinforced their perception that grime was anti-corporate and was a site of resistance.

Despite aligning to underground sensibilities, grime music crossed over into the mainstream almost immediately after its inception in the early 2000s with Dizzee Rascal's debut album *Boy in Da Corner* winning the Mercury Music Prize in 2003, selling over 250,000 copies worldwide in its first year of release. To cement his place in the mainstream, Dizzee Rascal has subsequently won a number of Brit Awards as well as featuring in the opening ceremony of the 2012 London Olympic Games performing his Number 1 song *Bonkers*. Similar accolades have been received by Tinie Tempah who has had hit records in the mainstream charts, won Brit Awards and, somewhat controversially, was the pre-match entertainment at the 2016 FA Cup Final at Wembley Stadium. More recently, the critical and commercial success of Skepta, JME and other artists on the independent Boy Better Know label has led to well received sets on the main stages at both Glastonbury and the Reading and Leeds festivals and a sold out show at London's Alexandra Palace in 2016. *Konnichiwa*, Skepta's album of the same year, was awarded the Mercury Music Prize and was certified as a gold selling album. Such live events, awards and unit sales are far from the genre's origins of distribution on various pirate radio stations such as Rinse FM, Déjà Vu FM and Mystic. Much in the same way that Radio Caroline acted as a cultural gatekeeper for the surge of youth oriented beat and pop music of the early 1960s, these stations have acted as cultural taste makers for grime and the illegal nature of this medium only added to the seeming anti-establishment feeling that was growing in the scene.

Software such as Fruity Loops helped determine the aural characteristics of grime such as low end bass rumbles and cutting snares which can be read as aural symbolism of the harsh reality of inner city London life. There is a clear aggressive tone to the sound of grime music, both in the vocal delivery and in the timbre of the electronic beats and bass lines used. The tempo of grime tracks is usually around 136-140 b.p.m. and the aural qualities of the tracks can be considered as lo-fi and somewhat crude and this is crucial to an understanding of grime's DIY ethos which links it closely to punk music in intent. The use of independent labels and seemingly anti-corporate mechanisms for distributing and circulating grime, along with a criticism of using overly simplistic melodic patterns which is often levelled at it, link to punk's ideals of raging against the machine and, in some ways, grime can be seen to be continuing this standpoint. A number of websites and internet forums have been established under the Grime Digital name — a non-profit organisation set up in 2008 to enable distribution networks for the scene, similar in manner to the underground fanzine culture of punk.

Those grime artists who have signed record contracts with major labels were termed by those in the field as selling out the fundamental aims of grime culture and diluting their sounds for a wider audience, thereby damaging any sense of credibility they possessed. The output of crossover artists such as Dizzee Rascal, Tinchy Stryder and Chipmunk, all of whom have had number one singles in the UK national charts, is markedly different from their work on early grime mix-tapes. The dilution of their original sound is a common theme for artists who wish to pursue commercial sales rather than artistic integrity.

Isaac: When Dizzee Rascal got signed, the label said to him 'You can leave grime behind. You can touch it once in a while but you've got to leave it behind. You do what we want you to do.'

This suspicion of record labels, and the control they enjoy over their roster, arguably stems from the research participants' need to perceive their music as simply theirs, and not the product of some distant industry over which they have no control. In this instance, resistance to major label output and their ways of working is demonstrated.

As mentioned earlier, the Lewisham group had a much greater connective affinity with grime music compared with the participants from other geographical locations and this attraction is largely as a result of the geographical proximity between the audience and performers. This resulted in the Lewisham group labelling grime music as theirs, as a part of their lifestyle possession. The focus group members were asked why they identified with grime culture:

Jemal: Because it's from here, innit?
Ash: It's something that we can be proud of, like. I mean, we can say that, yeah, it originated from London. It's what's happening and that. Like, if it gets big then, yeah, we can say, like people

can say 'ah, yeah, I like grime music from another country',
like. It originated from London; we're the ones that made it
so that's what makes grime music good.

Blackman (1995: 43) discusses the value of youth cultural identification and
focuses on the idea that 'the band is the bond'. He attempts to draw out socio-
cultural relations between musical artists and youth groups. In this study there
was a connection between symbolic identification and authentic engagement in
cultural production. Grime music was, and is, *their* music. The research subjects
did not see grime music as an aspect of black culture; instead they referred to
it as a culture belonging to a particular social class. For them, it belonged to
the inner city, poverty stricken boroughs of London and crossed racial, but not
social class, divides. They also recognised grime scenes were developing in other
British cities but made it clear in our discussions that they felt connected to
some of these artists because, as Ash stated, "*They ain't from round London but
they're living the same. As in, they are poor … and so don't make no difference their
colour*". The racial mixing that is evident in this study follows similar findings
of increased multiculturalism in the work of Hewitt (1986), Wulff (1995) and
Gidley (2007). In opposition to post-subculturalist theorists, the fieldwork data
suggests that from the perspective of those closely engaged with the culture,
authentic participation in grime culture is reliant on aspects of social class. Grime
culture celebrates the local in key elements such as lyrics and visual presentation
in videos and marketing material. Postcodes are very often included in tracks to
establish a sense of space and place, as markers of ownership and as a form of
allowing the wider world to know of the existence of that location.

Grime artists use English dialect and slang along with, for appropriate artists,
occasional lapses into Caribbean speech codes. The use of recognisable London
accents highlights the importance of space and place whilst the use of aspects of
patois infers an appreciation by the rapper of their cultural heritage whilst also
demonstrating London's multicultural nature. The use of 'road' (the street style
London accent and concomitant slang) combined with aspects of 'yard' (black
with Jamaican roots) also displays a linguistic dexterity crucial to success in the
grime scene. The lyrical content in grime tracks reinforces the culture's need
for 'authentic' protagonists as a focus is on autobiographical accounts of life 'on
road' and the ever present threat of intimidation and violence as a result of the
territoriality of city life. Central themes include the mandem (the rapper's gang
to whom a sincere sense of loyalty is projected), the *dissing* and *punking* of rival

MCs as a form of braggadocio which is often coupled with the threat to bring 'arms house' (violence, often with the use of weapons). A sense of rivalry between rappers and their crews has developed in the popular discourse of grime music which has been further enhanced by the artists who focus on declaring their supremacy in regards to their rapping ability and, on occasions when this will not suffice, their physical dominance (despite there being a recurring theme in a significant number of tracks that the artists are reluctant to resort to physical violence). A well publicised 'beef' (grudge) between Tinie Tempah and Chip (formerly known as Chipmunk) centred around the pair producing diss tracks to one another via BBC Radio 1 Xtra's *Fire in the Booth* slot on Charlie Sloth's show. Both artists have had commercial success and have been accused of selling out their grime roots to achieve this. *Fire in the Booth* is a popular segment on the BBC's urban music station which consists of rappers freestyling and thereby reinforcing their credentials as improvisers — an ability seen as fundamental to the credibility of artists in the realms of both hip-hop and grime. This original spat between Tinie Tempah and Chip evolved to include a number of other rappers including Big Narstie, Bugzy Malone, Devilman and Saskilla amongst others who all released tracks referring to some degree to this recurring disagreement. Not only does grime perpetuate itself by making reference to lines in other tracks in an almost insistent and immediate back and forth manner but there is also a tendency for dominance to be a key theme within the culture.

Clashing in grime is very much akin to battle raps in hip-hop and centres on two MCs challenging one another in a battle of lyrical dexterity. This aspect of the culture enables the performer to show their improvisatory skills, a key marker for authenticity and subcultural kudos. The *Lord of the Mics* series is one of the most popular platforms for such clashes with YouTube views in the hundreds of thousands for the various instalments. The *Lord of the Mics* events were started by grime scene elder Jammer and the early instalments were filmed in his basement, a location which is now as much a part of grime lore as 1520 Sedgwick Avenue is to hip-hop culture. Although the clash aspect of grime started on pirate radio, it was the filmed event between Wiley and Kano in 2004, the first in the 'Lord of the Mics' series, that more readily established clashing as an integral part of grime culture for a wider audience. The Lewisham group felt that clashing was a significant element of grime culture and rather than these events being seen as overtly hostile, they felt that participation acted as a way to celebrate the wider culture:

Emmanuel: Clashing is so, so important to grime. So important. To those
               who don't know it may look kind of like each man is showing
               their angst to the other but that ain't the case. Look at that
               Wiley and Kano clash and they both looking the same way,
               to camera. That means they're fronting [posturing] with their
               words, not their bodies. It says to me that they're challenging
               each other but there's no beef there. Like, they know the rules
               of the clash and the clash is good for grime. That's not to say
               that every clash ends well, though (laughs)

The demonisation of grime music as a violent culture which promotes anti-
social behaviour has been fairly consistent in mainstream media as well as in
the night time economy in cities where a number of nightclubs have banned
the playing of grime. The British tabloid press have often highlighted grime's
relationship with criminality in negative and sensationalist form, yet the reporting
of an incident which involved Dizzee Rascal being stabbed in Ayia Napa in 2003
arguably raised the profile of the genre into the public consciousness and the
link between grime and crime was fixed for many. This incident was reported
as being gang related and it was insinuated that Wiley was somehow involved, a
claim often and vigorously denied. This sense of 'beef' helped to establish grime
as the UK's answer to gangsta rap with the notion of grudges between performers
becoming commonplace in the raps of grime artists. Grime has a clear ability
to transmit certain emotions, including anger, which has helped it become the
sound of disenfranchised (often, but not always, black) youth as evidenced in the
use of Lethal Bizzle's *Pow! (Forward)* in the student protests on 9th, December
2010 in London, although few grime tracks actually deal with the political in an
explicit manner though narratives revolving around life in the poverty stricken
inner city and aspects of police harassment are becoming more evident as the
genre develops. Despite its seeming lack of overtly political content, grime has
become a politicised form of music as its protagonists, being mainly young, poor
and black, represent those groups most often demonised and marginalised by
the establishment. Grime has been used as something of a political platform,
however, for young people. The grime MC Novelist was elected to the position
of Deputy Young Mayor of Lewisham at the age of sixteen. This scheme started
in 2004 and was aimed at engaging more young people in political issues in the
London borough and ten out of the thirteen elections to date have seen young
people with some form of connection to grime culture being elected. Of course,

one way of reading this could well be that grime has a political centre, another could be that many young people in this area of London simply like grime and so this seeming over representation is to be expected.

Creative aspects of grime culture

The participants from the Lewisham group were all enrolled on the local college's music production course. Their student status meant that they could begin to develop their skills on computer software packages such as Logic and Reason which would have otherwise been inaccessible to them. All five members in the focus group produced and MCed on grime tracks of their own composition and they would often collaborate with others from both inside and outside the college environment in order to create a collective grime scene.

All five members of the group stated that their interest in hip-hop and grime music was the main driving force behind their enrolment onto a course of Further Education. Their life histories were very similar in the manner in which they came to embrace grime culture as illustrated here by Ash:

TD: So, how did you get into grime music?

Ash: Me, I just, like ... I was listening to garage, innit? I started listening to that but then after a ... because it got a bit boring, I started listening to more hip-hop than garage and hip-hop, like, that then turns into grime. In, like, Year 9 we used to do our own little rhymes, innit? Just playing about and that with little rhymes. So when grime came out I started listening to the rhymes and that. Stuff like Roll Deep and everything. We listened to that and our rhymes started to get better and, like, making sense and that. That's about Year 10 and 11. So I wanted to go full pelt with grime and everyone around me did, too. And we were, like, influencing each other. Giving each other the knowledge, see?

Allatt (1993: 154) discusses the 'skills of exchange' which sustain social relationships and allow social and cultural capital to be accrued. This notion is very much evident in Ash's last comment where knowledge of grime culture was accumulated as a collective. Social capital was gained by 'everyone around' Ash being interested in the same form of music.

The lyrical subject matter of choice for the focus group respondents centred on their own lives, what they knew and what they saw around them every day. The sense of authenticity maintained by a rap and grime MC was seen as a significant factor in regards to cultural acceptance throughout the focus group interviews. On numerous occasions it was claimed that their take on grime culture was much more authentic than other artists they were aware of. The fact that their work had so far not gained attention by record labels, or other such vehicles of the music industry, was seen as a marker of their ability to stay true to their art, not to sell out to a label that would perhaps alter their sound. On this point the following extract from the focus group is of interest:

TD:	If someone said to you, as an artist, if somebody listened to your track and said 'I like it and I want to sign you but you need to change your lyrics, you need to change the beats a little bit', how far would you go?
Dave:	I'd say 'no'. Depends what you mean by 'a little', though. Like, I wouldn't want to change my sound on someone's say-so but … like, if it was just to fiddle around with the lyrics or something then maybe … then maybe I'd agree. If it was more, like, advice than instruction.
Jemal:	Depends. If someone was saying that we needed to spit on, say, a slower beat then that's alright because most grime artists spit on slower beats but if they're trying to make us fit, like, our stuff onto a hip-hop beat for the tune to sell then I'd say no. Like, lots of grime artists or whatever try to make UK hip-hop sometimes and it sounds rubbish. It sounds bad. You have to stick with grime, innit, because, like, most grime artists have … grime is in their blood so when they try to spit on a hip-hop beat they just ain't up to it.
TD:	Would you change what you do for a guaranteed audience?
Jemal:	If I thought that more people would listen to my music if I changed then yeah.
Ash:	But then you might lose the audience that you have if they like the stuff that you're doing now. Say … like, if nobody was listening to grime then maybe I would try making something else but, like, if it was rubbish then, like switch back, eh?

There is a clear dilemma for the focus group participants when the issue of altering their work is addressed. From an artistic perspective there was a tendency to reject ideas of amending their own creativity yet, from a commercial viewpoint, they could all see a sense in changing their output. As a general rule, however, these respondents rejected the idea of working for a big record label as their view was that they would no longer retain control over their work in such a scenario. It was also clear in the discussions that they perceived major labels as being anathema to the concept of grime as a grassroots cultural form. The agency and creative elements of these research participants reflect their views on grime culture. According to this focus group, the major record labels that have signed grime artists do not fully understand grime culture and crossover acts quickly lose the respect of the grassroots culture. Grime culture belongs on the streets and there is wide ranging scepticism about media outlets who broadcast diluted or distorted aspects of the scene.

This creative fashioning of music away from mainstream commercial constraints demonstrates youth agency in the face of what Rupa Huq terms '... the negative version of globalisation whereby a top-down process of cultural homogenisation forcibly flattens cultural diversity ...' (2006: 110). The focus group participants show awareness that in order to gain a wider audience for their own music there may need to be some adjustment in their creativity. This appears contradictory with regard to their own stance on crossover artists who have, in their eyes, failed the subculture. One artist who was perceived as an exception to this general idea, however, was Skepta. One of the most respected grime MCs for the respondents in the fieldwork, Skepta (Joseph Adenuga) and his brother and fellow grime MC JME (Jamie Adenuga) were cited as influential figures as they not only continued to produce grime that was, according to Dave from the Lewisham group 'honest' and 'true to the origins of the scene', they were also labelled as astute businessmen as they run their own record label, Boy Better Know. This label has released a number of records by influential grime artists such as Wiley, Frisco, Jammer as well as work by JME and Skepta. In the eyes of those in the focus groups, both Skepta and JME were emblematic of the potential in grime music for people to elevate their lives away from their impoverished upbringings:

Ash: See, them boys (Skepta and JME) keep to the truth and their honesty is what you want to do in your own grime cuts, innit? Like, I see them as kind of brave because they're two

> young black men who had an idea, a sort of vision of what
> they wanted to do, and they went out there and just smacked
> it! If you can keep things true and make that kind of success
> then that's fair play. We look at that and think it can be done
> your own way and just look at them now. High rollers, man.
> That's what, at the end of the day, needs to be done which is
> stay true and see what happens.

There was an aspirational quality to artists such as Skepta and JME which
was seen as valuable in light of the dilution of sound for crossover appeal that
many artists had previously demonstrated. For example, artists such Dizzee
Rascal, Wiley and Tinie Tempah were often lambasted in the discussions for
their seeming betrayal of the grime scene although often the blame for this
was, as has been seen, attributed to record labels rather than directly at the
artists. It is of note that even in situations where artists were seen as altering
their sound to appeal to a wider audience it was often determined by the focus
group respondents that this was as a result of external pressures by big corporate
entities (despite, for example, Dizzee Rascal being signed to an independent
label in the UK). In this sense, this can be interpreted as another mechanism by
which those engaged in grime culture see themselves as opposed to mainstream
sensibilities, thereby marking grime as an authentic and honest form of musical
expression.

A range of markers were set by the fieldwork respondents to separate their own
cultural engagement and to distinguish between their own cultural competence
and that of others. It was important that there was a sense of ownership felt by
all of the research respondents to their own subcultural engagement but this
was even more evident with the grime affiliated group of Lewisham who were
more vociferous in claiming the cultural as their own. Similarly to Simon's earlier
declaration that the hip-hop purists make and therefore accordingly change
the cultural form, there was a determination within the Lewisham group that
they felt grime belonged to them and that interference from record labels was
unwelcome as it would often lead to the altering of the sound and ideas of the
culture — a position very close to those of the early hip-hop fans in the 1970s.
The truth of the grime scene, for these respondents, came from the lived every
day experiences of the MCs that could easily be related to by the audience
who faced similar obstacles in their lives. JME was cited regularly as a major
influence as it was felt that his lyrics, which focused on education and the general

mundanity of life as opposed to some artists who were seen to glamourise and overstate violence, were more honest and thereby authentic. The problematic concept of authenticity is more fully developed in a later chapter in this book. Here, however, it is significant to note that this idea, though contested, was a key determinant in identifying grime MCs with artistic integrity and worth.

Sites of consumption

Although grime culture has crossed over into the mainstream pop charts, the Lewisham group purported no real desire to consume the wider selling variants of the culture. Their preferred artists tended towards underground, niche acts who allowed the youth culture an opportunity to develop. They also claimed to know personally a number of grime MCs, such as Dot Rotten and Mic Ty, who they considered to be more artistically skilled than those with major label record deals. As grime artists themselves they considered grime culture to be about being involved actively, not being subjected to the ideas and messages of others. The Lewisham youth group felt that they could justifiably claim an ownership of grime culture due to their participation in creating aspects of the form for themselves.

Their sites of consumption tended towards platforms which were accessible to them for free as opposed to purchasing vinyl, CDs or legal downloads. Internet sites, notably YouTube, were used to sample new tracks and artists whilst the peer to peer file sharing network Pirate Bay was the preferred choice for downloading albums without paying although individual tracks were usually converted to MP3 format from YouTube. Their consumption was very much based on their own sense of active pursuit in terms of cultural knowledge. There were no evident grime taste makers from outside of the social circle of the focus group respondents. During the fieldwork, the Lewisham group repeatedly stated that they did not seek the advice of mediated sources of information such as magazines and national radio stations. Their perception was that in order to feel fully engaged with grime culture they needed to actively participate. If an MC or producer was seen to be creating music outside of the machinations of the standard aspects of the music industry, such as record labels and marketing departments, then they would have the notions of integrity and authenticity bestowed upon them. For the focus group respondents, grime was a word of mouth culture. Their geographical proximity to the scene meant that there was no need for them to rely on secondary sources of information.

Channel AKA is a British urban music station which specialises in British hip-hop and grime culture. Although this channel is dedicated to urban music with a significant emphasis on grime, the individuals in the focus groups watched the output in a sceptical manner. Ash stated in one interview session that he felt 'Channel AKA is making grime a laughing stock'. This was the general perception of the group who felt that this channel failed to represent the musicality of the genre, preferring to place emphasis on the street tough imagery that they saw as negative, an aspect developed later in this chapter. The Lewisham focus group constantly repeated the fact that money between the sums of £500 and £700 was needed in order to get a video on Channel AKA and that this fact denied the artists featured on the channel any sense of credibility. Other sites of distribution such as SoundCloud were seen as a much better option for the grime scene as the assumption was that the more democratic nature of this website, i.e. it is free to build a page and upload tracks, resulted in the focus being on the sound rather than any superficial visual aspects. SoundCloud, Bandcamp and other similar internet sites allowed talent to circumnavigate record labels in the eyes of the research respondents.

Ash: See, you watch them on that channel and your focus is less on the music which I think is a proper shame, like. So, most of us prefer to put our music on websites where the image is not there 'cos this way the audience are really focused on what you're saying, not what you're looking like.

Dave: Grime has its roots firmly in pirate stations — Rinse and Deja and all that — so it is a form of music first and last. This is why to stay true it's more important to listen, not to look.

Channel AKA was perceived by the Lewisham group as an outlet for aspects of grime culture that they did not relate to. Their idealised conception of grime as coming from, and belonging to, the streets of their particular localised areas was discredited by the output of this television channel. In their opinion, Channel AKA was for consumers of grime who had no real concept of its spatial location and cultural importance. This purist group perceived this broadcast channel, and similar media platforms, as serving the interests of peripheral grime consumers. As is clear from Ash and Dave's comments, the internet was seen as a considerably more favourable way of distributing their own tracks as this was perceived to be an extension of the audio nature of the scene's rise to prominence via pirate stations.

In an earlier chapter I discussed how the perceived threat of intimidation in the night time economy, at clubs and bars, resulted in many of the focus group respondents engaging with the culture through mediated means, whether television, radio or increasingly, and perhaps most significantly in terms of active cultural engagement, the internet. This fear of conflict, articulated in grime tracks by threats of violence and intimidation, perpetuated a sense of non-inclusivity to many in the research who felt that despite being geographically close to the 'scene' they were excluded due to not being associated with the right people. This then led to a fragmented, insular cultural form. It was also noted that grime music fans were not well served in pubs or nightclubs.

Dave: I know guys who have been given DJ slots at clubs and when they start spinning grime the owners get vexed and put a lock down on them. So many places won't allow grime to be played and it's mad.

At the grassroots level, this was a common issue raised by the focus group respondents, all of whom felt aggrieved that they were restricted in their choice (despite laying claim to threats of violence stopping them from going to clubs in the first place). In 2014, an event at The Barbican in London was cancelled, supposedly on police orders. The Just Jam event was a night of electronic music with a heavy emphasis on grime, although the headline act was Syrian artist Omar Souleyman. Just Jam was a part of a specially commissioned series of events at The Barbican but this was the only concert in the schedule to be pulled. Some commentators suggest that the Metropolitan Police regularly use the notorious Form 696 to racially profile music event audiences and take action to cancel events when deemed necessary. This form is essentially a health and safety warrant that promoters must complete twenty-one days before a live music event and submit to the police for inspection. The names, addresses and contact details of all artists and promoters are to be included along with a description of the genre of music at the event. Until 2008, the form also asked for a breakdown of the expected ethnic demographic of those attending. Form 696 has been seen as a way for the police force to stop minority groups from congregating en masse under the guise of a pre-emptive attempt to stop public disorder. In March 2016 another case was reported by local and national media about a South London club whose owner had been directly instructed by the police to stop hosting bashment (Jamaican dancehall) nights as they are seen as being associated with crime and disorder. Although the focus group members did not mention Form 696, they did mention how the perceived threat of violence which often stopped them from going out to such night time spaces came not just from other grime fans from different areas.

Dave	Well, maybe I'm not the one to say this as I'm white but I have seen a lot of shit that goes on in some clubs with bouncers and the five-O [police] towards the black kids which is unfair. We all get patted down and searched, like, but I've seen white kids been let through on some nights whilst the black or Turkish or Greek, Asian or whatever kids get a rough time. Some say it ain't racist, but …
Jemal:	*(interrupting)* It's racist! They're saying the black kids more likely to be carrying (a weapon) than others. That's what they're doing there — looking for trouble that ain't there. Then you got people in line getting hassled and feelin' like shit as the cops stare them down which causes grief. There's not much love for the po-po [the police] on nights like that.
Ash:	There ain't much love for the po-po—period!

The policing at such events, whether by the Met or bouncers at the clubs, was seen as confrontational. The threat of violence, therefore, came not just from people from different area codes but also from the authorities. This double edged affront reinforced the idea of engaging in grime music activities in safe spaces, whether that be on the street corner spitting bars with friends, in smaller groups or alone listening to mix tapes, pirate radio stations or accessing new tracks on the internet.

The appeal of pirate radio stations led many in the focus group to use this medium as a means of enhancing their own sense of cultural competence but they were vociferous in regards to their ability to actively engage with what they heard rather than passively consume grime in that way.

Isaac:	Pirate stations can be a bit, sort of, connected. Sort of too connected and safe for the rappers. I can't think of the word but I mean to say that they all seem to know each other so I

	listen but I'm sort of suspicious about how those people got to where they're at.
Dave:	It's cliques — that's the word. You listen and it seems that they're all this little group sort of celebrating themselves rather than reaching out to new artists in the street.
Isaac:	Maybe it's cos I listen on my ones [alone] and so I'm just jealous or whatever. I do enjoy listening to the stations, though, cos it's where the scene belongs. Radio allows you to focus on the bars and the punchlines and it's less about their swagger [visual representation] which makes radio important for me as I use it to learn and take into account what others are doing with their rhymes. But you just have to question what you're hearing.
TD:	Question in what way? What do you mean by that?
Isaac:	Like, I don't know these people and I don't know how that station broadcasts and I don't know if other people … sort of other people like record labels or people's management or whatever, pay for those stations to be there and play out [broadcast] so I always ask questions when I'm listening. I am listening more for what I can learn and I'm not too worried about the DJ or whoever telling me what is good.

Isaac's sentiments in the above comments were echoed by others in the group who saw their engagement with pirate radio as active and as a means of researching the culture to which they felt most connected. There was also a feeling that some of the presenters on pirate stations were not as knowledgeable about the street level of grime as they should be, as if their involvement in radio had allowed them to lose focus on that aspect of grime which was most vibrant and dynamic. Isaac's comments about the funding of these stations and how this could affect the output of the station once again testifies to the suspicions of these grime fans as they seek to negotiate mediated forms of the culture in order to consume purer, more authentic aspects of the culture. As a result of a lack of cultural gatekeepers who were trusted, these young grime subculturalists relied on the opinions of their immediate peer group rather than seemingly distant tastemakers. There existed an obvious distrust of anybody outside of their subcultural group, regardless of their perceived cultural engagement and experience of grime culture.

Visual components of grime

As discussed previously in this chapter, the most accessible television music channel which plays grime music on heavy rotation, Channel AKA, was viewed negatively as not truly representing the concerns of grime culture. However, the channel has helped to transmit a sense of dress code which could be labelled as grime. The visual component of grime reinforces the idea of the mandem and the rapper's 'ends' or 'gates' (their area) as central to the grime narrative. In this sense, the visual aspects of gangsta rap are being used as a marker to express a sense of pride in the artist's upbringing and the size and strength of their peer group. Being true to the area where you grew up and a sense of the collective is therefore essential in the presentation of grime artists and their subsequent validation by the audience. Videos often have the appearance of being in one take, as to enhance the degree of authenticity that the artist has in their ability to 'spit bars' (rap). The production values are low, again reinforcing the sense of a background of relative poverty. The video for Stormzy's track *Shut Up* is a prime example of the codes and conventions of grime music videos — Stormzy delivers his bars in one take, with a direct mode of address to the camera, as his mandem surround him and respond to his punchlines and also complete the end of each phrase or line. This call and response aspect has clear links to hip-hop and this aspect of grime can be considered to have links to Paul Gilroy's (1993) concept of the Black Atlantic wherein call and response, along with rhythmically and tonally simplistic drum patterns with an emphasis on repetition are key elements of the musical traditions of the African diaspora. Stormzy's video also uses a handheld camera technique akin to being filmed on the camera of a mobile phone and the rap is delivered live as opposed to lip synching which is the industry standard in most music videos. All of these elements — one take, handheld recording device, location, personnel, seemingly improvised lyrics — infer a sense of authenticity to the audience as there is an immediacy to the video which circumnavigates the falsity of the recording industry. In this example, grime has a need to stay true to the streets.

The previous chapter showed that the purists were less interested in visual appearance when compared to the peripheral groups and therefore the notion of a spectacular subculture could be seen to be outdated. The Lewisham group were vociferous, however, in the idea that grime culture is street culture, therefore the visual appearance of those actively engaged in the culture is nothing other than a true representation of life 'on road'.

TD: Is there a clear and identifiable grime look? Do people dress in a way that helps show them as belonging to the grime culture?

Emmanuel: Well … not really. I mean, not one that is so, like, totally different from anything else. So, you got your hoods and trackies [tracksuits]and treads [trainers] with caps and all that but that's just what people are wearing out on the street. That's not kind of a grime fashion because, to me, the word fashion has a kind of idea that people have thought about what they're wearing and put together all the pieces so that they look good and fit in together. To me, people on the street wear what people on the street wear and the fact that they're into grime and are doing grime don't mean that what they're wearing is grime.

Ash: You got this idea of 'swag', see. That is the way someone look, the way they walk and hold themselves up in public. Swag can be a hip-hop thing or a grime thing — it's all the same as they're music that came from the streets. These things are real so that's why you can see people in the street and think they're into grime but they ain't necessarily as that's just a street look.

Jemal: Yeah, but … see, I think there is a sort of grime look as there are bare [many] people who look grimey. You see them on the streets and I think it's how they wearing what they wearing rather than what, you know? Say, you see a rude boy and his mandem or his squad or whatever and they'll be wearing all those things what you (referring to Emmanuel) said but they're going to be wearing them a certain way. Hoods up, caps down. The sort of string around the hood going to be tight. All them bad men on street corners hanging in numbers dress like that but when they on their ones [on their own] they ain't looking like that 'cos the police may stop 'em or other kids going to be getting up in their face and challenging them if they dress all bad in their ends [local area].

There was a general reluctance in the focus group to establish a visual identity to grime which was in any way seen to be commodified or contrived. Instead, the dress code of those engaged in the culture was seen to be organic and as an extension of clothes worn by working-class youths in London. Jemal's comments above, however, suggest that a sense of posturing is important and again links to a sense of territorial ownership, confrontation and intimidation. Whereas hip-hop fashion is evident and, as argued previously, can be perceived as the domain of the peripheral groups who were concerned with projecting an image in a spectacular manner, this is not currently the case with grime. It could be argued that this is likely due to the more marginal place that grime holds in the cultural sphere when compared to hip-hop which is much more global in appeal and has subsequently been co-opted not just by record companies but fashion houses and clothes designers.

The issue of visual and spectacular subcultural performance has been criticised in a number of grime tracks, notably in Skepta and JME's *That's Not Me* which questions ostentatious displays of wealth via the wearing of fetishised clothing such as Gucci and other designer brands and in Skepta's *Shutdown* where a verse centres on no longer being impressed with certain brands (in this instance, Fendi products). However, an analysis of a number of grime album covers and other promotional materials show that there is a discernible dress code that grime artists and, by extension, the audience adhere to. Matching tracksuit top and jogging bottoms with trainers of the same brand are commonplace. Companies such as Puma have started to use grime as a marketing technique in collaboration with street wear shops such as ALIFE wherein artists such as P Money and Ghetts performed in Shoreditch, London, in May 2016 and Stormzy has echoed Run DMC's earlier hailing of Adidas as his brand of choice. He has referenced Adidas in a number of tracks and in the video for *Know Me From* as well as featuring in an advert for Adidas with Manchester United's Paul Pogba, at the time the world's most expensive footballer. When Stormzy also had his twenty-third birthday party in July 2016 at Alton Towers there were several carefully tweeted images of the Adidas party bags that all of the guests received. This sense of brand endorsement in grime may be new but will surely grow as its continued exposure in the mainstream develops.

Conclusion

Their own perceived sense of ownership over grime music was a fundamental issue for the research respondents with regards to their affiliation to the culture. These individuals eschewed UK hip-hop in favour of what they saw to be a form of musical expression which had immediate links to their own lives and geographical areas. As they all created forms of grime music, they aspired to distributing their music to a wide audience yet they were vehemently suspicious of record labels, pirate radio stations and television channels that were involved in the dissemination of grime music. Not only did such perceptions affect their forms of consumption and the sites which were used as vehicles for accessing grime, it also allowed for a reinforcement of subcultural values as rather than relying on the opinions of outsiders to those they saw as subcultural peers, the groups used their immediate social circle as markers of grime authenticity which cultural gatekeepers and other such agents did not, in their eyes, possess. The Lewisham focus group were familiar with the UK garage scene that had predated grime and it was clear from the focus group meetings that they perceived garage to suffer from interference from major labels or the national press which led to its implosion. Subsequently, these individuals were overly protective, perhaps to the point of paranoia, about the involvement of others in a culture to which they so vehemently felt a claim of possession.

The increased co-optation of grime culture in more recent years, by record labels and as a means for marketing teams to link their products to what may be termed as urban authenticity, may well lead to its success in terms of commercial sales yet could well hasten its demise as a significant subcultural form, notably for those with knowledge of grime's origins and links to the streets. The global appeal of rap music is evident as the form has been adopted and transformed in many parts of the world, yet it is difficult to say at this stage of its life cycle whether such international reception awaits grime music. Grime was seen by the Lewisham set as a platform by which they could celebrate their own existence as they felt that the wider world were becoming increasingly familiar with their area, lifestyle and concerns. Grime, therefore, has the potential to give a voice to those who are perhaps most disenfranchised in British society.

Chapter 6

Representing images in Hip-Hop

"I remember you was conflicted ... "[6]

Introduction

This chapter focuses on the interpretations of mediated aspects of hip-hop culture by the research participants. The literature shows a lack of studies in this field which focus on analysis concerning the decoding of mediated hip-hop and grime imagery by the consumers. Audience studies by Morley (1980), Ang (1985 and 1991) and Willis (1990) detail the uses of texts by the audience yet these tend to be within the parameters of 'ordinary', mainstream research subjects and not those individuals who may be termed subcultural. Writers on hip-hop such as Quinn (2005) and Perry (2004) do not offer empirical evidence in their work to contest their claims. This weakness is also apparent in the work of Kitwana (2005), Ogbar (2007) and Rose (2008) who offer a critical account of hip-hop from a purely theoretical and political position. This chapter offers a critical interpretation relating to how rap images and lyrics are interpreted by the focus group members with reference to the representation of gender and ethnicity through an application of the research data. By analysing the varying focus group perspectives this chapter also aims to illustrate further distinctions between the purist and peripheral groups, further drawing out the distinctions made in Chapter 4. I begin by analysing the data from two of the most relevant questions from the questionnaires before engaging with the qualitative findings from the focus group meetings.

Responses to hip-hop imagery

In this section I will detail the quantitative and then the qualitative findings from the field. Key areas of focus in the research linked to two of the three original research questions, namely the representation of images and the notion of authenticity. This book has attempted to show hip-hop as a commodified entity of black cultural expression and now moves on to focus on the reception of this culture by young people. The utilisation of grounded theory to explore how audiences interpret representations of blackness helps to further develop an understanding of the research participants' cultural engagement with hip-hop. There are potential distinctions between the grassroots level of hip-hop and grime culture for the research participants and the commodified variant of the culture which need to be considered. It is in this holistic and detailed portrayal of these cultures that a more developed appreciation of different reading positions and subcultural engagement can be elicited.

Quantitative data

As a part of this component to the research, the attitudes and opinions of 132 individuals, including rap fans and those who purported no specific engagement with the culture were collected from a range of sites. The data for all questions is presented in Appendix II page 223. There you can see that the responses to each question were analysed in line with the gender of the respondent and the relative degree of rap 'fandom' that they reported. Of the 132 respondents, 86 were male and 46 were female. On a five point Likert scale of fandom, 42 respondents 'totally agreed' that they were fans, 36 'slightly agreed', 6 were 'unsure' whilst 22 'slightly disagreed' and 26 'totally disagreed'. The focus in this section is on those statements from the questionnaire which directly relate to audience interpretations of mediated hip-hop.

The first most significant statement in this respect was *Women are treated fairly in rap music videos*. In total, 85 respondents (65%) disagreed with the statement. Of those who 'totally disagreed', 19 were male and 20 were female, so in terms of the relative percentages of those taking part in the survey, 43% of the female respondents strongly believed that the treatment of women in rap videos was unfair compared to 22% of the male participants. The data shows that 20 respondents (15%) either 'slightly agreed' (11 people) or 'totally agreed' (9 people) with the statement. Of the twenty people who agreed, only one was female. No women totally agreed as opposed to 9 men (10% of the male respondents). Twenty-seven of the respondents (20%) were unsure. It was found that, as a percentage, almost twice as many females compared with males tended to view the imagery of women in rap music videos in some way as 'unfair'. The quantitative responses provide an overview of the positions expressed in the questionnaires; in the qualitative data we are able to pursue issues raised in this way in more detail. For example in these questionnaire responses it is unclear which rap videos are referred to and detailed discussion of the topic in the focus groups can provide more information.

The data indicates a disparity between the opinions of the female and male respondents but, perhaps surprisingly, no difference between the opinions of fans and non-fans. The results mirror each other—12 of the fans (15% of the total

number of fans in the research) agreed or slightly agreed that women were treated
fairly in rap videos, 16 (21% of the total number of fans in the research) were
unsure whilst 50 (64% of the total number of fans in the research) either totally
or slightly disagreed. These were the same percentage figures produced from the
non-fans. This illustrates a general view that female participation in rap music
videos is perceived as disrespectful and, possibly, secondary. Rose states that '...
mainstream masculinity continues to treat women as fundamentally less valuable
than men ... and tries to control, label, and, at times, exploit women's sexuality ...'
(2008: 118). It would be unreasonable to assume such an interpretation, notably
the second half of Rose's quote, from the data produced in statement 5 discussed
above. Therefore the responses from question 8, *Rap music contains lyrics and
images that degrade women*, further advances an argument in this respect which
partially moves away from a focus on music videos.

The semantic focus of this question is arguably more direct than the one
previously discussed due to the inclusion of the word 'degrading'. Ninety-three
of all respondents (70%) agreed with this statement, either 'totally' (21) or
'slightly' (72 in total). Twenty-one people (16%) answered that they were unsure
whilst 18 respondents (14%) either 'totally' (3 people) or 'slightly' (15 people)
disagreed. Whereas the previous question drew significant differences out of
the attitudes between genders, this area raised little variance in response. Of the
male respondents, 59 (69% of the male respondents) agreed, either 'totally' (13
males in total) or 'slightly' (46 males in total) with the statement, whereas 34
of the female respondents (74% of the female respondents) fell into the same
category. Eight females (17% of the female respondents) agreed totally while
26 (57% of the female respondents) agreed slightly. The consensus between the
genders is slightly contrary to that from the previous statement. There may be
several reasons for this. The interpretation of the term 'fairly' could be of some
relevance as, for example, although a male respondent may perceive a degree
of misogyny in rap culture, the extent to which this may be attributable to the
dominance of masculine values in the mediated culture could be open to debate.
It can be suggested that the semantic properties of these two statements afforded
some degree of interpretation for the respondents.

On two of the questionnaires the statement about rap music degrading
women was amended by the research participants. Both altered the wording of
the statement to 'mainstream rap music'. These respondents went on to agree
with the statement. Both of these questionnaires were completed by members
of a music oriented website called *Drowned in Sound* and both contacted me

via email to say that they had altered the question to reflect their view that it was only mainstream hip-hop and rap music that perpetuated such negative representations of femininity. As will be discussed below, this was a position clearly voiced in the qualitative data by the majority in the purist groups whereas such a distinction was not raised by the peripheral groups of Rochester and Brighton.

From the 42 research respondents who 'totally agreed' that they were fans of hip-hop, 34 (81%) felt that the genre degraded women in its images and lyrics. Of the five variations of 'fan' in this research it was this group who most agreed with this notion. As both the quantitative figures presented here and the qualitative data which follow show, a major finding of this study is that there was a consensus among fans of hip-hop that the music they consume, along with its accompanying visual imagery, is degrading towards women. Before collecting the quantitative data from the questionnaire, I had assumed that fans of the genre would be more defensive on issues such as gender representations compared with non-fans. This was not the case and was therefore an area that needed further investigation with the focus group research subjects.

Qualitative data
In order to further develop an understanding of the quantitative findings, the data collected was analysed and taken into the focus group meetings. This triangulation of information not only serves to inform the validity of the quantitative data but also enables an elaboration of the key findings from one form of research to the other. The following section on the qualitative data is divided into three sections — masculinity, femininity and ethnicity.

The representation of masculinity
It was in the discussions of masculine imagery in rap music videos that the clearest disparities between the purist and peripheral groups were evident in terms of their perceptions of the constructed nature of mediated images. The Ashford and Canterbury groups (purists) viewed mainstream hip-hop's images of masculinity as contrived. The Lewisham group (purist) perceived a sense of poetic fictionality in hip-hop and rap music, although they were more reluctant to apply this notion to grime despite feeling, as has been shown in the previous chapter, that the imagery they were presented with in grime videos was somehow inauthentic. Neither of the peripheral groups demonstrated such a form of interpretation and they were much more inclined to view the representations of

masculinity within hip-hop as truthful. As will be seen in the following chapter, the notion of authenticity is regarded as a key determinant of the value of a performer in hip-hop and the following exchange from the Rochester group (peripherals) not only highlights this fact but also centres on their appreciation of masculinity within the genre. The discussion at this point centred on music video imagery with particular reference to 50 Cent's *Candy Shop* which Lou from the group screened for everyone else on his mobile phone.

Zac (R):　　I think 50 Cent is, like, the ultimate rapper because he's lived through it. He can't be beat for that kind of attitude he's got.

TD:　　What do you mean by that? What kind of attitude do you see him having?

Zac (R):　　He's just, you know, tough, man. Like, all of his stories and tales are right there and, you know, you wouldn't mess with him.

Dan (R): (laughs)　Like, in his videos he's seen as totally in control. He can do everything and you believe in him to do that. All surrounded by girls and cars and money. You know, for us that's like the ultimate success.

Lou (R):　　He earned everything by coming from the bottom. I think that's what makes him something to look up to as he, you know …

Zac (R): (interrupting)　And to us that's what being a strong man is all about, you know? He sort of says what it is to be down but to win at the end.

For Zac, there is a connection between the value of a performer and their masculine physicality. He claims that 50 Cent is the 'ultimate rapper' due to a combination of the reality of his raps and how 'tough' he is seen to be. This point is reinforced by both Dan, who links material and sexual possessions with the idea of control, and Lou who declares that he is seen as a role model. The peripherals within the focus groups did not perceive any sense of contrivance or constructiveness in the mediated performance of their favoured artists. Dan illustrates this clearly in the above extract by stating that the audience 'believe' in 50 Cent's capabilities to act in the manner that his persona would suggest. There is also a clear contradiction within this group in their interpretations of femininity and masculinity in hip-hop imagery. As will be shown in the next section, this group declared that the repetitious nature of mainstream rap videos could lead to the conclusion that such product was sexist and in this respect there is an assertion of patriarchal control. However, the above extract shows that when such imagery is connected to male domination there is not a tendency to view the artist as misogynistic. Dan asserts that one reason that 50 Cent is seen as a role model by this group is his sexual governance over the females in his videos. The focus is therefore on the assertive action of the male rather than the passive role of the female. This is developed in further comments from the Rochester group:

Lou (R):   Like, you see that *Candy Shop* video and what 50 is saying is that he has it all and that he can't be touched. He is in control of everything, see?

Dan (R)   And that's what I'm saying. He's got the swagger and the girls and that video presents to us what we want to see.

Notions of black masculinity transmitted via contemporary mainstream rap imagery centre on the male as hyper-masculine, hyper-sexualised and, in many rap texts, as hyper-criminalised (Rose, 2008; Asante Jr., 2008). There is also an emphasis towards a celebration of materialism and capitalist values, notably in gangsta rap. This, therefore, is in opposition to the anti-capitalist critique present in many underground forms of black expressive culture (Gilroy, 1992: 268). 50 Cent's persona, and the perceived manufactured nature of it, was discussed by the Canterbury group:

Catherine (C):   It's just a big game, isn't it? I mean, all of these rappers who always try to out-muscle each other all the time. It's kind of funny in a way and these constant public beefs [disagreements between rappers] are obviously ridiculous and made up.

Luke (C):   But are we the audience for this type of hip-hop? I'd say not, you know? He's [50 Cent] sort of more for, like, the kids to listen to. I'm not sure any adult can take that whole thing seriously. You know, he's sort of an image of a black man that maybe doesn't sit well with me.

The Canterbury group's resistance to mainstream hip-hop is illustrated by their perceptions of the commodification of black masculinity. Catherine's assertion that the publicised feuds between performers are contrived and are a part of a wider 'game' are of significance in terms of seeing this group as potentially resistant. Luke underlines this position further by suggesting that this form of commercial hip-hop is aimed at an audience who possess less subcultural knowledge than themselves. We may see his use of the term 'kids' as significant due to the clear implication that, in Luke's opinion, 50 Cent's target audience lack a level of interpretative understanding and maturity that characterises his own group. Quinn discusses the idea of poetic fictionalities, and suggests that the hip-hop audience is, in fact, intelligent enough and sufficiently culturally astute to be aware that these performers are acting as pop-cultural mediators (2005: 34). Perry states that one argument against the ability of the audience to distinguish between entertainment and reality is that the general audience for hip-hop is too young and unsophisticated to determine differences, whereas the argument is presented that the consumers of a differing variant of what is essentially a story-telling format, the American literary realists, have an ability to appreciate the fact that '... the depictions [in the narrative of the text] were ideologically loaded and artistically crafted ...' (2004: 90). Both of these theoretical positions are evident within the data from the Canterbury group as they clearly see themselves as sufficiently astute whilst asserting the view that the demographics of consumers who readily engage with 50 Cent's output are inexperienced and incapable of realising that he is presenting something other than reality. Samuels suggests that '... the more rappers were packaged as violent black criminals, the bigger their white audience became ...' (2004: 147). The above extract aligns the Canterbury group with Samuels' position due to the repetitious portrayal of rappers as hyper-sexualised, criminal and misogynistic.

These images portray a sense of hegemonic masculinity which signify males as powerful, dominant and competitive. Connor (1995: 31) states that the idea of 'cool' is evident in mainstream hip-hop artists as they reflect the ideas and concerns of the ghetto. In this respect, self protection comes from peers bestowing an individual with the label 'cool' which brings with it self-esteem. This cool affords an individual protection because the assumption is that with cool comes the knowledge of how to defend oneself. Michael Eric Dyson extends the point further by stating that '... violent masculinity is at the heart of American identity ...' (2007: 93) and that this idea is central to American democracy and cultural self-expression. What is of note here is that during the life course of hip-hop culture there has been a cycle of themes and messages running through the lyrics. As discussed in an earlier chapter, hip-hop's origins come from celebratory parties. The music and dancing were often used as a means to diffuse violent, gang related situations. Today's mainstream, major label controlled image of hip-hop can be seen therefore as somewhat in direct opposition to its cultural origins. Contemporary mainstream rap, according to the focus groups, centres on images of violence and guns, hatred towards women and excessive material consumption.

> *Josh (A):*　You have to ask yourself, sort of, who exactly are these images aimed at? I mean, nobody really enjoys some bloke shooting his mouth off about slapping or pistol whipping some girl, do they?
>
> *Rachel (A):*　I just think the whole image thing in hip-hop for men today is just totally ridiculous. Each rapper comes along with bigger muscles than the last and a meaner stare and, kind of, erm … you know, sort of a little bit more of whatever made the last guy sell records.
>
> *Matt (A):*　Yeah, I'd say that the whole image of men in hip-hop is pretty pathetic and I reckon it's mostly the little kids that are not only buying the records but also believing all that crap that goes with it.
>
> *Josh (A):*　I think that maybe hip-hop's changed, you know? There was a kind of difference in the way things were done back in the day and now sort of all the material is the same. Guns and bling and all that is sort of … yeah, it's sort of for the immature listener. I think, you know, maybe when the big [record] labels got involved with it they changed it.

Josh's last comment is hugely significant here, not just with regards to the notion of representation but also as a means of developing a further appreciation of the suspicion felt by the purists towards major record labels. As discussed in the previous chapter, purist groups tend to view the output from major labels as more contrived in its construction when compared with independent labels. It is this shift, from independent to major, that Josh attributes to an altering of the imagery of rap music. The co-optation of the culture by multinational conglomerates is perceived as a moment which affected the imagery and cultural messages. There is a degree of reflective inference in what is being said by Josh, possibly harking back to a nostalgic time when no hip-hop consumers could be termed as 'immature'. The selling of the culture by global companies has, for Josh, debased both the messages and the purity of the audience.

The protagonists of the pimp, thug and hustler have transferred to centre stage in contemporary hip-hop, in comparison with earlier politically conscious rap acts such as KRS-One, Public Enemy and X-Clan, as implied above by Josh. These characters '... are the perfect metaphor for American capitalism ...' (Hopkinson and Moore, 2006: 86), in that they can be seen to reflect the wider dominant ideology of empowerment through economic attainment. The previous comments from the Ashford group clearly illustrate the view that much of the output of commercially successful contemporary male rappers has, from a purist perspective, altered over the life course of the culture. The focus on criminality and misogyny is, in the view of this group, a relatively new phenomenon which has arisen through a need to maximise profit margins, thereby satiating the requirements of the audience and the commercial drive of major labels. The peripheral perspective, however, was less critical of the representation of masculinity:

Paul (B):   I don't really see anything hugely wrong with the way a lot of rappers use the word 'bitch' because, like, lots of the female rappers use that term so I'm not sure how people can be offended by it.

Kate (B):   Well, I don't really like it and I wouldn't want anyone to call me a bitch.

Paul (B):   But it's a sort of different culture, isn't it? I think maybe the terms mean different things or have slightly different ... erm ... different meanings and maybe not as harsh or something.

Kate (B):   Maybe. I just think it can be a bit too over the top sometimes.

Paul (B):   I just think a lot depends on the kind of context in which it's being used. When I listen to rap I don't sort of blush every time I hear that word. I think maybe at first people can get upset about it but maybe the power of the word is sort of lost after being said, like, a million times.

As can be seen from the following comments from the Rochester group, many within the group perceived the main role of women in hip-hop to centre on passivity in relation to masculinity and sexualised imagery for the male gaze. The ubiquity of such roles in mediated hip-hop culture reinforces its misogynist nature according to the Rochester group. This led many to be critical of the form, whereas others accepted it.

Jon (R):　A lot of rap videos have these days got sort of the same. Like, the same girls shaking their thing.

TD:　Do you see this as an issue?

Jon (R):　Erm … not really but I do find it kind of weird that that kind of image is everywhere in hip-hop and there's …

Sarah (R): (interrupting)　You don't get that with Eminem, though. He doesn't show himself like that so not everyone in hip-hop does that.

Dan (R):　No, that's not true. There's that video ['Without Me'] where he's in bed with some famous porn stars so that ain't right.

Sarah (R):　Well, all I'm saying is that not all hip-hop has those sorts of images and scenes in them.

Dan (R):　But you look at all the big names out there and you've got, like, Dre and Snoop through to 50 Cent, The Game, Jay-Z, Lil' Wayne and … I don't know … but they all have the same videos with girls all naked around them.

TD:　And what do you think of that?

Dan (R):　I don't know, really. I mean, say, I …

Sarah (R):　*(interrupting)* But do you (referring to Dan) not think it's sort of sexist?

Dan (R):　Yeah, maybe. I mean, yeah. This might sound a bit weird but I think if it was just a couple of videos then maybe I wouldn't say it was sexist but you have to admit that those scenes are pretty much all the time you see a hip-hop video. I think the fact that it happens a lot maybe makes it, you know, maybe more sexist.

TD: (to Sarah)　Do you think it's sexist?

Sarah (R):　God, yeah! They … well, they just don't do anything, do they?

Of note here is that Dan's statement relating to mainstream rap's perceived misogyny only comes after forceful questioning from Sarah. It was difficult for many of the peripheral focus group members to analyse the imagery from an objective perspective. The constructed nature of the imagery was not an aspect that they were particularly comfortable with, preferring to see the texts as products of an authentic cultural experience wherein the artists were concerned with the recounting of their own biographies. This point is developed further in the chapter that follows.

The qualitative data concerning the representation of masculinity, and the subsequent treatment of females, showed marked differences between the interpretative abilities of the purist and peripheral groups. There was, for the peripherals, a sense of reality to the imagery they viewed whilst the purists read a number of texts as works of fiction. It was found from the qualitative data that the purists held the position that such output, although they were opposed to it, was not to be taken as a literal portrayal of black culture. However, the male members of the peripheral groups in particular tended to deny any sense of fiction within the texts and rarely offered any notion of pretence in the personas of the rappers they discussed. The constant reference by the purists to those in the audience who they viewed as consuming mainstream images without question, along with the terms used to describe such individuals, can be seen as another tool of demarcation between themselves and those who are perceived to have less knowledge of hip-hop. In this respect, the emphasis for the purists in terms of interpretative use of the cultural output lies in the subject position of the empirical listener (Dibben, 1999).

The representation of femininity

A significant number of the research subjects tended to agree with the findings of the quantitative data as the majority felt there was an undeniable degree of misogyny present in mainstream hip-hop culture. The following extract represents an exception:

TD:	Do you feel that hip-hop images and lyrics can be seen to degrade women?
Dave (L):	Erm, I don't want to sound harsh here, like, but I don't think so, no. I mean, nobody's forcing them to dance in these videos so not sure how they can be said to be degraded. They're making money from it, eh?
TD:	And so the fact that they're making money makes it okay?
Dave (L):	Yeah.

This response furthers the previously suggested argument that there is a disparity in people's perceptions of the terminology of 'fair' and 'degrading'. Dave's views on this matter were, however, oppositional to the majority of participants across all five of the focus groups. Many of the male research subjects seemed hesitant to offer opinions on this matter, whereas the females were more vociferous. It is significant to note, in Dave's comments, how he perceives women in the culture. The question itself made no direct reference to the roles undertaken in hip-hop culture by women, yet Dave seems to naturally marginalise and restrict females to the role of dancers. This is clearly how he perceives the female presence within mediated hip-hop, as a visual component of the culture, thus ignoring the various roles that females have undertaken during the life course of hip-hop, from rappers, turntablists, producers and businesswomen. For Dave, there is no exploitation of women's sexuality. Instead, there is a financial gain to be achieved by these females which seemingly negates any sense of exploitative practice. As a member of a purist group, Dave's views are contradictory to others labelled the same. Rather than weaken the theoretical position of this demarcation it arguably reinforces the notion of complexity and contradiction which was evident in the field. The purist/peripheral model does not seek to reduce or homogenise the individual concerns and opinions of the research subjects.

As the quantitative data showed, the majority of respondents who termed themselves 'fans' stated that they perceived the representation of women in hip-hop videos to be somewhat degrading. However, when pressed on their consumption of a cultural form that consisted of images that they saw, to quote Rob from the Brighton group, as 'unnecessary' they tended towards the argument that there was very little that could be done about the situation.

TD: Do you select certain artists who you see to be degrading women and boycott their products?

Alice (B): Erm ... I think I should but, like, I don't. I mean, what difference will it make if just one person says 'I'm not going to buy this'? None. So, say a record company get a lot of people buying something then they'll keep pushing out the same old thing, right? If loads of people stopped buying music by rappers who they didn't necessarily agree with then maybe this kind of thing would stop. Thing is, it's always the real big acts that do stuff like this and you don't want to not know what they're rapping about at any given moment. Like, as a girl, I think that there's a lot of lyrics that I could protest against, or whatever. If you did that you'd look pretty stupid. I mean, what'd be the point?

TD: So, do you still listen to the music of certain rappers even if you think they may be sexist?

Alice (B):   I do, yeah. It ain't as easy as just saying that their lyrics are down on women. Maybe their flow is wicked and the beats, the production and whatever is amazing so you, you know, kind of forget the purpose of the lyrics. You get lost in the other things sometimes.

This somewhat compromised position was seen to be a common reason given by the research subjects who actively participate in aspects of the culture that they perceive as misogynistic. Rose (1994) offers this same explanation for the consumption of tracks where the lyrical content goes against her usual political views, claiming to be 'lost in the funk'. There is also a sense of helplessness in Alice's comments. It is more important for her to listen to popular rappers in order to accumulate knowledge rather than apply some form of personal politics to a piece of music. In this manner, the need to be receptive to the messages of commercially successful artists is more important than personal attitudes. Also of note is her declaration that it is 'always the real big acts' that portray women in a derogatory manner, suggesting that this form is perpetuated primarily by acts on major labels. The issue of the ownership of this imagery is therefore significant and is analysed in greater depth at the end of this chapter where the focus turns to hegemony and the notion of the commodification of hip-hop messages.

The issue of focus group members taking exception to certain lyrics was also discussed with the Canterbury group:

TD: Do you listen to tracks that maybe you find difficult? I'm thinking about tracks and artists that you may feel belittle women. Lyrics that go against your own opinions.

Catherine (C): I see myself as an intelligent woman and I often turn off tracks when I really focus on what's being said. But, you know what the funny thing is? I often get carried away when I listen to a track and can often find myself shouting out the lyrics

	before realising what I'm saying. I get swept along and have to say I feel a bit ashamed afterwards, you know?
TD:	What kind of things do you find yourself singing?
Catherine (C):	I'd be far too embarrassed to say to you (laughs). I find it weird how a good beat can suck me in, you know?
Simon (C):	To be fair to you (referring to Catherine), though, you do often take exception to lyrics that you feel are degrading or racist or homophobic or whatever. You don't always get carried away. I think she (referring to Catherine) has got quite a morally driven approach to what she listens to.
Catherine(C):	Yeah, maybe you're right. I do get worried about how I get suckered in, though. It sort of makes me think of all the people listening because not everybody will be critical of their favourite rappers, will they?
Simon (C):	You know what, though? I'm not really sure that many people pay too much attention to what's being said, like … exactly, you know?

Catherine's last point here is an important one. It was evident in the responses that the idea of others interpreting the culture with less knowledge than they possess was a significant one. This sense of otherness relates to people who they see as outsiders to the true essence of the culture, individuals who consume the music without all of the related lifestyle choices, and therefore the cultural competence, that goes along with serious involvement with hip-hop. As has been discussed, the purist groups felt that those who were more peripheral, or those on the outside of the culture, could in no way have the same interpretive mechanisms available to them when compared with those who more closely 'lived' the culture.

TD:	How do you perceive the role of women in hip-hop culture?
Rachel (A):	Depends what you mean by hip-hop culture. If you mean the big selling, mainstream chart acts then women get a pretty raw deal in hip-hop. But that's just an image that's sold, ain't it? I mean, like me, I'm a female rapper and it's funny when I get up on stage for a freestyle battle and the opponent and the whole crowd are just going mental at me 'cos I'm a girl. It's like we're not supposed to be on a stage rapping or whatever.

I get looked at all up and down and the other guy usually bangs on about me being a woman or whatever and then when it gets to be my turn I usually surprise a few people with what I can do. That's the real hip-hop right there but, like, in the mainstream images all you get is women being, like, the plaything of the male rapper.

Trevor (A): But that's what sells, right? Even female MCs sell their sex and that rather than their skills.

There is again the reference to commercial pressures ('that's what sells') from Trevor which reinforces the notion that artists have to take into consideration the marketplace when constructing mediated images of themselves. Rachel implies that the 'big-selling, mainstream' form of hip-hop culture constantly perpetuates an image of femininity within a subservient and passive framework which serves the requirements of the male artist. This arguably allows for a perception of female engagement within hip-hop production to fit neatly into the roles as prescribed by Dave in his previously discussed comments. There is a limiting of the potential roles for women in the culture towards powerless positions where aesthetic beauty and sexual availability are favoured over creativity. Such a position can be seen in evidence within the focus groups as illustrated by Trevor's remark that the industry market sex rather than talent.

Collins's (1990) notion of controlling images focuses on the representation of women and her position utilises a feminist framework. However, I will follow the lead of Ogbar (2007) in extending this phrase into the analysis of black culture in general, moving the term away from an essentially feminist focus. Contemporary mainstream female rappers such as Lil' Kim, Foxy Brown and Nicki Minaj represent a form of black femininity which emphasises the hyper-sexualised and commitment free nature of their personas. It has been argued that the majority of commercial hip-hop lyrics and images show black women in a disrespectful and contemptuous manner (Rose, 2008: 118), a position mostly held by the participants in this study. The three rappers mentioned above, along with many others, are seen to use their sexuality to commodify their appeal for a mass, mainly white audience. Their unapologetic and confrontational form of femininity which manifests itself through sexually explicit dress codes and lyrical content can be perceived as a challenge to traditional forms of masculinity inasmuch as capitalist gender roles could arguably be reversed. The findings from this study show that the hip-hop audience do not perceive that these individuals are presenting an alternative to capitalist patriarchy. Indeed, by falling into historically caricatured representations of black femininity one may reasonably argue that they are, in fact, reinforcing dominant perspectives by fetishising their bodies as spectacle for the male gaze (Mulvey, 1975).

Woldu (2006: 102) argues that financial, sexual and emotional independence is a cornerstone in women's rap and that female presence in contemporary hip-hop culture is more 'fully fleshed'. Flesh is indeed a key signifier of successful female rappers, though the research demonstrates that it is the amount of flesh on display by these performers that allows them the most attention according to the focus groups. This point is illustrated in the following extracts from the Ashford and Canterbury groups:

TD: What about so-called strong female rappers? I'm thinking of someone like Lil' Kim — someone who uses her female sexuality in a really visible way.

Rachel (A): I can't, like, see her as ... I can't see her as strong. Sorry. She just sort of panders to that whole 'whore' image. How is that a strong female?

Trevor (A): Can she be taken seriously, really? I mean she is ... erm ... sort of ...

Rachel (A): (interrupting) I just don't buy the whole thing, you know? She's, sort of ... I guess you could say I'm not the audience for it as I'm after hip-hop with a little bit more to it, you know? Sort of ... I need substance in the stuff I listen to. That whole Lil' Kim and ... erm ... Foxy Brown stuff is, I'd say, aimed at guys. I can't see that they're saying anything to me. So, no, I wouldn't call them strong.

Similar views were held by the Canterbury group when this issued was raised in connection with Nicki Minaj and Lil' Kim:

Simon (C): I think that they are ... erm ... I'd say that maybe they're not really anything more than sexualised for a male audience. I know a lot of girls that are into rap and I'm not sure if any of them would say they listened to this stuff. It's, I think, maybe a little too much about sexualised things ...

Catherine (C): (interrupting)   I don't know anyone that listens to that crap, female or male. I don't know but I'd say it's aimed at younger boys. You know, that kind of group who don't really listen to the lyrics but buy the stuff for the buzz of it. I don't know, I think that a lot of this is aimed at people who see the videos. Like, would they sell so many copies if nobody knew what they looked like?

Chris (C):   But who isn't that true of? Everything's visual these days so you can't just level that ...

Catherine (C): (interrupting)   No, of course, but I guess I'm trying to say that for a lot of people there's a substance to what they're saying but for Lil' Kim and Minaj then I'd say, you know, much of what they're about is just a bit porny, you know? That's what they are, basically — porn in music.

Luke (C):   It's that whole slut thing, isn't it? Like years ago Madonna was either a brilliant businesswoman or a dirty whore. It just sort of depended on your viewpoint. Now it's the same in hip-hop. Early hip-hop wasn't sort of like that, I think. Sort of Queen Latifah and that weren't as sexual but, I suppose, that's sort of the way things have gone.

It is clear from these comments that the output of many commercially successful female rappers is not held in high regard by those in the Ashford and Canterbury groups. Rachel implies that the target audience for such material are interested in superficial aspects of the culture. She states that her reason for not engaging with these artists is due to her desire to only listen to material which has, in her mind, substance. Her need to listen to music 'with a little bit more to it' is a clear rejection of what she perceives as the facile and one-dimensional nature of rap's more commercialised aspects. The sexualised representations of femininity as offered by these artists are not seen by these groups to be redressing patriarchal dominance; rather they are exploiting female sexuality in order to target a male audience who willingly consume such product. Catherine states that without a visual aspect to these artists they would not be successful, the inference being that aesthetic appeal is of more commercial significance than ability for those who consume mainstream forms of hip-hop.

A significant number in the focus groups perceived female rappers who exploit their sexuality as weak, lacking in substance and aimed at a male target audience who are perhaps not as culturally astute as they see themselves. Catherine's assertion that they are merely 'porn in music' emphasises the sexual over the artistic. However, there are many examples of female rappers who do not centre their persona on over-sexualised representations of femininity, although the focus groups were in agreement that such roles were restricted. The following extract illustrates, once again, that there is a perception within the focus groups that there is a targeted demographic (males) that the representations of sexualised femininity are aimed towards.

Rachel (A): There's a whole load of really strong females out there but I don't see them as much when I pick up a hip-hop magazine or flick through the [music television] channels. You've got Missy [Elliott] and old school stuff like Monie Love who, you know, will tell their stories. They don't just sell sex.

Matt (A): I don't know, though. A lot of Missy's lyrics are chatting about sex and that.

Rachel (A): Okay, yeah, but I think in maybe a different way. Sort of … I don't know … not playing up to the male audience or something.

As Rachel states, access to mediated platforms is in her view limited for those female rappers who do not centre their star image on sexuality. This was a common opinion expressed by many in the focus groups and a key theme in the discussion of the role of women in the culture. A significant number of the respondents felt that rap music was largely controlled by men and that the positioning of women was as a result of their relative weakness within the power structure of the culture. The following extract illustrates this point:

Luke (C): When you sort of look at who owns these record companies then it's obvious that women are going to get a raw deal. Like, I mean it's men who run the labels and say what will and won't be played on the music channels and maybe it's mostly men that buy the records. If, you know, if that's the case then it's little wonder that women are going to play a sort of … erm, a sort of role that is more about sex than power.

Simon (C): Yeah, it's kind of like not a surprise that men control the companies and so women don't have much say. I suppose they just, you know, go along with whatever is seen to be marketable or whatever as a sort of product.

This seeming passivity of female rappers is not, however, as all-encompassing as the focus groups suggest. Cheryl Keyes discusses 'the fly girl' as a sub-category of female performativity in rap music. She offers Salt 'N' Pepa as an example of fly girl posturing whose visual imagery centres on short skirts or shorts, make up, jewellery, long sculpted nails and voluptuous curves (2004: 269). In terms of the portrayal of women in hip-hop, the character of the fly girl, sassy and independent, may be seen as a precursor to the more sexually explicit form of independence as espoused by Lil' Kim, Eve and others. Missy Elliott is a full bodied, contemporary fly girl who uses sexually explicit lyrics. On the track *Work It*, from the album *Under Construction* (2002, Elektra), Missy addresses her lover and portrays herself as sexually dominant, though not sexually aggressive, with regards to her carnal demands. The lyrics show the active nature of Missy Elliott's sexuality. She is both the instigator of the sexual liaison and the dominant force during sex. This lyric challenges the patriarchal construction of femininity prevalent in various forms of popular music where '... women are portrayed as simultaneously submissive, innocent and childlike, yet sexually available ...' (Dibben, 1999: 336). In this respect, Missy Elliott subverts the traditional female role evident in contemporaneous hip-hop. In another example, the lyrics for *One Minute Man* from the album *Miss E ... So Addictive* (2001, Elektra) include Missy Elliott mocking a potential suitor for his lack of sexual prowess and ability, again asserting Missy Elliott as a fly girl due to her independent nature and no holds barred attitude. The general perception of Missy Elliott from the focus groups was that she presented an image of a strong independent woman, although the consensus was that that this was an uncommon trait for commercially successful female rappers.

> Rachel (A):   I think that, for me, Missy is right up there as someone to look up to. She's quite ... erm ... plump so she can't really just focus on the sex angle. Her lyrics are kind of out there and up front and she doesn't really take any prisoners with what she's saying. I think it's tough for any woman in an industry that's just run by men but I guess she stands up for herself.

All of the female respondents from the qualitative section in this study bemoaned the lack of similar artists to Missy Elliott in the mainstream consciousness and stated that this was as a result of women's relatively diminished status within the power structure of the recording industry. As Rachel's comments illustrate, the position of women in hip-hop is seen as subordinate to males who form the controlling élite. This reinforces the perception of the limited potential roles available to female rappers within the realms of the heavily commodified and marketed world of mainstream rap.

It has been argued that female voices in hip-hop have been sexualised by male ghostwriters over recent years (Hopkinson and Moore, 2006: 86). This is in contrast to the representation of female MCs in the early years of hip-hop culture who consciously resisted depicting themselves within the parameters of the Jezebel character (Ogbar, 2007: 78). However, even fly girl acts such as Salt 'N' Pepa used male composers, particularly in the early part of their career. The manager/producer of the group, Hurby 'Luvbug' Azor, wrote the majority of Salt 'N' Pepa's early big hits such as *Push It*, *Shake Your Thang* and *I'll Take Your Man* (Keyes, 2004: 270).

This is not to say, however, that there are not female rap performers who do not portray themselves within such standardised and stereotyped forms of black femininity. Lauryn Hill, Sister Souljah, Miss Dynamite, Speech Debelle and Lady Sovereign were all mentioned by the research participants during the focus group meetings as examples of artists whose performativity arguably opposes the emphasised femininity present in much of popular rap music. There have historically been a number of female personas that were not discussed in the focus groups. For example, the 'Queen Mother' category of female rap artist as proposed by Cheryl Keyes comprises those who see themselves as African-centred icons (2004: 266). The image of such rappers makes reference to Africa and the lyrical content focuses on socio-political issues as well as declaring themselves to be intelligent black women. Lipsitz (1994) uses Queen Latifah as an example of an artist who utilises such forms of representations. Her use of African imagery is seen as a subversion of common representations at the time of young, black females who were often shown as single mothers and strains on the welfare system. It was found from the data that such imagery is not foremost in the mind of consumers when they consider femininity in contemporary rap music.

The purist viewpoint on the representation of femininity in hip-hop was that the negative portrayals were largely as a result of the ownership and control of the culture by males for the edification of what was considered to be a largely male audience. By extending these terms to the representation of black culture by white major label corporations, an argument can be forwarded that the portrayal of stereotyped and caricatured black images contained within hip-hop culture maintain a form of projected subordination for those presented within such images.

The representation of ethnicity

The concept of ethnicity '... was invented partly in opposition to the idea of race, since it was taken to denote possibly malleable culture rather than biologically fixed characteristics ...' (Hochschild, 2009: 641). Mediated ethnic portrayals are often bound up in debates about racial/ethnic power hierarchies and subsequent forms of hegemonic control of minority groups (Cashmore, 1997). For Back and Solomos, '... the question of cultural production and the politics of identity are fast becoming an important area of contemporary debate ...' (2009: 20).

The Brighton group were unified in their opinion that mainstream rap images could be construed as negative:

TD:	When you say 'negative representations', where are they from? How do you know that they're negative?
Paul (B):	When you see the videos, for example, you might see guns or you see people fighting or you can tell they're doing drugs and things like that and that kind of gives you the impression that that is what they're like in real life. As we're British and white we don't hang around with as many sort of black people as you might in America so it kind of ... what you see on TV might influence how you think they actually are.
TD:	Is that the usual sort of imagery you would associate with hip-hop videos?
Alice (B):	Yeah. Violence, guns and probably women as well, like their femininity as well.
Kate (B):	Because there's been so many of them [music videos] from so many different artists ... you look at them and they're all ... not the same but they've all got the same elements like guns, drugs and sex.
Paul (B):	Yeah but, for example, Kanye West hasn't said at any point that, you know, 'I came up in a gangster lifestyle and got shot

> twenty-four times'. He's said that he's come from a wealthy
> family or whatever whereas 50 Cent has been shot ...
>
> *Kate (B): (interrupting)*   Yeah, but, I'm not saying that. I'm not saying
> whether it's true about being shot twenty odd times or
> whether they come from a wealthy background, I'm just
> saying the videos are all the same.

The Brighton research subjects clearly felt that the recurring imagery of mainstream rap videos was negative in its portrayal of black culture in general, and black femininity in particular. Paul's comment about not personally knowing many black people is of significance as he feels that such images could lead to an essentialising of the people represented in this mediated form. The imagery that the Brighton group refer to, and that they perceive as ubiquitous in mainstream rap, serves to devalue a sense of femininity as there is an all-encompassing portrayal of hyper-masculinity. This hegemonic representation of black cultural expression may serve to homogenise those who are portrayed within the texts. The question of '... the economic domination of Black music by non-Blacks (is) normalised beyond question ...' (Asante Jr., 2008: 102) and this is a perspective which the purist groups within this study held. This domination and control manifests itself as a transmitter of values that place the black performers of hip-hop as 'other'. This white supremacist ideology has historically placed black people as more animal than human, lacking the capacity to feel (hooks, 1991: 105).

There are, however, many instances wherein contemporary rap artists do not fall into the trap of portraying their ethnicity as subordinate. Such acts as The Roots, Jurassic 5, Mos Def and KRS-One, however, exist on the peripheries of mainstream hip-hop even though they have established themselves as well known performers within the genre. The black and Latino communities who created hip-hop culture have, in terms of mainstream commodification at least, relinquished control of the commercial appeal of the music and therefore have little, or no, determining voice in the portrayal of their culture to the audience (Rivera, 2003). The consumer demographic of hip-hop, according to statistics used by Rose (2008: 4), is 75% white and, therefore, one can safely say that in the mass marketed form of the culture, the representation of black people can be seen to suit the interests and values of the majority of the paying public. This 75% figure, often a little higher, is often repeated in the literature on hip-hop studies although there are obvious issues with this. Such data is collected to compile sales charts and is therefore often collected from large retailers rather than smaller independent shops and such a collection process also ignores other modes of consumption such as mixtape culture, peer to peer file sharing or audio streaming websites.

Regardless of the accuracy of this figure, it can be argued that mainstream hip-hop artists aid the perpetuation of racist images and ideals which are very much in line with the portrayal of black people from historical forms of entertainment such as the minstrel shows as well as from popular discourse during slavery. Ogbar states that it is not uncommon to see black actors in films and television roles as diverse as doctors, judges or street thugs and other equivalent roles, while hip-hop '... offers only the most narrow and problematic representation of black imagery ...' (2007: 10). He goes on to declare that the majority of platinum selling albums since the early 1990s have utilised portrayals of black people as oversexed, criminal and impulsive with a tendency towards nihilistic violence. This fact, coupled with hip-hop's insistence on 'keeping it real' would suggest that an audience would consume such mediated images and view them as being based on some form of reality. Samuels states that the appeal of hip-hop to a white audience '... rested in its evocation of an age-old image of blackness: a foreign, sexually charged, and criminal underworld against which the norms of white society are defined ...' (2004: 147).

Such views were expressed by the research groups, most significantly by purists. The consensus from the fieldwork was that those who benefit most from this form of ethnic representation are the white élite who control the commodified variant of the culture and also the majority white audience who consume it. Such a viewpoint has a long history, dating back to issues of ownership in minstrelsy as well as in the performance of self in daily life. The minstrel can be read as an inversion of the white man, wherein white America portrayed itself as bounded in advances within the fields of science and technology, in government and scholarship. The minstrel show allowed a rational inculcation for the notion of white supremacy for the audience, as the characters seen in the various shows, with their simplistic, often child-like views, would doubtless be considered as incapable of interacting appropriately in white 'civilised', democratic society. The buffoons on display reinforced the notion of race logic through the hegemonic vehicle of popular culture. Such images of blackness were created to suit the needs of the ruling élite. Although these representing images may have originated from black culture, it should be seen as a reaction to the needs of the dominant white culture. As these images were taken to the minstrel stage they became ideals of white racial subjectivity. As Pieterse notes '... the first role blacks were permitted to perform in white society, after that of slave or servant, was that of entertainer ...' (1995: 136).

The Canterbury group were amongst the most vocal in their disapproval of what they saw as an inherent racist ideology present within mainstream rap music:

Luke (C):   Well, I'd like to see more positive images of black men. Ones that don't just go on about having a big dick, thugging and bashing on some girl. The sort of view you get on men in this type of hip-hop [mainstream] is fairly, I would say, like ... restricted. Sort of ... all you get is sort of muscles and guns and tattoos. I'm not sure that's a really positive thing for many people to see as it sort of just links black men with crime.

Simon (C):   Yeah, I think that you have it there. Like, people get outraged when they see programmes or films from years ago and there's all this racist stuff in there but it's there in front of our noses every day. Like, the whole myth of black men just being sexually depraved is there for people to see on MTV every day if they want. It's more difficult seeing any sort of image of an intelligent black person in the big commercial side of the culture.

Simon finds similarities between historical representations of the black experience and hip-hop. Saxton states '... blackface minstrelsy epitomised and concentrated the thrust of white racism ...' (1996: 67). In this same manner, mainstream hip-hop can be perceived as a platform for the representation of black artists as 'other', reproducing images of black culture which centre on violent physicality, enhanced sexuality and a leaning towards criminal behaviour. Such images serve to perpetuate the idea of white mastery and are, for the Canterbury, Lewisham and Ashford groups, undoubtedly present in contemporaneous hip-hop images, notably within the gangsta rap sub-genre. In *Representing Race*, Ferguson states that to avoid seeing racial representation as either arbitrary or 'natural', one must take an historical perspective (1998: 78). The relational concept of difference, according to Hall is necessary and, indeed, essential (1997: 236) as humans can only construct a sense of meaning of the world through a dialogue with the 'other'. It is this sense of otherness that is important with regards to hip-hop culture, as is the notion of the control of such mediated representations. Pfeifer states that '… minstrel shows performed a 'service' to the institutional and systematic framework of the existing social order by reifying black cultural constructions of manhood, a practice that furthered the reproduction of racism …' (2007: 4). The Canterbury group, as illustrated in the above extract, aligned themselves with this view of the forms of ethnic representation present in contemporary hip-hop culture. Rose proposes that the 'keeping it real' rhetoric present in rap music, which is examined in further detail in the following chapter, is '… a cover for perpetuating gross stereotypes about black people …' (2008: 141) as the constant repetition of a narrow range of portrayals in mainstream hip-hop culture limits the representations present to negative ones.

The purist group demonstrated a resistant and oppositional reading to mainstream images of black culture whereas it was found that the peripherals tended towards an approach which centred on unquestioning acceptance of the representations offered by major label corporations. This highlights the distinctions between these two variances of subcultural engagement and the relative degrees of active interpretation evident from the field.

Hegemony and the commodification of music

The purist research respondents felt that the messages contained within the lyrics and images of current mainstream rap music serve the interests of the white patriarchal ruling élite, in line with the work of Cashmore (1997). The social process of making culture, and all of the texts that are significant in this respect, '… can circulate only in relationship to the social system, in our case that of white, patriarchal capitalism …' (Fiske, 1989: 1). The term 'black culture' must be superseded, therefore, with the term 'black American commercial culture' (Quinn, 2005: 18). As has been demonstrated, it was found in the fieldwork that many in the focus groups held the view that there was some credence to the position that an essentialising of black culture underpinned much of what was regarded as mainstream hip-hop culture. As highlighted in previous extracts from the qualitative data, there is a clear appreciation that such imagery influences audience perception and opinion.

Hegemony may be a useful concept to explore the commodification of music. The term refers to '… the 'spontaneous' consent given by the great masses of the population to the general direction imposed on social life by the dominant fundamental group …' (Gramsci, 1971: 12). For Osgerby, Gramsci contended that the ruling-class position within society was secured not only through '… the possession of economic power and coercive force but through producing a world view; a philosophy and a moral outlook that subordinate groups were *persuaded* to accept ...' (2004: 117, italics in original text). This world view is often seen in the form of spontaneous consent from the subordinated masses as they perceive such control as little more than a common sense interpretation of the world as they see it or, rather, as they are told it is. Hegemony, therefore, can be seen as a site of ideological struggle which is often perceived by the masses almost as a protective device, a safeguard handed down to them by the privileged with very little recourse to fight against the ideals being pushed towards them.

During the fieldwork different members of the research groups alluded to the idea of the hegemonic capabilities of hip-hop and the influence that the culture's messages had on its audience. Another theme was the ability of the research respondents to competently interpret and understand messages in hip-hop whereas others could not. As has been seen in the earlier section, terms such as 'little kids' and 'immature' were utilised as a means to demarcate subcultural positions from the textual readings of others who were perceived as being more easily influenced. The theme of the naturalising of forms of representation was discussed by the Lewisham group:

Isaac (L):   Like, for me, I'd say that there's issues over the sort of ownership of hip-hop today. So, like, say all people saw was guns and bling and, you know, crime and that then that's what the people will think is really out there.

Dave (L):   Obviously I know a lot of black kids from all areas who don't act all like pimps so I know what's going on but if you're some white kid somewhere who may be watching then so all you see is that black thug thing then ... that's what's going to make you think a certain way about people. You know, I think it's sort of interesting that when you look into this stuff then you see it's whites that own these companies that are putting out these tunes.

TD: So you're saying that hip-hop images can change the way people view others?

Dave (L):   Totally.

Jemal (L):   See, I don't know if others get it but people have told me they've seen folks cross the road to get out of their way, like, or else they're going to get all bashed up. Not one of them has ever done nobody no harm so somebody somewhere is getting a wrong sort of idea about what the youths are like, eh?

TD: Are you saying that rap music has got something to do with this? And what has this got to do with what you (referring to Isaac and Dave) were talking about? This issue of ownership is interesting.

Jemal (L):   Yeah, you know, I think what people see in hip-hop videos they may think sort of is like that in the real world. That's the sort of place where you see most black people, like, in the videos and that so this image that's sent out for people to buy is, you know … I'd say it's … yeah, an influence in the way of people's thinking. And, like was said over there, when we looked at who was putting out this stuff then there ain't really much black people in charge. I think that has to be important in the way we look at how these rappers show themselves.

TD: What do you mean by that?

Jemal (L):   Like, I think that maybe peoples are telling these big stars what to say and wear to make more money for them, eh?

The position offered by this group is informed by an aspect of their college course as Jemal states that the group have collectively looked into the issue of record company ownership. This fact was also evident from a number of posters on the walls in the room where these focus group discussions took place which showed the machinations of the recording industry as well as detailing aspects of such things as subsidiary labels. This group possessed knowledge of the industry but the most significant aspect of the extract is the fact that they felt that the ownership of the mediated culture influences the forms of representation offered and, by extension, the subject position of the text's material (Dibben, 1999). The purist groups, as has been discussed in this chapter, were concerned that the images synonymous with rap music influenced those with insufficient cultural knowledge. Jemal, in the above extract, states that mediated images of black violence have possibly been a significant reason for people's negative perceptions of what he terms as 'youths'. His opinion that hip-hop affords an opportunity for black faces to regularly be seen on television yet, due to the lack of black ownership within the industry, there is a packaging of an image ('sent out for people to buy') which includes representations that perpetuate negative images of black culture ('somebody somewhere is getting a wrong idea').

When dealing with the term commodification, the connotative level of the term revolves around not simply the idea of a product being packaged for a predetermined marketplace, but also infers some degree of exploitation along Marxist lines of ownership of control. Adorno states that '... an approach in terms of value judgements has become a fiction for the person who finds himself hemmed in by standardised musical goods. He can neither escape impotence nor decode between the offerings where everything is so completely identical ...' (1991: 30). Music, for Adorno, had moved away from an art form and had become a part of a commercial process of the culture industry that was little more than an assembly line, churning out formulaic works at a rapid rate. The writing of a song had become '... a mechanical operation motivated purely by commercial gain and social manipulation ...' (Negus, 1996: 37). According to Adorno (1991: 39), the commodity consists of a combination of use value and exchange value where the exchange value deceptively supersedes the use value as the important measure of worth. The regularity of the use of terms such as the 'hook' of a song, most usually observed within the chorus of popular songs, is in Adorno's opinion, used with a degree of self awareness in the sense of enticing and trapping the audience. The cultural product is, therefore, written and performed with an identified set of consumers in mind. This industry, for a number of the research subjects in the field, commodifies black musical expression for the political and ideological gains of the controlling white owners. The data shows that the purist groups' level of cultural engagement and interpretation challenges this notion of hegemonic control as they were critical of the mainstream output of the culture. Their creative engagement, creating new combinations of sounds and beats with turntables or writing their own music and lyrics, was outside of the control of record companies and allowed them space to explore the music without being constrained by matters of commodification.

Fiske (1992: 47) sees a link between the commodification of a musical artefact and the subordination of the audience as a result of reverence. The piece of music has been created, it is perceived, by 'special individuals' and it is this canonisation of the composer and/or artist which arguably helps to maintain a distorted view of the exchange value of a commodified work. Sanjek (2002: 60) suggests that the relationship between those who create and those who package cultural goods is neither a symbiotic nor a parasitic one, but both. As has been shown, the cultural engagement of the Canterbury group eschews any sense of artistic hierarchy as all members of the group were invited to DJ at parties irrespective of comparative skill levels and therefore negates any reverential treatment for performers.

The research findings suggest that the purist research respondents believe that mainstream hip-hop texts have been created with a specified demographic in mind. As has been shown, the purist groups from the fieldwork were critical of the recurring visual signifiers in rap videos and the representations inherent in the form. Issues of ownership and power relationships, along racial lines, were highlighted as possible reasons for this, as well as an understanding of the demographics of the audience and their particular set of needs. It can be suggested that the mass production and selling of black culture in recent years has been undertaken with the proviso that the performance is packaged to conform to whites' images of blacks (Cashmore, 1997: 1). Jacques Attali notes that music '... is all too often only a disguise for the monologue of power ...' (1985: 9). This power can be seen to manifest itself in hip-hop cultural expression through the incorporation of imagery that sustains a subordination of an identified racial group through hegemonic means. The cultivated controlling images allow for an engagement by the audience with 'the other' that makes up mediated black experience and cultural expression, whilst also fulfilling a stereotypically represented version of the diaspora that allows a white audience some sense of empowerment over the figures from the culture that they are investing time and money in. There is an argument that the degree of black expression and cultural value is lost in this processed packaging of the culture, an idea expressed by Garofalo (1993) and echoed in the opinions of the purists from the fieldwork.

Conclusion

This chapter has interpreted data from the fieldwork to illustrate that fans and non-fans feel that hip-hop represents femininity and ethnicity in a demeaning manner. Of significance is the hesitancy within many of the research subjects to actively boycott material deemed to be inappropriate. Popular music consumption relies on a form of knowledge and cultural competence from its audience and this is illustrated in this study as individuals from the different groups continue to consume, even though this leaves them in a somewhat compromised position. A number of the research subjects listened to material that they were morally opposed to in order to keep up to date with the culture as highlighted in the chapter by Catherine from the Canterbury group and Alice from the Brighton set. Here, their personal response and opinion was viewed to be less important than their continued consumption of products which are seen as significant to the culture and have been produced by those who are perceived with reverence by the audience (Fiske, 1992). Individual feeling in this respect can be seen to be secondary to acceptance into a subcultural collective.

The chapter has focused on the divide between the interpretations of the purist and peripheral groups with regards the poetic fictionalities present in mainstream hip-hop imagery. The purists regarded mainstream hip-hop imagery as a marketable construction whereas the peripherals did not. The findings in the study show that varying interpretive positions exist within the youth groups which reinforces the value of the non-essentialised purist/peripheral conceptual model. It was found that the purists viewed the representation of females in mainstream commercial hip-hop videos as limited and being concerned primarily with passive sexual appeal, thereby enforcing a sense of hegemonic femininity which portrays women as dependent (Connell, 2005: 83). According to the majority of the purist sample, this limiting of the creative space for females, coupled with the performance of black identity, has been allowed to happen by major label corporations who use the draw of commercial success to ensure that their artists exist in a manner which is most beneficial to the market.

Chapter 7

Youth groups and musical authenticity

"She was really the realest before she got into showbiz ... "

Introduction

Rappers constantly proclaim to be the 'real hip-hop' and there is an obvious theoretical issue with discussing the notion of authenticity as it is a contested and intangible idea, one that I would argue to be illusory. The concept of authenticity in terms of the fieldwork findings for this study, however, is inextricably linked to Pierre Bourdieu's notion of taste which defines the accomplished individual and can be seen to link to the practices and values of the collective groups. The aim of this chapter is to examine aspects of authenticity in commodified hip-hop from the perspective of the youth groups engaged with the culture and is therefore a continuation of the investigation of hip-hop consumers and mediated imagery. Authenticity will be examined from the perspective of the research participants and how this shaped their understanding of rap music. The chapter incorporates both quantitative and qualitative findings from the fieldwork before moving on to a discussion of the four markers of authenticity as defined by the research sample—locality, biography/narrative, vocal delivery and ethnic identity.

Hip-hop consumers and ideas of the authentic

The notion of authenticity is central to the discourse of representation as seen in the last chapter. The research participants negotiated an understanding of the imagery in hip-hop and grime culture in order to validate their own aesthetic tastes and subsequent subcultural capital. The purist group in this study perceived a sense of construction to the images of masculinity, femininity and ethnicity in mainstream texts. Such an idea compromises an artist's sense of authenticity and artistic integrity. Aspects of authenticity were also discussed in Chapter 5, where the contention was that Dizzee Rascal's record label had ensured that he moved away from his grime roots in order to become commercially successful. This 'dilution' of sound and image also affects the claims to authenticity which is central to the marketing strategies of rap and grime music. The links between authenticity and the other thematic lines of enquiry in this book are, therefore, apparent. It can be suggested that '... authenticities do not reside in the performance, but in the reading of the performance …' (Moore, 2001: 200) and therefore this chapter privileges the reception of rap music and its subsequent interpretation by the audience.

I will begin by analysing a number of the responses from the quantitative data before developing the topic areas further by incorporating the qualitative findings. In general the fieldwork found that consumers of hip-hop often seek a sense of authenticity from their performers to reassert the identification that they have with a particular artist and, as a result, with their subcultural group.

Quantitative data

In the questionnaires there were three statements of relevance to the notion of authenticity. The first statement of relevance is *The images and lyrics in hip-hop music are true to life.* In terms of those research subjects who considered hip-hop to be seen as a reflection of reality, only 4 of the respondents (3%) totally agreed with the statement whilst the most popular response was given by 47 individuals (36%) who slightly agreed. Twenty-six respondents (20%) were unsure, 38 respondents (29%) slightly disagreed whilst 17 (12%) totally disagreed. Of the respondents who slightly agreed with this statement, a tendency can be seen for fans to agree more than non-fans. From the 78 individuals within the fan category, 33 (42%) slightly agreed with this statement compared with 12 out of 48 (25%) of the non-fans. This could lead to an interpretation that fans of hip-hop music are more likely to perceive the narratives of rap artists in their tracks to be genuine to some extent, whereas non-fans are likely to disregard this factor. This appears somewhat contrary to the qualitative data presented in the previous chapter which highlighted the purist group perspective as encompassing an understanding of the construction of mainstream artists in hip-hop texts.

These results show that, as a percentage, non-fans are five times more likely to totally disagree with this statement compared with fans. Four fans (5%) marked this category of the statement compared with 12 non-fans (25%). This data suggests that fans of the genre are more likely to perceive, and perhaps require, a sense of truth, reality and authenticity in the hip-hop that they consume. As for the results from the non-fans, it would be negligent to suggest that their perception of the genre as somehow unrealistic is one reason why they do not engage with the musical form. Of note, however, are the variations between fans and non-fans in terms of their perception of hip-hop as an authentic documenter of reality.

The next question for analysis *A good rapper is one who has lived the life they rap about,* addresses ideas of authenticity by positing the notion that a judgement value (a good rapper) comes from a direct correlation between biography and lyrical content. For this statement, the percentage of non-fans was greater than the percentage of fans in each of the first three categories — 'totally agree', 'slightly agree' and 'not sure'. Overall, 36 fans (46%) either totally or slightly agreed with this statement compared with 25 non-fans (53%). It is of note that less than half of the fans positively connect the significance of lived biography to the assessment of the ability of a performer (as 'good'). This suggests that the constant declaration of rappers as 'the real hip-hop' is not necessarily reflected in the opinion of hip-hop consumers. However, there is a need, as shown by the qualitative data findings, for the biography of a rapper to inform and validate their work and this is one of the key elements of authenticity that was drawn from the field.

The data shows that 15 fans (19%) compared with 12 non-fans (25%) felt that 'not sure' was the statement that most closely matched their opinion. Twenty-two fans and 7 non-fans slightly disagreed with this statement and as a percentage this equates to almost twice as many fans as non-fans (28% compared to 15%). The data suggests that hip-hop fans do not see as much of a link between the value and the personal history of a rapper. Alternatively, the interpretation could be that those who consider themselves to be fans of the genre may possess a form of subcultural knowledge that means they are less likely to rely on the marketing techniques of record companies who often overstate the hardship that artists have been through. In this respect, and as discussed in the previous chapter, they are aware of the poetic fictionalities present in contemporary hip-hop. They possess sufficient cultural competence to interpret the genre as including poetic texts, not merely declarations of truths. As Dr. Dre states in an interview '… the shit I talk on records is just that: shit …' (cited in Quinn, 2005: 136).

The final statement of note in this section from the quantitative data is *Rap music explains to me how life is for black Americans.* The wording of the question can be seen to almost homogenise black cultural experience, yet none of the questionnaires were returned with amendments made to the wording of the question. Regardless of this area of contention, the results are still of note. Twenty-two out of the 48 non-fans (46%) totally disagreed with this statement whereas 18 out of the 78 (23%) fans also disagreed. At the opposite end of the response spectrum, only 5 non-fans (10%) slightly agreed with the statement in comparison to 16 fans (21%). The tendency for both fans and non-fans (and the 'unsures') was to respond to this question in either the slightly disagree or totally disagree categories. Forty-seven fans (60%) and 34 non-fans (70%) 'slightly' or 'totally disagreed'. This suggests that hip-hop is perhaps not seen as the social mirror that many academic and music commentators presume it to be. The nine per cent discrepancy between fans and non-fans also suggests that fans of the genre are more likely to accept the possibility that the messages contained in rap songs are informing the audience of some aspect of black cultural life.

Qualitative data

The five focus groups in this study all perceived authenticity to be at the centre of hip-hop discourse, yet each group varied in their definition and use of the term. Authenticity and the abstract notion of 'reality' were key terms utilised by the focus group respondents when distinguishing between their preferred performers and those that they perceived to have no artistic value. The more a rapper had the label of being 'real' bestowed upon them by hip-hop consumers, the more likely it was that the rapper would be seen in a favourable light. The quantitative data suggested that fans were able to separate a declaration of reality from the talent of the performer. This, therefore, was a key aspect of the focus group discussions. All of the groups stated that authenticity was hugely significant to them when they considered their musical choices. As discussed previously, the majority of the research groups favoured American rappers and this is similar to ethnographic work carried out by Briggs and Cobley who state that '… Americanness was seen by our cohort as the benchmark of authenticity …' (1999: 345). The following extract comes from a conversation with the Lewisham group. The discussion at this time centred on their favourite rap performers.

TD: … but going back to Tupac, what made you like him?

Isaac (L):   He spoke the truth, like. It was kind of gospel, what he said. That kind of … like, when you listen to it properly, when you listen to certain tracks and listen to them properly and listen to the words you can, like, see that he's speaking in the words of God. People can listen to it and you'll think 'yeah, I'm gonna follow that path and go the right way'.

The phrase 'listen to it properly' is used several times in this statement. Isaac is suggesting that there is a level of concentration and interpretation that is needed from audience members in order to fully appreciate the ideas in Tupac's lyrics. The interpretation of his favourite performer in almost hagiographic terms illustrates the fact that, for Isaac, Tupac's form of truth was more sacred, and therefore more valued, than others. His level of authenticity, and therefore his worth, is subsequently heightened. The 'truth' in Tupac's lyrics separates his output from other artists.

The following excerpt, from one of the Ashford participants, was a very common form of expression.

> *Adam (A):*   Hip-hop speaks to me because it's real. I don't live that life. I
>   don't know that life but I identify with it 'cos you're listening
>   to real life. It's not crappy love songs written by other people.
>   British hip-hop shouldn't talk about knives 'cos so few people
>   are actually carrying knives that it's wrong. Maybe it makes
>   people carry a knife, I don't know.

The personal identification that Adam feels with hip-hop is through its ability to connect with him through informing him of reality. He perceives the genre as 'real' even though he is clear that this is not his own sense of lived reality. He is allowed to access a form of escapism in his consumption of hip-hop. This sense of reality in the genre is reinforced by his claim that British hip-hop has an accountability to act responsibly in terms of lyrics that deal with issues surrounding knives. His argument is that the lyrical content of British hip-hop does not match his own personal experiences in this regard and, therefore, is somewhat false. Also of note is his assertion that mainstream music (referred to here as 'crappy love songs') is inauthentic because, as he perceives it, much of the musical output is not written by those who perform it. This was an essential part of authentic cultural performance for the focus group respondents who, on a number of occasions, discussed the fact that they required their preferred rappers to be autonomous in terms of their creativity.

One major finding from the fieldwork was that each youth group used the notion of authenticity not only to validate their own musical preferences but also as a means of centring their subcultural identity and activity on the idea of taste. This issue was raised several times in the focus group meetings as illustrated here by a selection of extracts:

Jemal (L):	The people I hang with pretty much all listen to the same, like, type of hip-hop and grime as me. Like, that's how you know that someone has something to offer you, you know? If you like the same MCs and that then you've got something to, like, chat about and that. Most of my crew are, you know, into the same things as me and that's why we do what we do. You can't just chat and spit bars with people who don't know what they're chatting on.
Kate (B):	I think that you can tell if you're going to get on with someone if they like the same type of music as you. Not just rap but the same type of rap, if that makes sense. I'm not sure I'd hang around with someone who didn't get real hip-hop stuff, you know?
Chris (C):	Our little group all kind of are into that East coast sound like De La Soul, A Tribe Called Quest, Souls of Mischief and more up to date hip-hop like Mos Def and El-P.
TD:	Is it important, do you think, that for people to be accepted into the group that they have to listen to certain forms of hip-hop and not others?
Chris (C):	Erm ... I think that sounds a bit harsh (laughs) but I do think that that is right. What we talk about, what we mix and what we play at parties are pretty consistent in that they're all, sort of, of a certain type. I think a lot of people who are more into the gangsta rap side of things are probably dickheads and really not that into hip-hop at all and so won't fit into our lot which is a bit more chilled than all that thug nonsense.

From the data we can see a clear exclusionary aspect where social and subcultural identity relies to a significant degree on engaging with a set of artists who are preferred by each group. In their comments we can identify a form of hierarchical taste values in evidence. Kate's use of the phrase 'real hip-hop' links to the notion of authenticity as does Chris' assertion that those individuals who consume sub-genres of hip-hop that vary from his listening tastes are 'really not that into hip-hop'. This understanding links to the idea of elitism within the groups, as discussed in the previous chapter. There is a considerable emphasis placed upon the '...'second nature' of their knowledges ...' (Thornton, 1995: 12). In discussion with the focus groups they asserted that it is not the responsibility of the youth group to educate an individual about the culture. For inclusion into a group, people needed to arrive fully informed and demonstrating an interest in the same form of the culture as the pre-existing group. Authenticity is used as a conceptual tool which distinguishes between those with and those without subcultural knowledge. In this way it can be seen as a key marker in relation to subcultural affiliation and activity and a means by which membership to subcultural groups is attained and sustained. This emphasis on subcultural knowledge can be seen to be exclusionary and a means to maintain a sense of collectivity. This evidence of distinct knowledge held by the youth groups can be seen in opposition to postmodern ideas of fluid boundaries in youth subcultural groups.

Dimensions of authenticity

The four dimensions of authenticity discussed in this section — locality, biography/narrative, vocal delivery and ethnic identity — are drawn from the empirical aspects of this research. In the focus group sessions, the groups discussed how important the idea of the authentic was to them and what an artist would need to present in order for their output to be considered as authentic and the elements discussed in the rest of this chapter are those aspects which were seen to be significant. In the four sections that follow I will outline each of the markers of authenticity in turn.

Locality—place and space

The sound of popular music and its geographical origins are often interconnected and have been seen as reliant on each other by academics. Studies include, for example, those focused on the Mississippi Delta blues (Hamilton, 2007), the 'Canterbury sound' of the late 1960s (Bennett, 2004), the Chicago blues (Grazian, 2004), rhythm and blues' relationship with inner-city urban America (Gillett, 1996) and the Bristol trip-hop sound of the 1990s (Wall, 2003). There is a sense of collective identity formation that occurs when such labels are utilised and it is clear that the sound and timbre of a music produced from a given local setting often imposes collectively defined meanings and a sense of significance about that space (Bennett, 2004: 3). Many of the focus group members discussed their musical preferences in terms of geographical factors, mostly focusing on the variation in sound to be found in American hip-hop. Those within the purist groups in particular distinguished between the output of areas such as the East coast, the Bay Area of San Francisco, Philadelphia, Southern rap, the West coast and St. Louis amongst others. Each of these areas represented a sub-genre of hip-hop such as the G-funk of the West Coast, crunk from Southern rap and hyphy from the Bay Area. This was a particular concern of the purist groups whereas the peripherals were largely unaware of such regional variations other than the widely reported East coast / West coast disputes.

> *Simon (C):* I can remember when the whole West coast sound broke over here. That kind of G-funk thing wasn't really for me, you know? It seemed a little bit … I don't know … maybe a little bit try hard, you know? I think they were just out to shock and that kind of changed the game a little bit and that's when I noticed a different audience getting into rap. Like, before with the political and kind of black consciousness East coast stuff it seemed that people were a little more genuine. I think, like, more kids got into rap as a result of the whole 'guns and bitches' thing that was being sold by West coast artists. It was a bit more exciting for people but, I think, maybe more based on stories rather than opinion and fact. I think that was the main difference.

This comment draws out a couple of significant points when dealing with the notion of authenticity, particularly with the use of the phrases 'try hard' and 'based on stories' which suggests that the West coast form of rap is, for Simon, a less genuine product than its East coast counterpart. Of note also is Simon's use of the word 'sold' when discussing the music from the West coast. This clearly aligns this form of hip-hop with a market and a 'for profit' motive. The labelling of the East coast audience as 'a little more genuine' can be interpreted as a nostalgic view of the early years of hip-hop and his own role in it or as a tool to separate different forms of the culture and their corresponding fans.

This theme of placing importance on locality was also seen in the Ashford and Lewisham groups although they would use this aspect in differing ways in order to confirm one region as more authentic, and subsequently better, than another. For example, the Lewisham group took the opposite view to Simon as they viewed the West coast rappers to be documenters of their own realities and experiences. They espoused the view that what they were hearing when they listened to artists such as Tupac, Dr. Dre, Ice Cube, The Game and others were the lived realities that these individuals had experienced first hand. Territory is an important factor and this is present in mediated hip-hop culture from the East coast / West coast rivalry to the ghetto being seen as the testing ground for the rappers to perfect their knowledge and skills (Forman, 2000). This sense of territory can be seen in other elements of hip-hop, including graffiti which is significant in matters of territoriality. 'Tagging' is when a graffiti artist places their personalised signature on a host of objects, including, and most significantly, city walls, subways, trains and similar places. This has been seen to be a marker of territory and can therefore illustrate the importance of locality in other strains of hip-hop culture.

References in raps to the artist's hometown or neighbourhoods serve to establish and reinforce the performer's credentials as authentic. Forman states that '... in the music and lyrics, the city is an audible presence ...' (2000: 66). This theme of place can be illustrated by the spoken opening line from the NWA album *Straight Outta Compton* (1988, Priority Records) which states that 'you are about to witness the strength of street knowledge', wherein the word street is synonymous and interchangeable with the idea of the city and connotes the recurring iconography of gangsta rap — the decaying post-industrial inner city, the ghetto. The following extract from the Rochester group illustrates this point:

TD: Why do you think rappers seem to always rap about where they live?

Jon (R):   That's what hip-hop's about, isn't it? It kind of sets out to tell people what these guys are seeing in their own lives. Like, when 50 Cent talks about being shot then you can tell it happened because of where he's from and the fact that his life was pretty tough. It makes sense for them to talk about the place they live because rappers write about what they see every day.

Zac (R):   Like, say someone raps about living in this place and then another MC comes along and kind of disses the first one because of where he lives then ... I ... erm ... I like that, you know?

Jon (R):   I was going to say ...

Sarah (R): *(interrupting)*   When you see all the videos and there's, like, someone like Snoop or someone hanging out in his 'hood then he's just representing the place and that's kind of like

one of the main ... erm ... aims of hip-hop, I suppose. You
know when you see him there that he's real.

Regardless of the mediated and constructed nature of hip-hop music videos,
the Rochester group demonstrate a desire for the music they consume to
declare a sense of identity through geography. Both 50 Cent and Snoop Dogg
are ascribed with authenticity by this group as a result of their association with
a particular recognisable space. It is the link between the rapper and the location
which allows the audience to perceive the rapper as authentic and to further
enhance a sense of engagement with the artist. There is a sense of metaphor
with the Rochester group and their interpretation of the spaces which surround
authentic hip-hop. The exact location is not as important as the idea of the place;
that is to say this peripheral group seem satisfied with an understanding of
hip-hop as an urban experience where territory is a key aspect which underpins
the credentials of the artist. There is perhaps in the extracts above an almost
romanticised idea of the urban setting of hip-hop and an ambiguity to the
defining of such a space.

Referring to Zac's comments, the history of hip-hop is littered with instances
of individual artists or groups laying claim to some degree of authenticity, or
belittling an 'opponents' claim to the same, as a result of geographical location.
Tricia Rose states that '... rappers' emphasis on posses and neighbourhoods has
brought the ghetto back into the public consciousness. It satisfies poor young
black people's profound need to have their territories acknowledged, recognised
and celebrated ...' (1994: 11). Although this may well have been the case for
the period from which Rose's writing originates, there is some credence to be
given to the idea that this portrayal has been exaggerated somewhat as a result
of the co-optation of the culture by mass media conglomerates whose interests
may not be to represent the lived experience of the black diaspora as much as
it is to sell such representations to an (arguably mainly white) audience. This
was a critical position which the purist groups held, as discussed in the previous
chapter. Neal (2004) discusses the East coast / West coast 'Civil War' in the mid
1990s — a 'conflict' that McPhaul (2005) implies was exaggerated by the media in
order to illustrate the false idea of the destructive nature of the balck personality.
Neal argues that the opposing factions used authenticity as a currency in an
attempt to establish a form of dominance over their 'enemy'. This 'Civil War'
would eventually lead to the deaths of both Tupac Shakur and Christopher
'The Notorious B.I.G.' Wallace, two successful rap performers of the mid-1990s

who were significant in terms of their East / West coast affiliations. It has been argued that '... at the core of the East coast versus West coast conflict was a fundamental belief that the experiences of those on one coast marked them as more authentic — more gangsta, more ghetto, more hardcore — than those on the other. In other words, one 'hood was deemed more authentically hip-hop, and by extension, more authentically black, than the other ...' (Neal, 2004: 58)

The use of the neighbourhood as a marker of identity can be heard on the Wu-Tang Clan track *Soul Power (Black Jungle)* from the 2001 album *Iron Flag* (Loud / Epic Records) which also serves as an example of a construction of authenticity. The close of this track features guest vocalist Flavor Flav from Public Enemy in 'conversation' with the Wu's Method Man recounting areas of New York where his extended family can be found while the beats of the track play on. When he realises that there is a degree of connection between his family and certain members of the Wu-Tang Clan, the bond between them in the 'narrative' of the track grows. This may be a typical example of different people finding that they have, in fact, something in common, though this whole scenario is, of course, played out in front of a microphone in the sound booth of the Wu-Tang Clan's recording studio, The 36 Chambers. The attempt has clearly been made to infer some degree of authenticity to this conversation, using the end of the record, where in a more traditional sense of popular music production a fade-out may occur. The audience is invited to eavesdrop on a conversation, linking these hip-hop practitioners, and a sense of accidental observation occurs for the listener as information about familial location is given by both parties. One could suggest that a degree of construction and contrivance is apparent here, yet the underlying trait is that the producers of the mediated text feel the need to incorporate such elements into their recording. This realisation reinforces, and even amplifies, the importance that geographical location has on the genre. McLeod (1999) details potentially dichotomous positions which are held by the rap audience and within the social locational scale the distinction falls between 'the street' and 'the suburb'. The successful and authentic hip-hop artist, in order to address the concerns of the audience, must come from the streets. As illustrated in the above focus group extract, Jon from the Rochester group states that the essence of 'what hip-hop's about' is this sense of locality and celebration of space.

Key studies on global hip-hop focus on the link between authenticity and location. Solomon (2005) details the significance placed on spatiality through the cultural utilisation of the word *yeralti* by the Turkish hip-hop community, a word which translates as underground. He states that '... this pervasive spatial metaphor encapsulates local notions of identity and authenticity …' (ibid.: 4). Kalyan's (2006) study of Hawaiian and Bolivian rap artists also highlights the importance placed on spatial dimensions as a tool to criticise the postcolonial context in which the artists found themselves. Italian hip-hop uses the *centri sociali occupati* (occupied social centres) as an index to authenticity (Mitchell, 1995: 339). The centri sociali were somewhat akin to a community of squatters, emerging in Italy in the mid-1980s. These were self-organised activity centres formed around refurbished, disused buildings, run along collective and co-operative lines. It was through experiencing life in the centri sociali occupati that rappers could lay claim to a notion of authenticity. Mitchell (ibid.) details a number of case studies where performers who gained popularity from routes outside of the centri sociali were criticised as inauthentic.

The notion of place is significant within rap music but so, too, is space in terms of time. A recurring theme of many recorded rap songs is to identify the year in which the recording was made. Examples include the line '2002 — represent the Wu' from the aforementioned *Soul Power (Black Jungle)* by Wu-Tang Clan (Loud/Epic Records), 'It's about to be the year 2000' by Missy Elliott on *Beat Biters* (Elektra/Atlantic), ''92, uh! One year later, Peace out Premier, take me out with the fader' on *DWYCK* (Wild Pitch Records/Virgin) by Gang Starr and 'This is how we chill in'93 til' …' from Souls of Mischief on the track '93 *Till Infinity* (Jive/Sony). The sense of authenticity can be derived from these in reference to the notion of MC battle raps wherein information may be delivered that is relevant to that exact moment in time or geographical location and this tradition has passed over to the recorded and commodified variant of the culture. The technique of placing temporal prominence and significance to a recorded track cannot only be seen as a way of making the track more authentic at the time of release but, it may be suggested, results in the track becoming more superfluous with the passage of time. The Lewisham group in particular saw this as a valued aspect of hip-hop and grime culture.

Dave (L):   I love all that '2 double 0 4' ['Pow' — Lethal Bizzle] stuff. If you go on the internet and hear someone chatting about the right here and now then that's pretty cool. Like, I hear stuff all the time but you want a kind of sense that it's happening right now and so I love it when I hear a shout out from the MC in a track that goes on about the date it was made.

Ash (L):   It kind of, like, makes it … immediate and that. Like, you don't hear that on many records that are out there because people want you to buy that stuff but I think if you listen to rap and grime all the time then you want to, like, keep up to date and that, innit? If an MC spits the date on a tune then you know that it's, like, for the people not to listen to.

There is, for both Dave and Ash, a sense of immediacy and a greater connection between the artist and audience in instances when a date is inserted into a lyrical performance. The instant access to cultural products afforded by websites such as SoundCloud, Bandcamp and formerly Myspace allows for cultural producers to place their creative output into the public domain without an intermediary such as a record label. It is this aspect which appeals to this group as Ash states the fact that 'people want you to buy that stuff' results in few moments on records when such declarations occur. This, again, separates the mediated form of the culture from that which is seen to be more 'street level', more authentic. It can be suggested that the practice of a declaration of the temporality of a track allows the audience to feel more involved in the culture as there is seemingly a negligible distance between the creative thought and the resulting product.

Biography and narrative

The biographies of hip-hop and grime performers' are often an important aspect of their marketing and potential acceptance by the audience. This was raised in the focus group sessions:

TD: How important is it for you to know about the background of an artist? Is this something you think about when you listen to a new artist?

Chris (C):   Yeah, I think it's really important. I don't think it's something that you really think about when you hear a new tune, I don't anyway. I'm much more likely to listen to their music and then if I like it I'll go and find out about them to see who they are and where they've come from.

TD: Have you ever liked an artist and then found out a fact about their life which has sort of made you go off them?

Chris (C):   You know what, I probably have, yeah. I can't think of an example right now for you but I have. Maybe it's like a subconscious thing rather than an obvious decision, like.

Simon (C):   I also think, though, with something like that you have to take into account what they're rapping about. I mean, if somebody came along and was rapping about something that 50 Cent would write about, like the ghetto and guns and that, and then people found out they were some middle-class posh kid then maybe, you know, maybe …

Catherine (C): (interrupting)   I think that would make lots of people stop listening to that artist. That's half the deal though, isn't it? With hip-hop you've got to not only be good at what you do but your story has to fit.

TD: What do you mean by 'the story has to fit'?

Catherine (C):   Like, if the rapper says that they've done this, that and the other then they need to either prove that they have or that they've at least had some form of experience of it.

Simon (C):   I think that's important, you know. Either that or they have to make it bloody obvious that they're making it up but I'm not sure that would sit well with a lot of people that listen to hip-hop. I mean, a lot of the kids can't really work out that 50 Cent isn't a gangster so they want their artists to be exactly as they say they are on the record.

Andy (C):   Maybe because we're older we can work out that they may not be being truthful 100% of the time. There still has to be some truth in it, though. Like that Ice Cube track ['You Can't Fade Me'] where he talks about getting a girlfriend pregnant and looking for a coat hanger to get rid of the baby and kicking her in the stomach … like, you know that's not real as such but you have to believe that of Ice Cube. His lyrics are, I'd say, not to be taken as pure fact.

This extract shows the significance placed upon biographical detail for the youth groups in the research. Chris' statement that his decision making may be done on a more subconscious level suggests that this aspect of hip-hop is culturally ingrained so as to become almost an autonomous element in the selection process of the music. There is some scope for poetic fictionality for this group as expressed by Catherine's comment regarding either the need for the rapper to have direct experience or some form of association with a lifestyle that is rapped about. However, it is clear that a career can be hindered if the artist claims a history that is later revealed as false. With this in mind, then, it is not surprising to see that the 'origin story' of many rappers is focused upon in the artists' own lyrics. The relevance here would be to address the issue of authenticity directly to the audience, claiming to have experience in the culture beyond that which the listener may be aware of. This aspect can be seen in Skinnyman's track *Fuck The Hook*, wherein he states that he '... might look young but I'm a real old timer / Been around ever since the days of Boogie Down [Productions] ...' (from the album *Council Estate of Mind*, Low Life / Talking Loud Records, 2002). Boogie Down Productions were pioneering hip-hop producers. The inference here is that Skinnyman has paid his dues within the underground hip-hop culture.

The notion of authenticity can often be linked with a sense of autobiographical information from the performer wherein '... an expression is perceived to be authentic if it can be traced to an initiatory instance ... (Moore, 2002: 213). There is seen to be an unmediated and negated distance between the mental origin of a performance and its subsequent physical manifestation. Although Moore was directly referencing rock and folk music in his article *Authenticity as Authentication* he himself makes the point that other generic musical formats can, and should, be considered in this manner. Neal (2004) makes the connection that claims of authenticity may lead to increased CD sales or heavy video rotation on music channels.

Patricia Hill Collins (1990) argues from a black epistemological perspective that having lived through an experience is more valued than having merely read about it. As Olson and Shobe Jr. state '... black epistemology rests on the value of personal experiences as they demonstrate the applicability of knowledge to the everyday world ...' (2008: 998). The idea of a credible biography for a rapper is an essential part of the marketing package needed for success in the contemporary recording industry, in line with both a black epistemological perspective and the needs of the audience. The focus group members in this research held this view as although a number were open to the possibilities of poetic fictionality there was a significant emphasis placed upon the biographical detail of an artist. This allows for the label of authenticity to be applied to those artists who match such criteria.

Narratives, the mode by which a story is told, are important in our everyday experiences as '… they furnish us with both a method of learning about the world and a way to tell others what we have learned …' (Berger, 1997: 10). Narrative has a number of identifiable traits and these significantly include the notion that there exists an '… artificial fabrication or constructiveness not usually apparent in spontaneous conversation. Narrative is 'worked upon'; sequence, emphasis and place are usually planned …' (Toolan, 2001: 4). Other factors include the presence of a teller of the story, no matter how invisible the narrator may be and a trajectory which commonly results in the conclusion to the tale. These factors are evident within rap lyrics — the use of rhymes can be seen as falling in line with the notion of construction, the rules of this particular form of narrative are abided by in the use and form of language incorporated into the text; the teller of the tale is often an individual within the structure of the story. Many of the narratives within hip-hop lyrics involve the use of the first person though it would be inaccurate to suggest all rap lyrics do this. The story telling technique in many hip-hop tracks includes what narrative theorist Todorov (1977: 111) would term a new-resolved equilibrium, a conclusion to the tale.

Vladimir Propp (1968: 79-80) formulated the notion that eight character types are present in narrative, though each character type does not need to appear and some characters within the narrative can fulfil more than one of these functions. These character types are: the hero (the seeker or victim), the hero's helper, the villain, the princess (reward for the hero), the princess' father (who bestows the reward on the hero), the donor (who gives the hero an 'object with magical properties' to aid them in their quest), the dispatcher (who sends the hero on the quest) and the false hero. In terms of a generalised view of hip-hop narratives, we may label the rapper as the hero who may seek such things as sexual gratification, material gain or respect from the neighbourhood, the character of the hero's helper can be seen as the main character's friends, his homeboys, or possibly even guest rappers who may appear on the track. The princess can conceivably be the girls within the narrative, although it should be noted that they are not held in the same regard as the fairytale princess. However, the counter claim can be put that the role of the princess as interpreted by Propp is an excessively passive role and therefore comparisons to the representation of hyper-sexualised but ultimately subservient women in some rap music videos are justified. The role of villain, one could argue, is largely taken up in rap narratives by the police or other institutions of ideological state power, for example the prison system.

The concept of narrative possibilities in rap is discussed by the Rochester group in the following extract:

Lou (R):   Lil' Wayne, for example, sometimes he talks about ... liked he's hyped up most of the time but, like, he can't talk about stories like Lupe Fiasco or something if he hasn't actually experienced anything, you know? He would be lying and it wouldn't really come from the heart.

Zac (R):   It actually depends on your background, like, what you can rap about.

TD: So you think that's important, then? The stories in their raps need to come from reality?

Zac (R):   Yeah. It has to come from the heart.

Jon (R):   You see, I'm not so sure. You know, I think people like feel good music so I don't think the lyrics are necessarily that important all of the time. There are people like Soulja Boy whose music makes us feel really good and so we don't really care so much for the lyrics. It's the beats. So, I think I prefer the beat, though. Lyrics are sometimes ... you know, I listen more to the beat.

The above discussion with Jon and Zac continued with the participants agreeing that rap lyrics are today perhaps a little more intelligent than in previous years. The Rochester group held the perception that more rappers were increasingly educated, in their words more rap artists were 'finishing school' and so they felt that lyrical wordplay and use of such tools as metaphors were more prevalent than ever before. The subject matter of more historical rap, which in the eyes of the Rochester respondents mostly dealt in the glorification of the drug trade, was as a result of the inherent connections between the rappers and their biographies before entering the entertainment industry. Irrespective of the subject matter of the lyrics, this group clearly recognised their own preferences for artists who delivered their messages 'from the heart'. Jon's comment that he often tends to prefer the beat over the lyrical content of the track was a perspective that was non-existent for the Canterbury, Ashford and Lewisham groups but was present within the individuals from Brighton and Rochester. The purist groups stated that for hip-hop tracks with vocals the lyrical content was more significant than the song's musical production whereas the Brighton and Rochester groups had members who did not actively listen to the lyrics. That is not to say that all members of the peripheral groups held this view but a significant number did. As an earlier chapter noted, Catherine from the Canterbury group was very clear that if she was offended by the lyrics of a rap song she would no longer wish to listen to the track, although a compromised position was in evidence. The Canterbury group also felt that although they personally placed a great emphasis on lyrics, many in the audience did not.

Vocal delivery and musical timbre

The 'grain of the voice' (Barthes, 1977: 181) of an artist was an important aspect for hip-hop consumers within the field. The geno-song and the pheno-song are the two main components of this theory whereby the former represents the musical performance's form of communication, representation and expression. The pheno-song, on the other hand, includes factors such as the volume of the singing and speaking voice and is the diction of the language. For Barthes, a successful performer is one who incorporates elements of the geno-song into their work. There is a difference here between meaningful singing and singing that makes meaning. In this respect, the grain of the voice does not evoke emotions or feelings from the vocal performance, it is those things. One example offered could be the case of the vocal style of Wu-Tang Clan member Ol' Dirty Bastard whose trademark hoarse vocal style exemplifies the characterisations present within his lyrical narratives, as opposed to simply evoking this aspect. The grain of the voice is an almost immeasurable phenomenon and one that arguably results from particular audience reception of vocal style.

It was found in the fieldwork that the idea of authenticity was often linked to vocal delivery. For example, Snoop Dogg portrays himself in music videos, album covers and song lyrics as a heavy marijuana user and his lackadaisical vocal style matches this representation, therefore a claim to authenticity can be made. This was a point taken up by Zac from the Rochester group:

Zac (R):   Snoop has this way of rapping that makes you know he's stoned. I mean, like, he drawls. You know, you can't fake that.
Lou (R):   That style is sort of like his own, man.
Sarah (R):   Yeah. If you heard someone try to copy it then you'd know they were just faking and ... erm ...
Lou (R):   (*interrupting*) In rap there's no room for fakers, see?

Dan (R):   The point is, you can't copy someone else's style. Snoop does his thing and tells his stories and they're his. If someone came along and just copied then he'd be shouted down because Snoop's, like, the real thing and anyone copying would be just a copy. Like, fake, you know?

The assertion by Dan that Snoop is 'the real thing' is linked with the performer's ability to project his character not just in the lyrical content of his songs but also in the vocal performance which further illustrates the artistic persona. A vocal performance which can be ascribed as authentic, therefore, is of paramount significance for acceptance by the members of the focus groups. Indeed, an artist whose delivery seems reminiscent of another, according to both Sarah and Dan in this extract, is likely to be considered as inauthentic by the audience and will potentially face being 'shouted down', that is to say that they will perhaps create resentment and possible hostility in the audience. In this respect, it can be seen that this group, as with others in the research, perceive a sense of originality and uniqueness to be key components to the labelling of an artist as authentic. The concept of 'keeping it real' is once again present as the audience may interpret a vocal performance as having all of the constituent parts to establish a badge of authentication to the recording or performance. This aspect was also addressed by the Ashford group:

Rachel (A):   When you hear some of those guys rap you can just hear their life story coming through their voice, you know? On a lot of Tupac's stuff his voice is, like … raw with the emotion of it all and then you know that what he's saying means a shitload to him.

Adam (A):   Yeah, I'd say the same. I'd say for, like, someone like Method Man the same kind of thing stands but in a different way. Like, he's sort of angry and sort of … well, just a bit pissed off half of the time and if his voice didn't kind of match his lyrics then it'd be a bit, like, not work and be …

Matt (A): (interrupting)   Same with Ice Cube, eh? He has this thing where he bangs on about hating this, that and the other and you can tell it's the way he feels because his voice is so … so fucking angry.

The nature of the vocal performance is aligned to the validation and authentication of the artist by the members of the group. The research subjects in the above extract demonstrate their subcultural knowledge by each discussing the particular vocal qualities of different rappers, suggesting a need in this group to show their cultural knowledge to one another in order to endorse their own, and each other's, place in the collective. The performances of raw emotion and anger highlighted by this group are linked to the personal feelings of the artists in question which further enhance the artists' credentials of authenticity. There is a sense that the vocalisation of feeling allows the audience to more fully comprehend the motivations of the artist and therefore creates a stronger connective bond between performer and consumer. Krims (2000: 39) discusses the idea of vocal delivery adding some degree of authentication to a performance and elaborates upon the actual sound of rap music, the music itself as a maker of meaning for the audience. The sonic force of hip-hop (Rose, 1994; Krims, 2000) also means that attention should not merely be paid to the vocal performance, but also to the timbre of the music and the meaning thus implied. The following extract from the Canterbury group highlights this point:

Luke (C):   One of the first rap acts I got into was Public Enemy. I just loved the way the music sounded as angry as Chuck D's lyrics. I think it's, erm, The Bomb Squad that produced a couple of those late '80s Public Enemy albums — that sound is so huge! I think, like, that whole conscious, angry political thing they were doing was really helped by the backing. You really get a sense when you listen to that that they're well pissed off.

Andy (C):   I think a lot of production can be so flat. I'm not sure if the producers think that the vocal is more important or what but if the sound of the track doesn't match whatever's being said then I can't see the point in that. A track needs to match the vocals and beats. So, like, it makes perfect sense for Public Enemy's beats to speak for themselves. That makes you realise that all of the people involved in that record were thinking along the same lines. It meant something to them, you know?

A level of authentication is ascribed here by Andy when he suggests a sense of collective purpose existed in the creation of Public Enemy's output. The perception of both of the research participants that the vocals and the beats of the tracks match in terms of intent suggests a level of collaboration which confirms a sense of authentication away from the procedural elements of music making.

Dimensions of ethnicity

The general consensus across all of the focus groups was that there was a valued place for white artists in hip-hop culture although endorsements from black hip-hop producers were seen as positive. The findings from Statement 11, *There is no place in rap music for white artists*, from the questionnaire show that 106 of the research respondents (80%) disagreed with the notion that hip-hop was a domain solely for black or Latino rappers: 39 (30%) slightly disagreed and 67 (51%) totally disagreed.

Of the 78 fans, 64 (82%) disagreed and of the 48 non-fans, 36 (75%) disagreed. There were similar results between fans and non-fans who totally disagreed with the statement: 41 fans (53%) and 25 non-fans (52%).

The white rapper Eminem was a very popular artist for many of the younger research subjects. The Canterbury and Ashford groups rarely mentioned him in conversation but the Lewisham, Rochester and Brighton groups would regularly discuss his work and significance. The following extended extract from the Lewisham group highlights a number of important points such as racial identity, the authentic notion of 'realness', the personal identification between artist and audience and the marketing of an artist and the patronage of a white rapper by a black 'mentor'.

Ash (L):	Personally, the thing that I thought was good about Tupac was that … no, I mean Eminem, is that he made … he made everyone know that hip-hop is not just for one particular people or you can be whatever race or whatever and do hip-hop and that. Or … or you can be however you want to be with hip-hop. He made hip-hop change, innit? Before, people used to think that hip-hop was only for black people and Eminem proved them wrong, like. He made it so, like, that's why I like him.
TD:	Jemal, what about you?
Jemal (L):	I was pretty much into Eminem as well because at the time … well, it was mostly childish, innit? Everything that he said just made me laugh. It was just a laugh.
TD:	Do you listen to Eminem in the same way now?

Jemal (L): No. Before, I was listening to Eminem because he was talking about beating up fat girls and all of that. Now I realise that that's childish but I realise he's a good lyricist, that his word play is good. I can listen to lyrics and know what they mean, and that.

TD: When you were younger listening to Eminem, did you think that what he rapped about was real?

Jemal (L): I knew it was a character he was playing because it was unrealistic. It was over exaggerated and that. It's like when you watch *The Simpsons* with all the mad things. You can make sense of what he's saying and he's saying it in a … …

Isaac (L): (interrupting) You can tell by the way he changes his voice because sometimes when he does it he changes his voice to make it more funny or something.

TD: So what do you think makes Eminem so popular?

Ash (L): Nowadays he's spitting truth about his daughter and what's going on around his house. That's how he's keeping his flow.

Emmanuel (L): It helps because his audience is, like, getting older so he's matching that.

TD: Do you think it helped him because he's white?

Jemal (L): I think it helped him to sell because no-one … no-one heard of a white rapper and it's like the whole Elvis thing, innit? Like, he wouldn't have sold unless he was white. He had the black people's voice but he had white skin and that. It's more, like, marketable, innit?

TD: It's interesting to me that you didn't reject him because he was white. You said earlier that it was a good thing as people were made to see that hip-hop wasn't just for black people.

Ash (L): Yeah.

TD: What do you think might have made you reject him?

Ash (L): If he came to the scene and started chatting bullshit and that. He was ordinary, like. He came to the scene as he was just, like, rapping and freestyling in battles and that's where he found his flow.

Isaac (L): That's why he did that film '8 Mile', innit?

Ash (L):   So, I guess he must have made a promo and Dr. Dre must
               have heard it and thought he was black. Dr. Dre must have
               thought he was black ...

Emmanuel (L): (interrupting)   But when you see him ...

Ash (L): (interrupting)   But when you see him and he's white it must have
               made Dr. Dre think different, innit? Like 'oh, it's not just only
               black people that are blessed with hip-hop'. White people are
               in it as well and that's what made him different.

TD: Do you think it helped Eminem to have Dre's backing?

Emmanuel (L): Yeah, because, like, Dre has been bare [many] people's
               mentor like Snoop Dogg and, like, even 50 Cent and ... like,
               The Game as well so that's what helped Dr. Dre move up his
               levels as well.

Jemal (L):   I think he's right. Like, the hardcore hip-hop fans must have
               thought that if Dr. Dre was into it then ... you know, other
               people would get into it, too.

From this exchange a number of key points are raised. Eminem, in the
perception of this group, has been accepted by the hip-hop community due to
a combination of his lyrical skills and his ability to 'tell the truth', his relationship
with Dr. Dre and the historical aspect of the marketable nature of white skin.
For Eminem at least, McLeod's (1999) binary opposites of real (black) and fake
(white) are not applicable as far as this group is concerned. Indeed, Ash makes
the point that the general consensus before Eminem was that there was perhaps
no place in rap music for white artists. The comments from this group suggest
that Eminem changed people's mentalities in regards to racial authenticity in
hip-hop. Factually it is useful to note that McLeod's work dates from 1999, the
same year that Eminem released his first major studio album *The Slim Shady
LP* (Interscope / Universal). Using Ash's terms, if a white rapper was to 'chat
bullshit' then the audience would not perceive them as authentic or credible.
Of significance from the above extract is the pivotal role played by Dr. Dre in
Eminem's acceptance by hip-hop fans. This audience approval by association
is understood by this group to be a determining factor for Eminem's success.

Tony Mitchell suggests that the contemporary version of hip-hop culture
'... cannot be viewed simply as an expression of African American culture; it
has become a vehicle for global youth affiliations and a tool for reworking local
identity all over the world ...' (2001: 1). However, any sense of authenticity

bestowed on a hip-hop performer needs to be considered within the parameters of a black epistemological context. White rappers need to forge their own sense of identity and value within preordained borders but this is also somewhat true for black artists. McLeod (ibid.) suggests that the racial boundaries of black/white distinguish between the notions of real/fake. The findings from the fieldwork for this study suggest this is a more complex issue. As Mitchell's above quote testifies, hip-hop culture today exists within a global framework with a number of localised variations of the culture. Contemporary hip-hop can be seen as a fluid and dynamic culture whose parameters have stretched beyond the simple bifurcation of black and white. Ogbar (2007: 38) suggests that the United States of America is a race obsessed country and that a popular understanding of authenticity is predicated in highly racialised terms. It can be suggested that, in terms of hip-hop at least, the link between ethnicity and authenticity is very much in evidence.

The appeal and consumption of a black musical form and its associating culture in an area of the United Kingdom which is seen to be 95% white was discussed by Andy Bennett (1999c, 2001). He assesses the fact that '... a central assumption in much sociological work examining white British appropriations of black musical styles is that they take place in settings where a prominent black population serves as a continual point of reference for such appropriations ...' (2001: 99). His study, based in Newcastle, investigates the consumption of hip-hop and how it is used by the inhabitants of the city to aid their own form of self-identification and subcultural belonging. The use of hip-hop amongst these individuals is seen as an important signifier in the demarcation of their own cultural formation and sense of localised cultural space. In fact, the use of hip-hop and the lack of a real black presence in the area has led to what might be termed deflected racism by many in the community towards these 'hip-hoppers'. A couple of Bennett's interviewees in his study, two local rap fans, contest this view of hip-hop as a construction of localised space and place by suggesting that there is no such thing as 'white hip-hop', that hip-hop composed and performed by Caucasian people should not be taken seriously and should not be considered authentic. It was found in the research for this study that such an opinion was not held by the research subjects. The popularity of Eminem, which occurred after Bennett's study, and other white rappers such as El-P, Bubba Sparxxx and Professor Green seems to have eroded such a sensibility in the hip-hop audience.

Tricia Rose (1994) suggests that hip-hop is about giving a voice to a black community which is otherwise under-represented and serves as a tool for the expression of the diasporic experience. This notion, however, does not reflect accurately what has happened to hip-hop in the marketplace with the huge numbers of units being sold by white rap artists in recent years. It has been claimed that it was only when white artists began to perform rap that wide-scale public attention and recognition was given to the genre (Olson and Shobe Jr., 2008: 994). Debbie Harry's rap in Blondie's *Rapture* (1980, Chrysalis Records), along with the presence of Aerosmith on Run DMC's crossover hit *Walk This Way* (1986, London Records) and the international success of the Beastie Boys a couple of years later all testify to this notion. Also, in terms of UK acts, Malcolm McLaren's tracks *Buffalo Gals* and *Double Dutch* (1982 and 1983, Charisma Records), which featured on his collaboration album with the World's Famous Supreme Team called *Duck Rock*, were a commercial success on both sides of the Atlantic.

The links between consumer and producer has been discussed by Krims (2000) who suggests that the significance of audience identification with an artist is based on the social and cultural backgrounds of the consumers, as well as the sub-genre of rap that is being presented. In terms of record sales, hip-hop has a majority white audience (Rose, 2008) and therefore the personal identification gained by the audience could, arguably, be greater with a performer from the same ethnic group as the members of the audience. This was not the case with either the purist or peripheral groups in this study's fieldwork. The extract above from the Lewisham group about Eminem highlights the reluctance by the research respondents to consider ethnicity as a significant marker of authenticity. It was found that skin colour was not taken into account when deciding a rapper's aesthetic and cultural value whereas performance ability and a biography based on truth were key to the labelling of an artist as authentic.

Authenticity and ideology

The idea of authenticity was used by the young people in the fieldwork as a form of division between their own subcultural opinions and attitudes and others who are mostly labelled as 'mainstream'. Such a demarcation reinforces subcultural distinction via aesthetic taste and value and places the emphasis on authenticity on the judgements of those engaged in the culture rather than from a musicological or external perspective. The construct of authentic texts and their consumption by individuals is central to the understanding of the accrual of cultural knowledge by the youth groups who sought to separate their own values from others. In this respect, degrees of cultural resistance are in evidence for peripherals as they utilise the term to acknowledge and identify their desire to be seen to be valued cultural consumers. For purists, emphasis also lies in their own degree of cultural creativity, in MCing and DJing, not simply in their patterns of consumption. In such distinctions, forms of agency are evident amongst the purist groups. The subcultural knowledge that each group possesses enables them to make informed choices about what they perceive to be authentic cultural expression and the variations between each group can be seen to be an illustration of the complexity of ideas of the authentic, as well as its contested nature.

Authenticity, for the research participants, had many meanings. It is clearly a contested notion, not easily defined by the individuals in the fieldwork, which goes some way in determining the value of the musical form being consumed as well as enabling the research participants to establish the parameters of friendship networks, and thereby the ideology of their collective. In this respect, authenticity should be seen as an abstract conceptual tool which engenders a sense of worth for the audience. There is an ideological impetus to the construct of authenticity which is arguably elitist and centres on a marker of separation between mainstream product and artistically valued pieces of music. For the purist groups there was a sense that authentic hip-hop and grime was anti-commercial in primary purpose, but this did not necessarily mean the artists were not relatively successful in terms of sales, adding further complexity and contradiction to the concept. Commerce and artistic integrity were dichotomous positions found in the fieldwork in terms of enabling an artist to be labelled as authentic though such terms were contested and there were often degrees of compromise involved in the consumption of some artists for some of the research participants. Thus, the participants would struggle over ideas of authenticity on a daily basis as a part of their hip-hop culture.

McLeod (1999: 139) suggests that the notion of authenticity within hip-hop culture is as a reaction to the threat of assimilation of the cultural practice by the larger, mainstream culture. His conceptual apparatus of semantic dimensions incorporates binary oppositions and the key terms here are the political-economic dimension which place 'the underground' and 'commercial' against one another. Commercial crossover records, according to some in the focus groups, often entail an altering of the sound from that of the original underground output. The emphasis on authentic hip-hop also reinforces the concept of consistent distinctiveness as a key element of subcultural substance and should be seen as a marker of subcultural identity.

Another aspect of authenticity which was highly valued by the purist groups was that of live performance. Here, the artistic ability can be assessed without the complex corrections and adjustments to performance that can occur using modern recording technology such as multi-tracking, overdubs and auto-tune. There was a clear hierarchical relationship between those performers who partook in live rap and grime shows and those who did not. MC battles, the spontaneous construction of raps in a live setting against an 'opponent', were seen for many to be the ultimate expression of authenticity for vocal performers. This once again places the emphasis on the direct and unobstructed connection between performer, performance and audience. For the purist groups this form of hip-hop culture was celebrated as a throwback to the origins of the culture, where the focus was on live events rather than recorded material. This highlights another form of subcultural knowledge that they possess over others as they see this as a deeper understanding of the culture and its historical roots, aspects that others who engage with rap music were seemingly unaware.

Mainstream texts were seen as repetitious and formulaic whereas authentic works were those that were somehow seen to be moving the genre forwards and had a greater sense of connectivity between artist and audience. One of the attractive aspects of using the internet as a means of accessing the culture was the seemingly negligible gap between producer and consumer. This was a point raised on a number of occasions by the focus groups, highlighted in the following extract:

> *Ash (L):*   Like, using web pages for artists is good, like, 'cos on the radio it's up to other people what you hear but on the internet you can go looking for stuff. Like, people like JME and Skepta can put their tunes out there as they want them to sound without radio messing with it all. They can see a thing, write about it and pretty soon it's up for people to hear, like.

The immediacy of this technology is attractive to Ash for two reasons. First, he views the internet as a platform through which artists can circumnavigate the cultural gatekeepers of the broadcast industries. There is also a sense that this tool allows the artist more freedom as they can negate the traditional gap between composition and consumption that the record industry affords. It is this creative immediacy which retains the purity of the artistic expression and therefore its authenticity. Emphasis is placed in the above quote on the ability of the composer to base their work on their personal experiences. Ash states that the catalyst to creativity for grime artists such as JME and Skepta is the fact that they 'see a thing' before expressing this event in their chosen musical form. There is a perception here that the output is created as a direct result of a personal event and that the internet is a means to connect the audience with the genuine experience of the artist with almost immediate effect. This increases the sense of authenticity attributed to an artist as such an event would serve as the initiatory instance as expressed by Moore (2002). This extract highlights the sceptical view held by many of the research subjects towards record labels or broadcast organisations who are viewed as a potential hindrance to the artist's freedom of expression. Such cultural gatekeepers were seen in the field as a significant factor in an artist's decision to alter their sound which, in turn, is detrimental to claims of authenticity.

Conclusion

The data illustrates that the notion of authenticity, from the audience's perspective, is hugely significant and highly contested. In general it was found that for the research participants, utilising the idea of the authentic protects them from what they perceive as the all-encompassing machinery of the recording industry. For the youth groups in this study there was an attempt to use their own definitions of authentic performance in order to not only validate their cultural consumption but also to allow subcultural allegiances and affiliations to be formed. Consuming forms of hip-hop and grime that are seen to be authentic is a means of attaining subcultural status within peer groups and allows for acceptance in a number of practices as well as rigidly enforcing a sense of collective identity through the practice of excluding those who do not appear to have the required level of cultural knowledge.

Hip-hop culture surrounds itself with the mantra of 'keeping it real' although, as a commodified global entity, it is difficult to say exactly how such things are reflective of reality. From the different positions of authenticity in the data we can identify the problematic nature of the concept as a tool to express more valid, and valued, artistic worth. The cultural and subsequent market value placed on an artist labelled as authentic is significant for record labels. For the youth groups it was found that the perceived immediacy of some platforms of consumption, for example the utilisation of websites such as myspace, Bandcamp and SoundCloud allow the artist a more pronounced connection with the audience compared with other mediated forms. Thus, for the research participants in this study, such rappers appear as more authentic as their creativity has seemingly not been diluted prior to consumption by a recording industry which is seen to be driven by commercial rather than creative or artistic interests.

Rap music, for many in the research set, maintained a sense of verisimilitude whilst others, notably in the purist group, more readily accepted the idea of poetic fictionalities within the cultural texts. As in the previous chapter on representing images, an analysis of the notion of the authentic further established the different perspectives held by the purist and peripheral groups, thereby affirming the theoretical applicability of this conceptual model. The qualitative data highlighted the different reading positions held by these groups. The purist group members tended towards a sceptical interpretation of commodified mainstream imagery. It was this group in particular who used the notion of authenticity to form subcultural affiliations with those who they saw to be likeminded in outlook. The purist groups in this study exhibited aspects of resistance similar to those in the structural work of the CCCS whereas the seemingly more *laissez-faire* approach taken by the peripheral groups aligns them more with the post-subcultural turn.

Chapter 8

Conclusion

Purists and peripherals

Hip-hop is an enigma. It is a multi-faceted, vibrant and vital form of cultural expression for many young (and not so young) people around the world. It is a mainstay of contemporary society, fulfilling a wide array of roles including as a vehicle for the transmission of capitalist values, as a means of expressing anti-establishment sentiment and as a hotly debated scapegoat for society's ills. Hip-hop is shaped by those who engage, create and breathe the culture and can be seen as a positive influence in the lives of countless people around the globe. Hip-hop educates, inspires and is used as a means towards collective social engagement whilst also vilifying those at the margins of society through the focus and glamorisation of criminality.

Hip-hop is in a state of constant flux outside of the concerns of the recording industry whilst simultaneously it can be argued that the rap game is being held in a seeming state of stasis by the interests of major record labels. The commercial success of American gangsta rap arguably perpetuates a one dimensional portrayal of the black experience to a global audience, yet recently, artists such as Kendrick Lamar, Young Thug, and to a degree Skepta in grime, can be seen to be challenging such derogatory images.

The complexities and issues of analysing human action and audience opinion, the main aims of this book, are numerous. I have not intended to portray engagement with hip-hop and grime here as some form of homogeneous entity, rather the work here shows a snapshot of varying degrees of subcultural engagement by five groups of young people whose opinions were being amended, shaped and perhaps more fully considered as a result of engaging with the research process. There are some contradictory opinions given by the research participants in this book, ones which I did not feel were worthy of highlighting in the main bulk of the text. However, rather than omitting these opinions or trying to suggest reasons for them I have left these open for interpretation by the reader. It is, I think, enough to say at this stage that people are often contradictions of their earlier selves and ideas and such things are also likely to be in evidence during focus group interviews, with all of the forced interaction that comes with this research method.

The purist/peripheral model of subcultural engagement needs further analysis and application before it can be considered a valid means of evaluating the divisions and separations within varying subcultural groups and subsequent depth and forms of engagement. However, in its defence I feel that the developing model more closely describes forms of subcultural activity that were evident to me in the field as a researcher but also through my own longstanding engagement in various musical spheres, including that of hip-hop. I believe that the purist/peripheral model will prove of value to those investigating a range of subcultures so long as the model's terms are not seen as a deterministic and dichotomous means of subcultural separation but that these labels are either end of a continuum, a sliding scale of cultural engagement. Neither should these labels be used to ascribe a set of presumed traits for those in either group or seen as value imbued terms. Researchers in the field should look at those who they are studying and work out whether distinctions such as purist and peripheral are of value to them in their own work from a grounded perspective. Not all subcultural groups could be labelled as purist and/or peripheral and I would hope that future work in this field does not seek to undermine this model simply because it may not fit each and every specific subcultural occurrence.

Finally, the purist/peripheral model should not be used as a tool for researchers to pre-emptively categorise subcultural groups as they enter the field but could be useful from a grounded theory perspective once positive relationships between the researcher and those they are studying has been achieved. It is much more important, in my view, to treat those under investigation as individuals first and foremost before attempting to establish common and identifiable means of identity formation with peer groups. Previous works in this field have suffered due to a reliance on homogenising those young people being analysed and the work is often then written in a way which neglects to include any real complexity or any acknowledgement that what is being presented is nothing other than a snapshot of a group of people at a particular moment in time. Although I have argued here that longevity of cultural engagement allows the social scientist to look beyond the rigid parameters of 'youth' when discussing cultural engagement, I do not pretend that those who have engaged for longer are somehow the 'finished product'. Those who have engaged with hip-hop and grime over extended periods of time remain in a state of dynamic engagement as they continue to enhance their cultural skills and knowledge to maintain their place within their peer group.

The dynamic nature of these cultural forms is evident, particularly with grime at present with regards to how fast the culture and its performers are moving into the mainstream. A number of grime acts campaigned for Jeremy Corbyn, leader of the Labour Party, in the UK General Election in 2017 and the twitter hashtag #Grime4Corbyn allowed grime artists including JME a platform to voice their support for Labour policies whilst also lambasting issues of austerity which were seen as central to the Conservative Party's economic viewpoint. It would be difficult to ascertain just how significant such things were in regards to the increase in youth voters in the election yet the point remains true that this hashtag trended repeatedly on Twitter as well as being picked up by mainstream news outlets and therefore placed grime within the political discourse of the country. My focus group research had finished before these events and it would have been interesting to see how such things influenced the political participation and opinions of those in the discussion groups. One aspect with which I feel is entirely under-represented in this work is that of the galdem - the female equivalent of the mandem. This is largely due to the demographic of the Lewisham group but also due to the fact that few female grime artists were in prominence at the time of our focus group meetings. In the last year or so more female grime artists are establishing themselves and the role of the galdem (often written as gyaldem) would be a valuable contribution to the field in future studies. Grime is a vibrant, charged cultural form with the ability to embolden, encourage and make visible those who previously felt ignored within the cultural landscape of the UK.

Appendix 1
Qualitative Data Set

The information here relates to the individuals who took part in the focus group interviews. Their age is in relation to how old they were in the first group meeting and the ethnic grouping named is in line with their own forms of self-identification.

Canterbury

	Age	Gender	Ethnicity	Nationality
Catherine	26	Female	White	British
Luke	38	Male	Black	British
Andy	29	Male	White	British
Chris	32	Male	White	British
Simon	31	Male	White	British

Lewisham

	Age	Gender	Ethnicity	Nationality
Ash	16	Male	Black	British
Jemal	18	Male	Black	British
Isaac	18	Male	Black	British
Emmanuel	18	Male	Black	British
Dave	19	Male	White	British

Ashford

	Age	Gender	Ethnicity	Nationality
Josh	19	Male	White	British
Rachel	19	Female	White	British
Adam	21	Male	White	British
Trevor	18	Male	White	British
Matt	23	Male	White	British

Rochester

	Age	Gender	Ethnicity	Nationality
Zac	19	Male	Black	Ghanaian
Dan	18	Male	Black	South African
Lou	16	Male	Black	Nigerian
Sarah	16	Female	White	British
Jon	18	Male	White	British

Brighton

	Age	Gender	Ethnicity	Nationality
Kate	17	Female	White	British
Rob	18	Male	White	British
Paul	18	Male	White	British
Alice	18	Female	White	British
Tony	18	Male	White	British

Appendix 2
Quantitative Data Set

Number of respondents: 132

Male: 86   Female: 46:

Ages of respondents*																
	16	17	18	19	20	21	23	24	25	26	28	29	30	32	33	35
Female	7	21	5	4	3	0	0	0	2	1	1	0	2	0	0	0
Male	13	29	18	3	1	1	1	2	2	1	0	1	0	1	2	1

*no respondent reported their age to be either 22, 27, 31 or 34
11 questionnaires were returned with no age reported.

1. I would consider myself to be a fan of hip-hop and rap music.

Totally agree   [42]
Slightly agree   [36]
Not sure   [6]
Slightly disagree   [22]
Totally disagree   [26]

2. I regularly buy or download rap music.

		Total		I would consider myself to be a fan of hip-hop and rap music				
				Totally agree	Agree slightly	Not sure	Slightly disagree	Totally disagree
I regularly buy or download rap music	Totally agree	24	M	21	2	0	0	0
			F	0	1	0	0	0
	Slightly agree	27	M	8	8	0	0	0
			F	3	8	0	0	0
	Not sure	8	M	2	0	0	1	0
			F	2	3	0	0	0
	Slightly disagree	25	M	5	2	3	5	0
			F	1	5	1	2	1
	Totally disagree	48	M	0	3	2	11	13
			F	0	4	0	3	12

3. The images and lyrics in hip-hop music are true to life.

		Total		I would consider myself to be a fan of hip-hop and rap music				
				Totally agree	Agree slightly	Not sure	Slightly disagree	Totally disagree
The images and lyrics in hip-hop music are true to life	Totally agree	4	M	0	2	0	1	0
			F	0	1	0	0	0
	Slightly agree	47	M	18	5	1	10	0
			F	3	7	1	1	1
	Not sure	26	M	4	3	1	3	3
			F	1	5	0	2	4
	Slightly disagree	38	M	11	4	2	2	4
			F	2	8	0	1	4
	Totally disagree	17	M	3	1	1	1	6
			F	0	0	0	1	4

4. A good rapper is one who has lived the life they rap about.

		Total		I would consider myself to be a fan of hip-hop and rap music				
				Totally agree	Agree slightly	Not sure	Slightly disagree	Totally disagree
A good rapper is one who has lived the life they rap about	Totally agree	16	M	3	3	1	4	1
			F	1	1	0	1	1
	Slightly agree	47	M	10	5	1	6	4
			F	4	9	0	1	1
	Not sure	29	M	5	3	2	4	6
			F	0	7	0	1	1
	Slightly disagree	29	M	14	3	0	2	2
			F	1	4	0	1	2
	Totally disagree	11	M	4	1	1	1	0
			F	0	0	1	1	2

5. Women are treated fairly in rap music videos.

				I would consider myself to be a fan of hip-hop and rap music				
		Total		Totally agree	Agree slightly	Not sure	Slightly disagree	Totally disagree
Women are treated fairly in rap music videos	Totally agree	9	M	1	3	1	1	3
			F	0	0	0	0	0
	Slightly agree	11	M	5	2	0	3	0
			F	0	1	0	0	0
	Not sure	27	M	4	3	1	2	5
			F	1	8	0	0	3
	Slightly disagree	46	M	16	5	2	7	3
			F	1	6	1	2	3
	Totally disagree	39	M	10	2	1	4	2
			F	4	6	0	3	7

6. You do not have to be very clever to be a successful rapper.

				I would consider myself to be a fan of hip-hop and rap music				
		Total		Totally agree	Agree slightly	Not sure	Slightly disagree	Totally disagree
You do not have to be very clever to be a successful rapper	Totally agree	34	M	8	5	0	3	9
			F	1	4	0	1	3
	Slightly agree	39	M	11	4	3	4	0
			F	2	11	0	0	4
	Not sure	17	M	4	1	1	1	1
			F	1	3	1	1	3
	Slightly disagree	27	M	7	3	1	7	1
			F	1	2	0	2	3
	Totally disagree	15	M	6	2	0	2	2
			F	1	1	0	1	0

7. Rap videos are excessively violent.

		Total		I would consider myself to be a fan of hip-hop and rap music				
				Totally agree	Agree slightly	Not sure	Slightly disagree	Totally disagree
Rap videos are excessively violent	Totally agree	1	M	0	1	0	0	0
			F	0	0	0	0	0
	Slightly agree	30	M	3	3	1	4	4
			F	3	4	0	2	6
	Not sure	29	M	6	1	2	7	5
			F	0	6	0	0	2
	Slightly disagree	56	M	20	10	2	4	3
			F	1	9	1	1	5
	Totally disagree	16	M	7	0	0	2	1
			F	2	2	0	2	0

8. Rap music contains lyrics and images that degrade women.

		Total		I would consider myself to be a fan of hip-hop and rap music				
				Totally agree	Agree slightly	Not sure	Slightly disagree	Totally disagree
Rap music contains lyrics and images that degrade women	Totally agree	21	M	7	3	1	1	1
			F	0	4	0	1	3
	Slightly agree	72	M	21	6	1	11	7
			F	6	9	1	2	9
	Not sure	21	M	4	3	1	2	4
			F	0	5	0	0	2
	Slightly disagree	15	M	3	3	1	3	1
			F	0	2	0	2	0
	Totally disagree	15	M	1	0	1	0	0
			F	0	1	0	0	0

9. Rap music explains to me how life is for black Americans.

			I would consider myself to be a fan of hip-hop and rap music				
		Total		Totally agree	Agree slightly	Not sure	Slightly disagree	Totally disagree
Rap music explains to me how life is for black Americans	Totally agree	0	M	0	0	0	0	0
			F	0	0	0	0	0
	Slightly agree	22	M	10	3	1	4	0
			F	2	1	0	0	1
	Not sure	25	M	2	3	1	4	1
			F	2	8	0	1	3
	Slightly disagree	44	M	14	7	2	4	2
			F	1	7	1	0	6
	Totally disagree	41	M	10	2	1	5	10
			F	1	5	0	4	3

10. Rap music is racist towards white people.

			I would consider myself to be a fan of hip-hop and rap music				
		Total		Totally agree	Agree slightly	Not sure	Slightly disagree	Totally disagree
Rap music is racist towards white people	Totally agree	6	M	0	2	0	1	1
			F	1	0	0	0	1
	Slightly agree	26	M	0	8	0	6	4
			F	3	2	0	1	2
	Not sure	29	M	4	2	2	2	6
			F	0	4	0	4	5
	Slightly disagree	38	M	11	3	3	6	1
			F	0	10	0	0	4
	Totally disagree	33	M	21	0	0	2	1
			F	2	5	1	0	1

11. There is no place in rap music for white artists.

		Total		I would consider myself to be a fan of hip-hop and rap music				
				Totally agree	Agree slightly	Not sure	Slightly disagree	Totally disagree
There is no place in rap music for white artists	Totally agree	6	M	0	0	0	0	1
			F	0	0	0	0	0
	Slightly agree	26	M	1	1	0	2	1
			F	1	2	0	0	1
	Not sure	29	M	2	5	0	3	2
			F	0	2	0	1	1
	Slightly disagree	39	M	7	4	5	4	0
			F	3	9	0	2	5
	Totally disagree	67	M	26	5	0	8	9
			F	2	8	1	2	6

12. American rap is better than British rap music.

		Total		I would consider myself to be a fan of hip-hop and rap music				
				Totally agree	Agree slightly	Not sure	Slightly disagree	Totally disagree
American rap is better than British rap music	Totally agree	20	M	12	1	0	2	1
			F	1	2	0	0	1
	Slightly agree	42	M	14	6	2	3	2
			F	2	8	0	2	3
	Not sure	40	M	2	2	1	8	6
			F	2	8	0	2	9
	Slightly disagree	15	M	5	4	1	1	0
			F	1	2	0	1	0
	Totally disagree	15	M	3	2	1	3	4
			F	0	1	1	0	0

13. Grime music is better than rap.

				I would consider myself to be a fan of hip-hop and rap music				
		Total		Totally agree	Agree slightly	Not sure	Slightly disagree	Totally disagree
Grime music is better than rap	Totally agree	8	M	2	3	1	1	0
			F	0	1	0	0	0
	Slightly agree	17	M	2	5	0	0	1
			F	2	4	0	1	2
	Not sure	59	M	7	2	2	11	11
			F	2	10	1	3	10
	Slightly disagree	17	M	5	3	2	2	0
			F	1	4	0	0	0
	Totally disagree	31	M	20	2	0	3	1
			F	1	2	0	1	1

14. Rap music promotes anti-social behaviour.

				I would consider myself to be a fan of hip-hop and rap music				
		Total		Totally agree	Agree slightly	Not sure	Slightly disagree	Totally disagree
Rap music promotes anti-social behaviour	Totally agree	16	M	2	3	1	2	2
			F	0	2	0	1	3
	Slightly agree	52	M	7	6	2	9	6
			F	3	9	0	2	8
	Not sure	28	M	4	1	0	5	5
			F	2	9	0	2	0
	Slightly disagree	24	M	12	5	2	1	0
			F	0	1	1	0	2
	Totally disagree	12	M	11	0	0	0	0
			F	1	0	0	0	0

15. The subject content in rap music has resulted in an increase in gang violence in Britain.

				I would consider myself to be a fan of hip-hop and rap music				
		Total		Totally agree	Agree slightly	Not sure	Slightly disagree	Totally disagree
The subject content in rap music has resulted in an increase in gang violence in Britain	Totally agree	21	M	3	5	2	3	2
			F	0	2	0	2	2
	Slightly agree	42	M	6	9	2	5	7
			F	3	5	2	2	6
	Not sure	35	M	8	1	1	3	4
			F	1	11	0	2	4
	Slightly disagree	25	M	11	0	2	6	0
			F	8	3	1	0	1
	Totally disagree	9	M	8	0	0	0	0
			F	1	0	0	0	0

Endnotes

1   from *The Real Holy Place* by Boogie Down Productions from the album *Sex and Violence* (1992, Jive Records)

2   from *Making Progress* by Blackalicious from the album *Nia* (1999, Mo' Wax)

3   from *Hip Hop* by Dead Prez from the album *Let's Get Free* (2000, Loud Records)

4   from *Concrete Schoolyard* by Jurassic 5 from the album *Jurassic 5* (1998, Pan Records)

5   from *JME* by JME from the album *Blam!* (2010, Boy Better Know)

6   from *King Kunta* by Kendrick Lamar from the album *To Pimp a Butterfly* (2015, Top Dawg Entertainment/Aftermath)

7   from *I Used to Love H.E.R.* by Common from the album *Resurrection* (1994, Relativity Records)

Bibliography

Adorno, T. (1973) *The jargon of authenticity,* London: Routledge

Adorno, T. (1976) *Introduction to the sociology of music*, New York: The Seabury Press

Adorno, T. (1991) *The culture industry,* London: Routledge

Adorno, T. (2004) *aesthetic theory*, London: Athlone

Alexander, V. D. (2008) *Analysing visual materials* in Gilber, N. (ed.) Researching Social Life, London: Sage, 462-482

Allan, S. (1998) News from nowhere: Televisual news discourse in Bell, A. and Garrett, P. (eds.) *Approaches to Media Discourse*, Oxford: Blackwell Publishers:105-141

Allatt, P. (1993) Becoming priviledged: The role of family processes, in Bates, I. and Riseborough, G. (eds.) *Youth and inequality,* Buckingham: Open University Press:139-159

Althusser, L. (1971) *Lenin and philosophy and other essays,* New York: Monthly Review Press

Anderson, N. (1923) *The hobo* Chicago: Chicago University Press

Ang, I. (1985) *Watching Dallas: Soap opera and the melodramatic imagination*, London: Methuen

Ang, I. (1991) *Desperately seeking the audience,* London: Routledge

Angrosino, M. V. and Mays de Perez, K. A. (2003) Rethinking observation: From method to context, in Denzin, N. K. and Lincoln, Y. S. (eds.) *Collecting and Interpreting Qualitative Materials (2nd ed.),* London: Sage: 107-154

Asante Jr., M. K. (2008) *It's bigger than hip-hop: The rise of the post-hip-hop generation,* New York: St Martins Press

Attali, J. (1985) *Noise: The political economy of music*, London: University of Minnesota Press

Back, L. (1996) *New ethnicities and urban multiculture: Racisms and multiculture in young lives*, London: UCL Press

Back, L. (2007) *The art of listening,* Oxford: Berg

Back, L. and Solomos, J. (eds.) (2009) *Theories of race and racism – A reader* (2nd. ed.), London: Routledge

Bailey, C. A. (1996) *A guide to field research,* Thousand Oaks, California: Pine Forge Press

Barbour, S. and Schostak, J. (2005) Interviewing and focus groups, in Somekh, B. and Lewin, C. (eds.) *Research methods in the social sciences:* 41-48

Barthes, R. (1972) *Mythologies,* London: Cape

Barthes, R. (1977) *Image, music, text*, London: Fontana Press

Basu, D. and Lemelle, S. J. (eds.) (2006) *The vinyl ain't final – Hip-hop and the globalisation of black popular culture,* London: Pluto Press

Baudrillard, J. (1994) *Simulacra and simulation,* Ann Arbor: University of Michigan Press

Becker, G. S. (1964) *Other side: Perspectives on deviance,* New York: The Free Press of Glencoe

Becker, H. (1963) *Outsiders: Studies in the sociology of deviance*, New York: Free Press

Bell, A. (2010) The subculture concept: A genealogy, in Shoham, S. G, Knepper, P. and Kett, M. (eds.) *International handbook of criminology* Boca Raton: CRC Press: 153-183

Benjamin, W. (1936/2008) *The work of art in the age of mechanical reproduction,* London: Penguin Books

Bennett, A. (1999a) Subcultures or neo-tribes? Rethinking the relationship between youth, style and musical tastes, *Sociology*, 33(3): 599-617

Bennett, A. (1999b) Hip-hop am Main: the localization of rap music and hip-hop culture, in *Media, Culture and Society*, 21(1): 77-91

Bennett, A. (1999c) Rappin' on the Tyne: White hip hop culture, in Northeast England – An ethnographic study, *Sociological Review*, 47(1): 1-24

Bennett, A. (2000) *Popular music and youth culture: Music, identity and place*, London: Macmillan Press

Bennett, A. (2001) *Cultures of popular music*, Maidenhead: Open University Press

Bennett, A. (2005) In Defence of Neo-tribes: A Response to Blackman and Hesmondhalgh, in *Journal of Youth Studies*, 8(2): 255-259

Bennett, A. (2006) Punk's not dead: The continuing significance of punk for an older generation of fans, *Sociology*, 40(2): 219-235

Bennett, A. (2007) As young as you feel: Youth as a discursive construct, in Hodkinson, P. and Deicke, W. (eds.) *Youth Cultures: Scenes, subcultures and tribes*, London: Routledge:23-36

Bennett, A. (2009) Spectacular soundtracks: Youth and music, in Furlong, A. (ed.) *Handbook of youth and young adulthood: New perspectives and agendas*, London: Routledge: 263-268

Bennett, A. (2011) The post-subcultural turn: Some reflections 10 years on, in J*ournal of Youth Studies*, 14(5): 493-506

Bennett, A and Kahn-Harris, K. (eds.) (2004) *After subculture: Critical studies in contemporary youth culture*, Basingstoke: Palgrave Macmillan

Bennett, A. and Hodkinson, P. (eds.) (2012) *Ageing and youth cultures: Music, style and identity*, London: Berg

Bennett, A. and Peterson, R. A. (eds.) (2004) *Music scenes: Local, transnational and virtual* Nashville: Vanderbilt University Press

Bennett, A., Shanks, B. and Toynbee, J. (eds.) (2006) *The popular music studies reader*, London: Routledge

Bennett, A. and Stratton, J. (eds.) (2010) *Britpop and the english music tradition*, Farnham: Ashgate Publishing

Berger, A. A. (1997) *Narratives in popular culture, media and everyday life*, London: Sage Publications

Berger, A. A. (1998) *Media research techniques (2nd. ed.)*, London: Sage Publications

Black, T. (1993) *Evaluating social science research: An introduction*, London: Sage Publications

Black, T. R. (1999) *Doing quantitative research in the social sciences: An integrated approach to research design, measurement and statistics*, London: Sage

Blackman, S. J. (1995) *Youth: Positions and oppositions*, Aldershot: Avebury

Blackman, S. J. (2004) *Chilling out: The cultural politics of substance consumption, youth and drug policy*, Maidenhead: Open University Press

Blackman, S. (2005) Youth subcultural theory: A critical engagement with the concept, its origins and politics, from the chicago school to postmodernism, *Journal of Youth Studies*, 8(1): 1-20

Blackman, S. J. (2007) 'Hidden ethnography': *Cr*ossing emotional borders in qualitative accounts of young people's lives, in *Sociology*, 41(4): 699-716

Blackman, S. and France, A. (2001) Youth marginality under 'postmodernis', in Stevenson, N. (ed.) *Culture and citizenship*, London: Sage, 180-197.

Bourdieu, P. (1986) *Distinction: A social critique of the judgement of taste,* London: Routledge

Bourdieu, P. (1993) *The field of cultural production,* Cambridge: Polity

Bourdieu, P. and Wacquant, L. J.D. (1992) *An invitation to reflexive sociology,* Chicago: University of Chicago Press

Bozza, A. (2004) *Whatever you say i am: The life and times of Eminem,* New York: Three Rivers Press

Brake, M. (1980) *The sociology of youth culture and youth subcultures,* London: Routledge and Kegan Paul

Brake, M. (1985) *Comparative youth culture: The sociology of youth cultures and youth subcultures in America, Britain and Canada,* London: Routledge and Kegan Paul

Bramwell, R. (2015) *UK Hip-Hop, Grime and the City: The aesthetics and ethics of, London's rap scenes,* London: Routledge

Brewer, J. D. (2000) *Ethnography,* Buckingham: Open University Press

Briggs, A. and Cobley, P. (1999) 'I Like my shit sagged': Fashion, 'black musics' and subculture, *Journal of Youth Studies,* 2(3): 337-352

Brill, D. (2007) Gender, Status and Subcultural Capital in the Goth Scene, in Hodkinson, P. and Deicke, W. (eds.) *Youth cultures: Scenes, subcultures and tribes,* London: Routledge: 111-126

Brown, A. (2007) Rethinking the subcultural commodity, in Hodkinson, P. and Deicke, W. (eds.) *Youth cultures: Scenes, subcultures and tribes,* London: Routledge: 63-78

Bryman, A. (2004) *Social research methods* (2nd ed.) Oxford: Oxford University Press

Bulmer, M. (1984) *Sociological Research Methods – An Introduction,* London: MacMillan

Bulmer, M. (1984) *The Chicago School of Sociology,* Chicago: University of Chicago Press

Burgess, R. G. (1984) *In the field: An introduction to field research,* London: Routledge

Burnett, R. (1996) *The golden jukebox: The international music industry,* London: Routledge

Butler, J. (1990) *Gender trouble,* London: Routledge

Callinicos, A. (1989) *Against postmodernism: A Marxist critique,* London: Polity

Carrington, B. and Wilson, B. (2004) Dance nations: Rethinking Youth Subcultural Theory, in Bennett, A. and Kahn-Harris, K. (eds.) *After subculture: Critical studies in contemporary youth culture,* Basingstoke: Palgrave MacMillan: 65-78

Carson, T., Pearson, M., Johnston, I., Mangat, J., Tupper, J. and Warburton, T. (2005) Semiotic approaches to image-based research, in Somekh, B. and Lewin, C. (eds.) *Research Methods in the Social Sciences,* London: Sage: 164-171

Cashmore, E. (1997) *The black culture industry,* London: Routledge

Cashmore, E. (2005) America's paradox, in Guins, in R. G. and Cruz, O. Z. (eds.) *Popular culture: A reader.* London: Sage: 159-167

Chambers, I. (1986) *Popular culture: The metropolitan experience,* London: Methuen

Chaney, D. (2004) Fragmented culture and subcultures, in Bennett, A. and Kahn-Harris, K. (eds.) *After subculture: Critical studies in contemporary youth culture,* Basingstoke: Palgrave MacMillan: 36-50

Chang, J. (2005) *Can't stop, won't stop: A history of the hip-hop generation,* London: Ebury Press

Chapple, S. and Garofalo, R. (1977) *Rock 'n' roll is here to pay: The history and politics of the music industry,* Chicago: Nelson Hall

Charles, M. (2016) Grime central! Subterranean ground-in grit engulfing manicured mainstream spaces, in Andrews, K. and Palmer, L. A. (eds.) *Blackness in Britain,* London: Routledge: 89-100

Clark, D. (2003) The death and life of punk, the last subculture, in Muggleton, D. and Weinzierl, R. (eds.) *The post-subcultures reader,* Oxford: Berg: 223-238

Clarke, G. (1981) Defending ski-jumpers: A critique of theories of youth subcultures, in Gelder, K. and Thornton, S. (eds.) (1997) *The subcultures reader,* London: Routledge: 175-180

Clarke, J. (1975) The skinheads and the magical recovery of community, in Hall, S. and Jefferson (eds.) (1975/1993) *Resistance through rituals: Youth subcultures in post-war Britain,* London: Routledge: 99-102

Clarke, J. (1975) Style, in Hall, S. and Jefferson (eds.) (1975/1993) *Resistance through rituals: Youth subcultures in post-war britain,* London: Routledge: 175-191

Clarke, J., Hall, S., Jefferson, T. and Roberts, B. (1975) Subcultures, cultures and class: A theoretical overview, in Hall, S. and Jefferson (eds.) (1975/1993) *Resistance through rituals: Youth subcultures in post-war Britain,* London: Routledge: 9-74

Cloward, R. and Ohlin, L. (1960) *Delinquency and Opportunity: A theory of delinquent gangs,* New York: Free Press

Coffey, A. (1999) *The ethnographic self: fieldwork and the representation of identity,* London: Sage

Cohen, A. K. (1955) *Delinquent boys: The culture of the gang,* London: Collier-Macmillan

Cohen, P. (1972/1980) Subcultural conflict and working-class community, in Hall, S., Hobson, D., Lowe, A. and Willis, P. (eds.) *Culture, media, language,* London: Hutchinson and Co.: 78-87

Cohen, P. (1997) *Rethinking the youth question,* London: MacMillan

Cohen, S. (1972) *Folk devils and moral panics: The Creation of the mods and rockers,* London: MacGibbon and Lee

Cohen, S. (1993) Ethnography and popular music studies, *Popular Music,* 12(2: 123-138

Collins, P. H. (1990) *Black feminist thought: Knowledge, consciousness and the politics of empowerment,* London: Routledge

Collins, P. H. (2006) *From Black Power to hip-hop: Racism, nationalism, and feminism,* Philadelphia: Temple University Press

Colosi, R. (2010) A return to the Chicago School? From the 'subculture' of taxi dancers to the contemporary lap dancer, *Journal of Youth Studie*s, 13(1):1-16

Condry, I. (2006) *Hip-hop Japan: rap and the paths of cultural globalization,* London: Duke University Press

Connell, R. W. (2005) *masculinities* (2nd. ed.) Cambridge: Polity Press

Connor, M. K. (1995) *What is cool? – Understanding black manhood in America,* Chicago: Agate Publishing

Craige Lewis, G. (2009) *The truth behind hip-hop* Camarillo, California: Xulon Press

Cressey, P. G. (1932) *The taxi-hall dance: A Sociological study in recreation and city Life,* Chicago: University of Chicago Press

Creswell, J. W. (2003) *Research Design – Qualitative, quantitative and mixed methods* (2nd ed.) London: Sage

Darlington, Y. and Scott, D. (2002) *Qualitative research in practice – Stories from the field,* Buckingham: Open University Press

de Jong, A. and Schuilenburg, M. (2006) *Mediapolis: Popular culture and the city,* Rotterdam: 010 Publishers

Den Tandt, C. (2002) Globalization and identity: The discourse of popular music in the Caribbean, in Young, R. (ed.) *Music, Popular Culture, Identities,* Amsterdam: Rodopi: 85-100

DeNora, T. (2000) *Music in everyday life,* Cambridge: Cambridge University Press

Denzin, N. K. and Lincoln, Y. S. (eds.) (1998) *The landscape of qualitative research–Theories and issues,* London: Sage

Denzin, N. K. and Lincoln, Y. S. (eds.) (2003) *Strategies of qualitative inquiry,* 2nd. ed. London: Sage Publications

Dey, I. (1993) *Qualitative data analysis: A user-friendly guide for social scientists*, London: Routledge

Dibben, N. (1999) Representations of femininity in popular music, *Popular Music,* 18(3):331-354

Dimitriadis, G. (1996) Hip-hop: From live performance to mediated narrative, *Popular Music*, 15(2):179-193

Dimitriadis, G. (2009) *Performing identity/performing culture: Hip-hop as text, pedagogy, and lived practice,* Oxford: Peter Lang

Dolan, E. (2010) '... This little ukulele tells the truth': Indie pop and kitsch authenticity, *Popular Music*, 29(3):457-469

Downes, D. (1966) *The delinquent solution: A study in subcultural theory*, London: Routledge and Kegan Paul

Downes, D. and Rock, P. (2011) *Understanding deviance* (6th ed.) Oxford: Oxford University Press

Durkheim, E. (1893/1984) *The division of labour in society*, Basingstoke: MacMillan Publishers

Durkheim, E. (1895/1964) *The rules of sociological method,* London: Collier-Macmillan

Dürrschmidt, J. (2000) *Everyday lives in the global city,* London: Routledge

Dyson, M. E. (2007) *Know what i mean: reflections on hip-Hop*, New York: Basic Civitas Books

Eminem (2000) *Angry blonde,* New York: Regan Books

Eminem (2009) *The way i am,* New York: Plume Books

Epstein, J. S. (ed.) (1998) *Youth Culture: Identity in a Postmodern World,* Oxford: Blackwell Publishers

Fairclough, N. (1995) *Media discourse,* London: Arnold

Ferguson, R. (1998) *Representing race: Ideology, identity and the media,* London: Arnold

Fernando Jr., S. H. (1994) *The new beats: Exploring the music, culture and attitudes of hip-hop,* New York: Anchor Books

Ferraro, G. P. and Andreatta, S. (2009) *Cultural anthropology: An applied perspective* (8th ed.) Belmont: Wadsworth Publishing

Fiske, J. (1989) *Reading the popular,* London: Routledge

Fiske, J. (1992) Cultural studies and the culture of everyday life, in Grossberg, L., Nelson, C. and Treichler, P. (eds.) *Cultural studies*, London: Routledge):154-173

Ford Jr., R. (1979) Jive talking N.Y. DJs Rapping away in black discos–*Billboard Magazine*, May 5, 1979 in Forman, M. and Neal, A. (eds.) (2004) *That's the joint–The hip-hop studies reader,* London: Routledge):43-44

Forman, M. (2000) Represent: Race, space and place in rap music, *Popular Music*, 19(1):65-90

Forman, M. and Neal, M. A. (eds.) (2004) *That's the joint: The hip-hop studies reader,* London: Routledge

Förnas, J. and Bolin, G. (1995) *Youth culture in late modernity,* London: Sage

Frankfort-Nachmias, C. and Nachmias, D. (1996) *Research methods in the social sciences,* London: Edward Arnold

Frith, S. (1978) *The sociology of rock,* London: Constable

Furlong, A. and Cartmel, F. (2007) *Young people and social change: New perspectives,* (2nd ed.), Maidenhead: Open University Press

Gans, H. J. (1979) *Deciding what's news: A study of CBS Evening News, NBC Nightly News, 'Newsweek' and 'Time',* New York: Pantheon Books

Garofalo, R. (1993) Black popular music: Crossing over or going under? in Bennett, A., Frith, S, Grossberg, L., Turner, G. (eds.) *Rock and popular music – Politics, policies, institutions,* London: Routledge):231-248

Gates Jr., H. L. (1988) *The signifying monkey: A theory of African-American literary criticism,* Oxford: Oxford University Press

Geertz, C. (1973) Thick description: Toward an interpretive theory of culture, in Geertz, C. (1993) *The interpretation of cultures: Selected essays,* London: Fontana: 3-30

Gelder, K. (2007) *Subcultures: Cultural histories and social practice,* London: Routledge

George, N. (1988) *The death of rhythm and blues,* New York: Pantheon

George, N. (2004) Hip-hop's founding fathers speak the truth, in Forman, M. and Neal, A. (eds.) *That's the joint – The hip-hop studies reader,* London: Routledge

George, N. (2005) *Hip-hop America,* London: Penguin

Giddens, A. (1976) *New Rules of Sociological Method – A Positive Critique of Interpretative Sociologies,* London: Hutchinson

Giddens, A. (1984) *The Constitution of Society,* Cambridge: Polity Press

Gidley, B. (2007) Youth culture and ethnicity: Emerging youth intercultures in South, London, in Hodkinson, P. and Deicke, W. (eds.) *Youth cultures: Scenes, subcultures and tribes,* London: Routledge: 145-160

Gilbert, N. (2008) *Researching social life* (3rd ed.) London: Sage

Gillespie, M. and Toynbee, J. (2006) Textual power and pleasure in Gillespie, M. and Toynbee, J. (eds.) *Analysing Media Texts,* Maidenhead: Open University Press: 1-8

Gillett, C. (1996) *The sound of the city: The rise of rock and roll,* London: Souvenir

Gillham, B. (2005) *Research interviewing – The range of techniques,* Maidenhead: Open University Press

Gilroy, P. (1992) *There ain't no black in the Union Jack,* London: Routledge

Gilroy, P. (1993) *The black atlantic – Modernity and double consciousness,* Cambridge, Massachusetts: Harvard University Press

Gittins, I. (2001) *Eminem,* London: Carlton Books

Glaser, B. and Strauss, A. (1967) *The discovery of grounded theory,* Chicago: Aldine

Godlovitch, S. (1999) Performance Authenticity – possible, practical, virtuous, in Kemal, S. and Gaskell, I. (eds.) *Performance and authenticity in the arts,* Cambridge: Cambridge University Press: 154-174

Gramsci, A. (1971) *Selections from the prison notebooks,* London: Lawrence and Wishart

Grazian, D. (2004) The symbolic economy of authenticity in the Chicago blues scene, in Bennett, A. and Peterson, R. A. (eds.) *Music scenes – Local, translocal and virtual,* Nashville: Vanderbilt University Press: 31-47

Griffin, C. E. (2011) *The Trouble With Class: Researching Youth, Class and Culture Beyond the 'Birmingham School,'* in Journal of Youth Studies, 14(3):245-259

Gunter, A. (2010) *Growing Up Bad – Black Youth, Road Culture and Badness in an East, London Neighbourhood,* London: Tufnell Press

Haenfler, R. (2010) *Goths, Gamers, and Grrrls: Deviance and Youth Subcultures,* Oxford: Oxford University Press

Hall, S. (1980) Cultural Studies and the Centre: Some Problematics and Problems, in Hall, S., Hobson, P., Lowe, A. and Willis, P. (eds.) *Culture, Media and Language*, London: Hutchinson: 3-33

Hall, S. (1981) Notes on Deconstructing the Popular, in Samuel, R. (ed.) *People's History and Social Theory*, London: Routledge and Kegan Paul: 227-239

Hall, S. (1992) What is This 'Black' in Black Popular Culture? in Dent, G. (ed.) *Black Popular Culture*, Seattle: Bay Press: 21-35

Hall, S. (1997) R*epresentation – Cultural Representations and Signifying Practices*, London: Sage Publications

Hall, S. and Whannel, P. (1964) *The Popular Arts*, London: Hutchinson Educational

Hall, S. and Jefferson, T. (eds.) (1975/1993) *Resistance through rituals – Youth Subcultures in Post-War Britain*, London: Routledge

Hammersley, M. and Atkinson, P. (1983) *Ethnography – principles in practice*, London: Routledge

Hammond, M. and Wellington, J. (2012) *Research Methods: The Key Concepts*, Abingdon: Routledge

Harker, D. (1980) *One for the Money: Politics and Popular Song*, London: Hutchinson

Harker, D. (1985) *Fakesong – The Manufacture of British 'Folksong' 1700 to the Present Day*, Milton Keynes: Open University Press

Harrison, A. K. (2006) 'Cheaper than a CD, plus we really mean it': Bay Area underground hip-hop tapes as subcultural artefacts, *Popular Music*, 25(2):283-301

Harrison, A. K. (2009) *Hip-Hop Underground – The Integrity and Ethics of Racial Identification*, Philadelphia: Temple University Press

Harvey, D. (1997) *Justice, Nature and the Geography of Difference*, New York: Wiley and Sons

Hasted, N. (2009) *The Dark Side of Eminem*, London: Omnibus Press

Hawkins, S. (1996) Perspectives in Popular Musicology: Music, Lennox and Meaning, in 1990s *Pop, Popular Music*, 15(1):17-36

Heatley, M. (2012) *Eminem: Survivor*, London: Flame Tree Publishing

Hebdige, D. (1975) The Meaning of Mod, in Hall, S. and Jefferson (eds.) (1975/1993) *Resistance through rituals: Youth Subcultures in Post-War Britain*, London: Routledge: 87-96

Hebdige, D. (1979) *Subculture – The Meaning of Style*, London: Routledge

Hebdige, D. (1988) *Hiding in the Light*, London: Routledge

Hesmondhalgh, D. and Negus, K. (eds.) (2002) *Popular Music Studies*, London: Arnold

Hesmondhalgh, D. (2005) Subcultures, Scenes or Tribes? None of the above, *Journal of Youth Studies*, 8(1):21-40

Hewitt, R. (1986) *White Talk Black Talk: Inter-racial friendship and Communication Amongst Adolescents*, Cambridge: Cambridge University Press

Hirsch, P. (1972) Processing Fads and Fashions: An Organisational Set Analysis of Cultural Industry Systems, *American Journal of Sociology*, 77(4):639-659

Hochschild, J. L. (2009) Racial Trends in the United States, in Back, L. and Solomos, J. (eds.) *Theories of Race and Racism* (2nd ed.) London: Routledge: 639-651

Hodkinson, P. (2002) *Goth: Identity and Style*, Oxford: Berg

Hodkinson, P. (2005) 'Insider Research' in the Study of Youth Cultures, *Journal of Youth Studies*, 8(2):131-149

Hodkinson, P. (2007) Youth Cultures: A Critical Outline of Key Debates, in Hodkinson, P. and Deicke, W. (eds.) *Youth Cultures: Scenes, Subcultures and Tribes*, London: Routledge: 1-22

Hodkinson, P. (2011) Ageing in a Spectacular 'Youth Culture': continuity, change and community among older goths, *British Journal of Sociology*, 62(2):262-282

Hodkinson, P. (2012) Beyond Spectacular Specifics in the Study of Youth (Sub)Cultures, *Journal of Youth Studies*, 15(5):557-572

Hodkinson, P. and Bennett, A. (2012) *Ageing and Youth Subcultures: Music, Style and Identity*, Oxford: Berg

Hollands, R. (2002) Divisions in the Dark: Youth cultures, transitions and segmented consumption spaces in the night-time economy, *Journal of Youth Studies*, 5(2):153-171

hooks, b. (1991) *Yearning: Race, Gender and Cultural Politics,* London: Turnaround

hooks, b. (1992) *Black Looks: Race and Representation* Boston: South End Press

hooks, b. (1994) *Outlaw Culture: Resisting Representations*, London: Routledge

hooks, b. (2004) *We Real Cool: Black Men and Masculinity,* London: Routledge

Hopkinson, N. and Moore, N. (2006) *Deconstructing Tyrone – A New Look at Black Masculinity in the Hip-Hop Generation* San Francisco: Cleis Press

Horn, D. (2011) *Birthday Thoughts on 'Popular Music'*, *Popular Music*, 30(3):471-472

Hughes, J. (1990) *The Philosophy of Social Research* (2nd ed.) London: Longman

Hutnyk, J. (2000) *Critique of Erotica: Music, Politics and the Culture Industry,* London: Pluto Press

Huq, R. (2006) *Beyond Subculture: Pop, Youth and Identity in a Postcolonial World,* London: Routledge

Huq, R. (2007) Resistance or Incorporation? Youth Policy Making and Hip-Hop Culture, in Hodkinson, P. and Deicke, W. (eds.) *Youth Cultures: Scenes, Subcultures and Tribes,* London: Routledge: 79-92

Jefferson, T. (1975) Cultural Responses of the teds: the defence of space and status, in Hall, S. and Jefferson, T. (1975/1993) (eds) *Resistance through rituals: Youth Subcultures in Post-War Britain,* London: Routledge: 81-86

Jenks, C. (2005) *Subculture: The Fragmentation of the Social*, London: Sage

Johnson, L. K. (1976) Jamaican Rebel Music, *Race and Class* 17(4:397-411.

Jones, S. (1988) *Black Culture, White Youth: From JA to UK,* London: Macmillan

Jones, M. L. (2012) *The Music Industries: From Conception to Consumption,* London: Palgrave MacMillan

Judy, R. A. T. (2004) 'On the Question of Nigga Authenticity' in Forman, F. and Neal, M. A. (eds.) *That's the joint – The hip-hop studies reader,* London: Routledge: 105-118

Kahn-Harris, K. (2004) Unspectacular Subculture? Transgression and Mundanity in the Global Extreme Metal Scene in Bennett, A. and Kahn-Harris, K. (eds.) *After Subculture: Critical Studies in Contemporary Youth Culture*, Basingstoke: Palgrave MacMillan: 107-118

Kalyan, R. (2006) Hip-Hop Imaginaries: a Genealogy of the Present, *Journal of Cultural Research,* 10(3):237-257

Kelley, N. (ed.) (2002) *Rhythm and Business – The Political Economy of Black Music*, New York: Akashic Books

Kelley, R. D. G. (1994) Kickin' Reality, Kickin' Ballistics: Gangsta Rap and Postindustrial Los Angeles, Perkins, W. E. (ed.) *Droppin' Science: Critical Essays on Rap Music and Hip-Hop Culture*, Philadelphia: Temple University Press: 117-158

Kellner, D. (1995) *Media Culture: Cultural Studies, Identity and Politics Between the Modern and the Postmodern,* London: Routledge

Keyes, C. L. (2004) Empowering Self, Making Choices, Creating Spaces: Black Female Identity via Rap Music Performance, in Forman, M. and Neal, M. A. (eds.) *That's the joint: The hip studies reader*, London: Routledge: 265-276

Kim, H. (2014) *Making Diaspora in a Global City: South Asian Youth Cultures, London* London: Routledge

Kirk, J. and Miller, M. L. (1986) *Reliability and Validity in Qualitative Research,* London: Sage

Kitwana, B. (2002) *The Hip-Hop Generation–Young Blacks and the Crisis in African-American Culture*, New York: BasicCivitas Books

Kitwana, B. (2005) *Why White Kids Love Hip-Hop–Wankstas, Wiggers, Wannabes and the New Reality of Race in America*, New York: Basic Civitas Books

Knight, N. (1982) *Skinhead,* London: Omnibus Press

Kress, G. and Mavers, D. (2005) Social Semiotics and Multimodal Texts in Somekh, B. and Lewin, C. (eds.) *Research Methods in the Social Sciences*, London: Sage: 172-179

Krims, A (2000) *Rap Music and the Poetics of Identity*, New York: Cambridge Press

Krims, A. (2003) Marxist Music Analysis Without Adorno: Popular Music and Urban Geography, in Moore, A. F. (ed.) *Analyzing Popular Music,* Cambridge: Cambridge University Press: 131-157

Krueger, R. A. and Casey, M. A. (2009) *Focus Groups–A Practical Guide for Applied Research* (4th ed.) London: Sage

Laughey, D. (2006) *Music and Youth Culture* Edinburgh: Edinburgh University Press

Lash, S. and Urry, J. (1988) *The End of Organised Capitalism*, Cambridge: Polity

Layder, D. (1993) *New Strategies in Social Research*, Cambridge: Polity Press

Leach, E. E. (2001) 'Vicars of 'Wannabe': authenticity and the Spice Girls', *Popular Music*, 20(2,):143-167

Lee, R. M. (2000) *Unobtrusive Methods in Social Research,* Buckingham: Open University Press

Lewin, C. (2005) Elementary Quantitative Methods, in Somekh, B. and Lewin, C. (eds.) *Research Methods in the Social Sciences*, London: Sage: 215-225

Lincoln, S. (2004) Teenage Girls' 'Bedroom Culture': Codes versus Zones, in Bennett, A. and Kahn-Harris, K. (eds.) *After Subculture: Critical Studies in Contemporary Youth Culture*: 94-106 Basingstoke: Palgrave MacMillan

Lincoln, S. (2012) *Youth Culture and Private Space,* Basingstoke: Palgrave MacMillan

Lipsitz, G. (1994) *Dangerous Crossroads: Popular Music, Postmodernism and the Poetics of Place,* London: Verso

Lott, E. (1995) *Love and Theft–Blackface Minstrelsy and the American Working Class,* New York: Oxford University Press

Lott, T. L. (1999) *The Invention of Race–Black Culture and the Politics of Representation,* Oxford: Blackwell Publishers

Lunt, P. and Livingston, S. (1996) Rethinking the Focus Group in Media and Communications Research, *Journal of Communication*, 46: 79-98

MacDonald, N. (2001) *The Graffiti Subculture: Youth, Masculinity and Identity in London and New York,* Basingstoke: Palgrave MacMillan

MacDonald, R. and Marsh, J. (2005) *Disconnected Youth: Growing Up in Britain's Poor Neighbourhoods*, Basingstoke: Palgrave Macmillan

MacDonald, R., Shildrick, T., Webster, C., Johnston, L. and Ridley, L. (2001) Snakes and Ladders: In Defence of Studies of Youth Transition, *Sociological Research Online*, 5(4).

MacRae, R. (2004) Notions of 'Us' and 'Them': Markers of Stratification in Clubbing Lifestyles, *Journal of Youth Studies*, 7(1):55-71

MacRae, R. (2007) 'Insider' and 'Outsider' Issues in Youth Research, in Hodkinson, P. and Deicke, W. (eds.) *Youth Cultures: Scenes, Subcultures and Tribes*, London: Routledge: 51-62

MacWeeney, I. (2008) *Imagining the Real: Chicano Youth, Hip-Hop, Race, Space and Place*, London: Goldsmiths University

Maffesoli, M. (1996) *The Time of the Tribes: The Decline of Individualism in Mass Society*, London: Sage

Mair, S. (2008) B-Boys and Bass Girls: Sex, Style and Mobility in Indian American Youth Culture, in Nair, A. (ed.) (2008) *Desi Rap: Hip Hop and South Asian America* Plymouth: Lexington Books: 41-70

Malbon, B. (1998) The Club: Clubbing, Consumption, Identity and the Spatial Practices of Every-Night Life, in Skelton, T. and Valentine, G. (eds.) *Cool Places: Geographies of Youth Cultures*, London: Routledge: 266-287

Marchart (2003) Bridging the Micro-Macro Gap: Is There Such a Thing as a Post-subcultural Politics? in Muggleton, D. and Weinzierl, R. (eds.) *The Post-Subcultures Reader*, Oxford: Berg: 83-100

Martin, P. J. (2004) Culture, Subculture and Organization, in Bennett, A. and Kahn-Harris, K. (eds.) *After Subculture – Critical Readings in Contemporary Youth Culture*, London: Palgrave MacMillan: 21-35

Mason, J. (2006) Mixing Methods in a Qualitatively Driven Way, *Qualitative Research*, 6(1):9-25

Matza, D. (1964) *Delinquency and Drift*, New York: John Wiley and Sons

May, T. (1997) *Social Research: Issues, Methods and Process* (2nd ed.) Buckingham: Open University Press

McCall, G. J. and Simmons, J. L. (eds.) (1969) *Issues in Participant Observation: A Text Reader*, London: Addison-Wesley Publishing Company

McLeod, K. (1999) Authenticity Within Hip-Hop and Other Cultures Threatened with Assimilation, *Journal of Communication*, 49(4):134-150

McPhaul, T. (2005) *The Psychology of Hip-Hop*, New York: Universe Books

McRobbie, A. (1993) Shut Up and Dance: Youth Culture and Changing Modes of Femininity, *Cultural Studies*, 7: 195-206

McRobbie, A. and Garber, J. (1975) Girls and Subcultures: An Exploration, in Hall, S. and Jefferson, T. (eds.) *Resistance through rituals: Youth Subcultures in Post-War Britain*, London: Routledge: 209-222

Measham, F. and Moore, K. (2009) Repertoires of Distinction: exploring patterns of weekend polydrug use within local leisure scenes across the English night time economy, *Criminology and Criminal Justice*, 9(4):437-464

Meer, S. (2005) *Uncle Tom Mania – slavery, minstrelsy and transatlantic culture in the 1850s*, Athens, Georgia: University of Georgia Press

Merrill, B. and West, L. (2009) *Using Biographical Methods in Social Research*, London: Sage

Merton, R. K. (1938) Social Structure and Anomie, *American Sociological Review*, 3(5):672-682

Middleton, R. (1990) *Studying Popular Music*, Milton Keynes: Open University Press
Middleton, R. (2011) 'Popular Music' is Growing Old(er), *Popular Music*, 30(3):472-473
Miles, S. (2000) *Youth Lifestyles in a Changing World*, Buckingham: Open University Press
Miller, J. (1997) *Autobiography and Research*, London: University of London Institute of Education
Miller, W. (1958) Lower Class Culture as a Generating Milieu of Gang Delinquency, *Journal of Social Issues*, 14(3):5-19
Mitchell, T. (1995) Questions of Style: Notes on Italian Hip-Hop, *Popular Music*, 14(3):333-348
Mitchell, T. (ed.) (2001) *Global Noise–Rap and Hip-Hop Outside the USA*, Connecticut: Wesleyan University Press
Moore, A. (2002) Authenticity as Authentication, *Popular Music*, 21(2):209-223
Moore, A. F. (2001) *Rock: The Primary Text–Developing a Musicology of Rock* (2nd. ed.), Aldershot: Ashgate
Moore, A. F. (2003) *Analyzing Popular Music*, Cambridge: Cambridge University Press
Moore, A. F. (ed.) (2007) *Critical Essays in Popular Music*, Aldershot: Ashgate
Moore, D. (1994) *The Lads in Action: Social Processes in an Urban Youth Subculture*, Aldershot: Ashgate Publishing
Morley, D. (1980) *The Nationwide Audience: Structure and Decoding*, London: BFI
Morgan, J. (1999) *When Chickenheads Come Home to Roost: My Life as a Hip-Hop Feminist*, New York: Simon and Schuster
Morgan, D. L. (1998) *Planning Focus Groups*, London: Sage
Morgan, D. (2008) *Hip-Hop Had a Dream:, vol. 1–The Artful Movement*, Milton Keynes: AuthorHouse
Muggleton, D. (1997) The Post-Subculturalist in Redhead, S., Wynne, D. and O'Connor, J. (eds.) *The Club Cultures Reader*, Malden: Blackwell: 167-185
Muggleton, D. (2000) *Inside Subculture: The Postmodern Meaning of Style*, Oxford: Berg
Mulvey, L. (1975) Visual Pleasure and Narrative Cinema, *Screen*, 16(3): 6-18
Munday, J. (2006) Identity in Focus–The use of focus groups to study the construction of collective identity, *Sociology*, 4(1):89-106
Mungham, G. (1976) Youth in Pursuit of Itself in Mungham, G. and Pearson, G. (eds.) *Working Class Youth Culture*, London: Routledge and Kegan-Paul
Murdock, G. and Phelps, G. (1972) Responding to Popular Music: Criteria of Classification and Choice Among English Teenagers, *Popular Music and Society*, 1(3):144-151
Nair, A. (ed.) (2008) *Desi Rap: Hip Hop and South Asian America* Plymouth: Lexington Books
Neal, M. A. (1999) *What the Music Said–Black Popular Music and Black Public Culture*, New York: Routledge
Neal, M. A. (2004) No Time for Fake Niggas: Hip-Hop Culture and the Authenticity Debates, in Forman, F and Neal, M. A. (eds.) *That's the joint–The hip-hop studies reader*, London: Routledge: 57-50
Neff, A. C. (2009) *Let the World Listen Right: The Mississippi Delta Hip-Hop Story*, Jackson: University Press of Mississippi
Negus, K. (1992) *Producing Pop: Culture and Conflict in the Popular Music Industry*, London: Edward Arnold
Negus, K. (1996) *Popular Music in Theory–An Introduction*, Oxford: Polity Press
Negus, K. (1999) *Music Genres and Corporate Cultures*, London: Routledge
Nelson, D. (2008) *My Son Marshall, My Son Eminem*, London: John Blake Publishing

Neuman, W. L. (2011) *Social Research Methods – Qualitative and Quantitative Approaches* (7th ed.) London: Pearson

Ntarangwi, M. (2009) *East African Hip-Hop: Youth Culture and Globalization* Chicago: University of Illinois Press

O'Reilly, K. (2004) *Ethnographic Methods,* London: Routledge

Oakley, A. (1981) *From Here to Maternity: Becoming a Mother,* Harmondsworth: Penguin

Ogbar, J. O. G. (2007) *Hip-Hop Revolution – The Culture and Politics of Rap,* Lawrence, Kansas: University Press of Kansas

Olson, P. J. and Shobe Jr., B. (2008) White Rappers and Black Epistemology, *The Journal of Popular Culture,* 41(6):994-1011

Osgerby, B. (2004) *Youth Media,* London: Routledge

Osgerby, B. (2008) *Fashion and Subculture: A History,* Oxford: Berg

Paddison, M. (2004) Authenticity and Failure in Adorno's Aesthetics of Music in Huhn, T. (ed.) *The Cambridge Companion to Adorno,* Cambridge: Cambridge University Press: 198-221

Pennay, M. (2001) Rap in Germany: The Birth of a Genre, in Mitchell, T. (ed.) *Global Noise – Rap and Hip-Hop Outside the USA,* Connecticut: Wesleyan University Press: 111-133

Perkins, W. E. (ed.) (1996) *Droppin' Science – Critical Essays on Rap Music and Hip-hop Culture,* Philadelphia: Temple University Press

Perry, I. (2004) *Prophets of the Hood – Politics and Poetics in Hip-Hop,* Durham: Duke University Press

Pfeifer, T. (2007) *A Visual Cultural Analysis of Blackface Minstrelsy and the Hip-Hop 'Wigga' as Neo-Minstrel* paper presented at a meeting of the American Sociological Association, New York City, 11/08/2007 [Online] Available at: http://citation.allacademic.com/meta/p_mla_apa_research_citation/1/8/5/2/8/pages185283/p185283-1.php

Peterson, R. A. and Bennett, A. (2004) Introducing Music Scenes, in Bennett, A. and Peterson, R. A. (eds.) (2004) *Music Scenes: Local, Translocal, and Virtual,* Nashville: Vanderbilt University Press: 1-16

Pieterse, J. N. (1995) White on Black – Images of Africa and Blacks, *Western Popular Culture,* London: Yale University Press

Pike, K. (1967) *Language in Relation to a Unified Theory of the Structure of Human Behaviour,* The Hague: Mouton

Platt, J. (1998) Chicago Methods: Reputations and Realities, in Tomasi, L. (ed.) *The Tradition of the Chicago School of Sociology,* Aldershot: Ashgate: 89-103

Polhemus, T. (1996) *Style Surfing: What to Wear in the 3rd Millennium,* London: Thames and Hudson

Polhemus, T. (1997) In the Supermarket of Style, in Redhead, S., Wynne, D. and O'Connor, J. (eds.) *The Clubcultures Reader: Readings on Popular Culture,* Oxford: Blackwell: 130-133

Pollert, A. (1981) *Girls, Wives, Factory Lives,* London: MacMillan

Polsky, N. (1971) *Hustlers, Beats and Others,* Harmondsworth: Pelican Books

Propp, V. (1968) *Morphology of the Folk Tale,* Austin: University of Texas Press

Quinn, E. (2005) *Nuthin' but a 'G' Thang – The Culture and Commerce of Gangsta Rap,* New York: Columbia Press

Ramsey Jr., G. P. (2003) *Race Music – Black Cultures from Bebop to Hip-Hop,* Berkley: University of California Press

Redhead, S. (1993) *Rave Off–Politics and Deviance in Contemporary Youth Culture,* Aldershot: Avebury

Redhead, S. (1997) *From Subcultures to Clubcultures: An Introduction to Popular Cultural Studies,* Oxford: Blackwell

Reinharz, S. (1992) *Feminist Methods in Social Research,* Oxford: Oxford University Press

Richards, C. (1998) *Teen Spirits: Music and Identity in Media Education,* London: Routledge

Rietveld, H. C. (1998) *This is Our House – House Music, Cultural Spaces and Technologies,* Aldreshot: Ashgate

Riley, A. (2005) The Rebirth of Tragedy out of the Spirit of Hip-Hop: A Cultural Sociology of Gangsta Rap Music, *Journal of Youth Studies,* 8(3):297-311

Rivera, R. Z. (2003) *New York Ricans from the Hip-Hop Zone,* Basingstoke: Palgrave MacMillan

Robins, D. and Cohen, P. (1978) *Knuckle Sandwich: Growing Up in the Working-Class City,* Harmondsworth: Pelican Books

Robinson, C. (2009) Nightscapes and Leisure Spaces: An Ethnographic Study of Young People's Use of Free Space, *Journal of Youth Studies,* 12(5): 501-514

Rose, D. and Sullivan, O. (1996) *Introducing Data Analysis for Social Scientists,* Buckingham: Open University Press

Rose, T. (1994) *Black Noise – Rap Music and Black Culture in Contemporary America* Middletown: Wesleyan University Press

Rose, T. (2008) *Hip-Hop Wars – What We Talk About When We Talk About Hip-Hop and Why It Matters,* New York: Basic Civitas Books

Rubinstein, D. (2001) *Culture, Structure and Agency,* London: Sage Publications

Samuels, D. (2004) The Rap on Rap: The 'black music' that isn't either, in Forman, M. and Neal, M. A. (eds.) *That's the joint – The hip-hop studies reader,* London: Routledge: 147-154

Sanjek, D. (2002) Tell Me Something I Don't Already Know: The Harvard Report and Soul Music Revisited, in Kelley, N. (ed.) *Rhythm and Business – The Political Economy of Black Music,* New York: Akashic Books: 59-76

Savage, J. (2007) *Teenage: The Creation of Youth 1875-1945* London: Pimlico

Saussure, F. de (1915/1959) *Course in General Linguistics,* New York: Philosophical Library

Saxton, A. (1996) Blackface Minstrelsy, in Bean, A.; Hatch, J. and McNamara, B. *Inside the Minstrel Mask – Readings in nineteenth-century blackface minstrelsy,* Connecticut: Wesleyan University Press: 67-85

Schloss, J. G. (2009) *Foundation: B-Boys, B-Girls and Hip-Hop Culture in New York,* Oxford: Oxford University Press

Schostak, J. (2006) *Interviewing and Representation in Qualitative Research,* Maidenhead: Open University Press

Schrøder, K., Drotner, K.; Kline, S. and Murray, C. (2003) *Researching Audiences,* London: Arnold

Scott, D. B. (ed.) (2009) *The Ashgate Research Companion to Popular Musicology,* Farnham: Ashgate

Scott, J. C. (1990) *Domination and the Arts of Resistance: Hidden Transcripts,* London: Yale University Press

Shaffir, W. and Stebbins, R. (1991) *Experiencing Fieldwork: An Inside View of Qualitative Research,* Newbury Park: Sage

Shapiro, P (2005) *The Rough Guide to Hip-Hop – the definitive guide to hip-hop from Grandmaster Flash to Outkast and beyond* (2nd ed.), London: Rough Guides

Sharma, N. T. (2010) *Hip-Hop Desis: South Asian Americans, Blackness, and a Global Race Consciousness* Durham: Duke University Press

Sharpley-Whiting, T. D. (2007) *Pimps Up, Hos Down: Hip-Hop's Hold on Black Women,* New York: New York University Press

Shaw, C. R. and McKay, H. (1942) *Juvenile Delinquency in Urban Areas,* Chicago: University of Chicago Press

Shildrick, T. and MacDonald, R. (2006) In Defence of Subculture: Young People, Leisure and Social Divisions, *Journal of Youth Studies*, 9(2):125-140

Shils, E. A. (1948) *The Present State of American Sociology*, New York: Free Press

Short, J. F. and Strodtbeck, F. L. (1965) *Group Process and Gang Delinquency* Chicago: Chicago University Press

Shuker, R. (1998) *Key Concepts in Popular Music,* London: Routledge

Shuker, R. (2004) Beyond the 'high fidelity' stereotype: defining the contemporary record collector, *Popular Music*, 23(3):311-330

Smith, A. (2005) Blues, Criticism, and the Signifying Monkey, *Popular Music*, 24(2):179-191

Solomon, T. (2005) Living Underground is Tough: Authenticity and locality in the hip-hop community in Istanbul, Turkey, *Popular Music*, 24(1):1-20

Southern, E. (1997) *The Music of Black Americans – A history* (3rd ed.), New York: Norton and Co. pub.

Stahl, G. (2003) Tastefully Renovating Subcultural Theory: Making Space for a New Model, in Muggleton, D. and Weinzierl, R. (eds.) *The Post-Subcultures Reader*, Oxford: Berg: 27-40

Stones, R. (2005) *Structuration Theory*, Basingstoke: Palgrave MacMillan

Storey, J. (1996) *Cultural Studies and the Study of Popular Culture: Theories and Methods* Edinburgh: Edinburgh University Press

Stratton, J. (1997) On the Importance of Subcultural Origins, in Gelder, K. and Thornton, S. (eds.) *The Subcultures Reader*, London: Routledge: 181-190

Strauss, A. L. (1987) *Qualitative Analysis for Social Scientists,* Cambridge: Cambridge University Press

Strauss, A. and Corbin, J. (eds.) (1997) *Grounded Theory in Practice*, London: Sage

Straw, W. (1991) *Systems of Articulation, Logics of Change: Communities and Scenes, Popular Music* in Cultural Studies, 53: 368-388

Straw, W. (1997) Sizing Up Record Collections: Gender and Connoisseurship in Rock Music Culture, in Whiteley, S. (ed.) *Sexing the Groove*, London: Routledge: 3-16

Sturges, F. (2005) 'A Life of Grime', *The Independent, July 9th 2005* [Online] Available at: http://www.independent.co.uk/arts-entertainment/music/features/a-life-of-grime-498018.html. (Accessed: 20 February 2010)

Swedenburg, T. (2001) Islamic Hip-Hop vs. Islamophobia: Aki Nawaz, Natacha Atlas, Akhenaton, in Mitchell, T. (ed.) *Global Noise – Rap and Hip-Hop Outside the USA*, Connecticut: Wesleyan University Press): 57-85

Sweetman, P. (2004) Tourists and Travellers? 'Subcultures', Reflexive Identities and Neo-Tribal Sociality, in Bennett, A. and Kahn-Harris, K. (eds.) *After Subculture: Critical Studies in Contemporary Youth Culture*, Basingstoke: Palgrave MacMillan: 79-93

Tagg, P. (1982) Analysing Popular Music, *Popular Music*, 2: 37-67

Tashakorri, A. and Teddlie, C. (1998) *Mixed Methodology: Combining Qualitative and Quantitative Approaches,* London: Sage

Tate, G. (ed.) (2003) *Everything but the Burden – What White People are Taking from Black Culture*, New York: Harlem Moon

Taylor, J. (2010) Queer Temporalities and the Significance of 'Music Scene' Participation in the Social Identities of Middle-aged Queers, in *Sociology*, 44(5):893-907

Taylor, T. D. (1997) *Global Pop: World Music, World Markets*, London: Routledge

Taylor, I. and Wall, D. (1976) Beyond the Skinheads: Comments on the Emergence and Significance of the Glam Rock Cult, in Mungham, G. and Pearson, G. (eds.) *Working Class Youth Culture*, London: Routledge and Kegan Paul: 105-123

Thomas, W. I. and Znaniecki, F. (1918) *The Polish Peasant in Europe and America*, Boston: The Gorham Press

Thornton, S. (1995) *Club Cultures – Music, Media and Subcultural Capital*, Cambridge: Polity Press

Thornton, S. (1997) Introduction to Part One, in Gelder, K. and Thornton, S. (eds.) *The Subcultures Reader*, London: Routledge: 11-15

Thrasher, F. (1927) *The Gang*, Chicago: Chicago University Press

Tiongson, A. (2013) *Filipinos Represent: DJs, Racial Authenticity and the Hip-Hop Nation*, London: University of Minnesota Press

Todorov, T. (1977) *The Poetics of Prose*, New York: Cornell University Press

Tonkiss, F. (2004) Using Focus Groups, in Seal, C. (ed.) *Researching Society and Culture (2nd ed.)*, London: Sage: 193-206

Tönnies, F. (1887/1957) *Community and Society* East Lansing: Michigan State University Press

Toolan, M. (2001) *Narrative – a critical linguistic introduction* (2nd ed.), London: Routledge

Toop, D. (1984) *Rap Attack 2 – African Rap to Global Hip-Hop*, London: Pluto Press

Toynbee, J. (2000) *Making Popular Music: Musicians, Creativity and Institutions*, London: Arnold

Toynbee, J. (2002) Mainstreaming, from Hegemonic Centre to Global Networks in Hesmondhalgh, D. and Negus, K. (eds.) *Popular Music Studies*, London: Arnold: 149-163

Urla, J. (2001) 'We Are Malcolm X!' – Negu Gorriak, Hip-Hop, and the Basque Political Imaginary in Mitchell, T. (ed.) *Global Noise – Rap and Hip-Hop Outside the USA*, Connecticut: Wesleyan University Press: 171-193

Wall, T. (2003) *Studying Popular Music Culture*, London: Hodder Arnold

Wallace, C. and Kovatcheva, S. (1998) *Youth in Society: The Construction and Deconstruction of Youth in East and West Europe*, Basingstoke: Palgrave

Watkins, S. C. (2005) *Hip-Hop Matters: Politics, Pop Culture, and the Struggle for the Soul of a Movement* Boston: Beacon Press

Watson, R. (1997) *Ethnomethodology and Textual Analysis*, in Silverman, D. (ed.) *Qualitative Research: Theory, Method and Practice*, London: Sage: 80-98

Watt, P. and Stenson, K. (1998) The Street: 'It's a Bit Dodgy Out There,' in Skelton, T. and Valentine, G. (eds.) *Cool Places – Geographies of Youth Cultures*, London: Routledge: 249-265

Webb, P. (2007) Hip-Hop Musicians and Audiences in the Local Musical 'Milieu,' in Hodkinson, P. and Deicke, W. (eds.) *Youth Cultures: Scenes, Subcultures and Tribes*, London: Routledge   pp.175-188

Weinstein, D. (2002) Progressive Rock as Text: The Lyrics of Roger Waters, in Holm-Hudson, K. (ed.) *Progressive Rock Reconsidered*, London: Routledge: 91-110

Weinzerl, R. (2000) *Fight the Power: A Secret History of Pop and the Formation of New Substreams*, Vienna: Passagen-Verlag

Weinzerl, R. and Muggleton, D. (2003) *The Post-Subcultures Reader*, Oxford: Berg

Westerfil, J. (2012) *Biography of Eminem,* New York: Hyperlink

White, A. (1996) 'Who Wants to Watch Ten Niggers Play Basketball?' in Perkins, W. E. (ed.) Droppin' Science – Critical Essays on Rap Music and Hip-hop Culture, Philadelphia: Temple University Press: 192-208

Whyte, W. F. (1943) *Street Corner Society: The Social Structure of an Italian Slum,* Chicago: Chicago University Press

Whyte, W. F. (1984) *Learning from the Field: A Guide from Experience,* London: Sage

Williams, C. (2001) Does it Really Matter? Young People and Popular Music, *Popular Music,* 20(2):223-242

Williams, J. P. (2011) *Subcultural Theory: Traditions and Concepts*, Cambridge: Polity Press

Willis, P. (1972) *Pop Music and Youth Groups,* unpublished Book study, Centre for Contemporary Studies University of Birmingham

Willis, P. (1977) *Learning to Labour: How Working Class Kids Get Working Class Jobs,* Farnborough: Saxon House

Willis, P. (1978) *Profane Culture,* London: Routledge and Kegan Paul

Willis, P. (1990) *Common Culture,* Buckingham: Open University Press

Wilson, B. (2006) *Fight, Flight or Chill – Subcultures, Youth and Rave Into the Twenty-First Century,* Montreal and Kingston: McGill-Queen's University Press

Wolcott, H. F. (1992) Posturing in Qualitative Inquiry, in LeCompte, M. D., Millroy, W. L. and Preissle, J. (eds.) *Handbook of Qualitative Research in Education,* San Diego: Academic Press: 3-52

Wolcott, H. F. (1994) *Transforming Qualitative Data – description, analysis, and interpretation,* Thousand Oaks, California: Sage Publications

Woldu, G. H. (2006) Gender as Anomaly: women in rap, in Peddie, I. (ed.) *The Resisting Muse: Popular Music and Social Protest*, Aldershot: Ashgate Publishing: 89-102

Wood, R. T. (2006) *Straightedge: Complexities and Contradictions of a Subculture,* New York: Syracuse University Press

Wulff, H. (1995) Inter-racial Friendship: Consuming Youth Styles, Ethnicity and Teenage Femininity in South London, in Amit-Talai, V. and Wulff, H. (eds.) *Youth Cultures: A Cross-Cultural Perspective*, London: Routledge: 63-80

Wyn, J. and White, R. (1997) *Rethinking Youth,* London: Sage Publications

Young, L. (1996) *Fear of the Dark: 'Race', Gender and Sexuality in the Cinema*, London: Routledge

www.ingramcontent.com/pod-product-compliance
Lightning Source LLC
Chambersburg PA
CBHW070905270326
41927CB00011B/2460